The Influence of Airpower
upon History

THE INFLUENCE OF AIRPOWER UPON HISTORY

Statesmanship, Diplomacy, and Foreign Policy since 1903

Edited by
ROBIN HIGHAM
AND MARK PARILLO

Foreword by
GENERAL RICHARD B. MYERS, USAF (RET.)

UNIVERSITY PRESS OF KENTUCKY

Scholarly publisher for the Commonwealth,
serving Bellarmine University, Berea College, Centre College of Kentucky, Eastern
Kentucky University, The Filson Historical Society, Georgetown College,
Kentucky Historical Society, Kentucky State University, Morehead State University,
Murray State University, Northern Kentucky University, Transylvania University,
University of Kentucky, University of Louisville, and Western Kentucky University.
All rights reserved.

Editorial and Sales Offices: The University Press of Kentucky
663 South Limestone Street, Lexington, Kentucky 40508-4008
www.kentuckypress.com

17 16 15 14 13   5 4 3 2 1

Library of Congress Cataloging-in-Publication Data

The influence of airpower upon history : statesmanship, diplomacy, and foreign
policy since 1903 / edited by Robin Higham and Mark Parillo ; foreword by
General Richard B. Myers, USAF (Ret.)
   p. cm.
  Includes bibliographical references and index.
  ISBN 978-0-8131-3674-5 (hbk. : alk. paper) -- ISBN 978-0-8131-3675-2 (pdf) --
ISBN 978-0-8131-4072-8 (epub)
  1. Air power—Case studies. 2. International relations—Case studies. 3. Military
history, Modern—20th century. I. Higham, Robin. II. Parillo, Mark P., 1955-
  UG623.I54 2013
  358.4009'04—dc23   2012043104

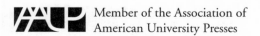 Member of the Association of
American University Presses

Contents

Foreword

The rapid rise of airpower—just a little over one hundred years old—has had a profound effect on world events. As this work points out, the use of airpower frequently resulted in controversy at the highest levels of government, as national leaders and statesmen debated how airpower might contribute to their particular vital national interests and to shaping world events.

Specifically, this work gives an important historical context to how various nations have viewed the development of airpower. As Higham and Parillo point out, from the earliest days of airpower, geography, national interests, diplomacy, and economics all have shaped how a nation views this vital capability. Indeed, airpower is about how military, commercial, and civil aviation all come together. These components are mutually reinforcing and mutually dependent, and a nation needs to be aware of the health of all three to understand the power, flexibility, and limitations of airpower.

As the reader moves through the various chapters, a fascinating mosaic emerges of specific nations making specific airpower choices to meet their overall security needs. For the military components alone this contribution is invaluable: the authors remind the reader that airpower is not the exclusive domain of one military service. Carrier-based aviation, as it did in the past, today still plays an important role in world events. And armies rely on airpower in the form of helicopters for tactical mobility and offensive firepower.

Moreover, the book also offers an important reminder of how fast things change in this technologically dependent domain. Stealthy aircraft and precision weapons are excellent late twentieth-century models. A twenty-first-century example is the increasing reliance on remotely piloted vehicles, which have replaced manned aircraft for a variety of missions. In addition, there is a developing imperative to integrate better the air, space, and cyber capabilities. This all comes at a relatively high price, and an effective military always has to balance the expense and challenge of exploiting new technologies with the looming danger of obsolescence.

In its significance for those at the highest level of government, this work is also a cautionary tale. Senior advisers must be able to offer their president or prime minister meaningful airpower options without asking their nation to spend lavishly to realize next-generation capabilities. Specifically for the United States, it highlights the need to advise the president accurately on what airpower capabilities can *and* cannot do when the government is looking for unique, innovative options with which to address national security challenges

This responsibility only grows with time. Looking at our nation's last fifteen years, we see that airpower has been called on in unique ways and has emerged as a force that can at times unilaterally shape the outcome of world events. The Kosovo conflict is an excellent example. The NATO bombing campaign started in March 1999 to force the Federal Republic of Yugoslavia to settle its differences with Kosovo peacefully. Although there was pressure in some quarters to use ground forces as well, President Clinton decided to use airpower exclusively, and in relatively short order President Milošević agreed to a peaceful way forward. NATO's assistance to rebel elements in Libya in overthrowing Muammar Gaddafi's government is another recent example of airpower's being the deciding force in the rebels' success. In Libya airpower achieved what might have been attempted by U.S. Marines in another era.

In my role as the principal military adviser to the U.S. president and National Security Council, I frequently found myself in discussions about the most effective way to apply military force in pursuit of national objectives. What a president or prime minister always wants is a variety of options. Airpower in particular offers many unique options in most security scenarios, given its inherent flexibility and agility. Historical context is also important when advising senior civilian leadership. In that vein, this book is must reading for those who will be discussing the application of airpower to today's complex security and diplomatic challenges.

In short, this volume does an excellent job of helping us think about airpower in its constituent parts—commercial, civil, and military. Only by thinking about all three of these mutually reinforcing capabilities does one get the comprehensive view of how airpower can contribute to a country's national strategic objectives. It also highlights the capabilities and limitation of the air domain. Parillo and Higham have done a great service to world leaders and their military advisers by outlining airpower's historical development so they can fully understand and articulate the various opportunities for using this powerful force effectively.

General Richard B. Myers, USAF (Ret.)
Chairman, U.S. Joint Chiefs of Staff,
2001–2005

Introduction

Robin Higham

Even as early man gazed up at the winged creatures soaring above him and first contemplated the wonders of flight, he began to grapple with the concept of airpower. The primal warrior could imagine the advantages of towering above his enemy, not only to observe his every plan and artifice but also perhaps to humble him with thunderbolts striking down.

Flight entered ancient Greek mythology as the domain of Daedalus's genius and the fatal allure that triggered Icarus's demise. In 328 or 327 B.C. Alexander the Great cowed into surrender the defenders of the Rock of Sogdiana, a mountain stronghold, just by having unarmed volunteers scale the heights surrounding the fortress. The besieged garrison commander was so unnerved by the sight of the Macedonians perched above his troops that he capitulated at once. In ancient China the kites that were created some three thousand years ago were being cleverly used for military purposes. In about 200 B.C., during the Han Dynasty, General Han Xin dispatched a kite over city walls—a virtual reconnaissance—in order to determine how deep were the city's defenses.

So it was that centuries before the Wright brothers ever mastered the currents of the ether, the various "monsters of the purple twilight," along with their uses in war and diplomacy, had entered human consciousness. Visionaries began to conceive the potentials of airpower, and the first true airpower theorists appeared in the early twentieth century. Ever since, those holding the reins of political control—the statesmen of the twentieth century and beyond—have had to develop their own sense of the uses, limits, and consequences of this evolving capability.

Before the advent of airpower, grand-strategic thinking had been built on theories of sea power. Vice Admiral Sir Herbert Richmond's

The French aviation pioneers Roland Garros (*right*) and Gustav Hamel with an early Morane monoplane, circa 1914. Early air shows provided visibility for national airpower. (SHAA B887-3568)

Statesmen and Sea Power (1946) and his unfinished *Navy as an Instrument of Policy I* (1953) built on Alfred Thayer Mahan's *The Influence of Sea Power upon History, 1660–1783* (1890) and *The Influence of Sea Power upon the French Revolution and Empire, 1793–1812* (1892) by focusing on the grand-strategic aspects of the employment of the Royal Navy—aspects limited by the geography of seas and coasts.

Ships can stop their engines and float; aircraft—other than airships—cannot. But the invention of the internal combustion engine and of the airframe quickly changed the dimensions of grand strategy from surface and subsurface capabilities to a full three dimensions. Yet airpower as an instrument of policy was a two-edged sword; it took some years to develop the technology and organization for effective air defense, let alone the legislative will to finance it. Thus, both potential belligerents—air and sea power—were vulnerable, which Giulio Douhet and like theorists pointed out. As the Royal Navy discovered when confronted by the U-boat, Britain was potentially at risk; the nation became aware that it was endangered by quite small enemy forces, which from 1915 to 1918 were hard to parry. And later, in both Britain and Germany between 1935 and 1945, this vulnerability required efforts costly in manpower as well as other resources.

The dimensions of the "air menace" were reshaped after 1945 by the nuclear threat. The double-edged nature of nuclear force—its massive power, its "overkill"—eventually made apparent that it had to become the unusable weapon. In addition, global conflicts in time would change, becoming ever more asymmetrical owing to the unequal strengths and vast differences between the world's haves and have nots. The "sword"—the fighting might or power—of insurgent masses or struggling minorities had no infrastructure of munitions or machines; rather, it became an ideological instrument of policy, often just as expensive in all its calculations to a nation.

Nevertheless, despite the changing nature of conflicts, instruments of diplomatic policy are in continual play, as is true of any element of national grand strategy. Air forces in peacetime may be weak and unusable, yet strong enough overall as a deterrent to maintain that peace, much like a wartime instrument. Airpower can carry the same weight for furthering national policy in wartime, and its application may range from the development of airliners and commercial air routes and contacts to massive bombing. Aerial reconnaissance (the Photo-Reconnaissance Unit, or PRU) can aid in tracking other economies, whereas diplomatic foreign aid (such as that to Turkey during World War II) can determine neutrality in place of either alliance or belligerency.

From Vision to Reality

Early on, the transformation of the visionary's imagination into a practical reality was the process of a dream slowly becoming a nightmare. The time from the Wright brothers' flight in 1903 to the first air crossing of the English Channel in 1909 to the bombing of London in 1917 was only a fourteen-year span. With the Channel shield broken, Brit-

A wartime Vickers Vimy similar to that in which Alcock and Brown flew in 1919 from Newfoundland to Ireland. (Vickers)

ish national defense quickly had to become focused on the air menace, which led to an independent Royal Air Force as an offensive bomber deterrent with a fighter defensive role, as opposed to what had been an offensive role over the Western Front trenches. The Air Ministry came into being on 1 January 1918, and the Secretary of State for Air had a seat in the Cabinet.

The psychological effect of a few bombs raining from the English skies was enormous. Death lists, wounded lying in the streets, and post-war depression ended smug Victorian assumptions about security from foreign threats. The short-lived 1904 Anglo-French relationship fathered by King Edward VII was replaced in the early 1920s by animosities over the Ruhr and the presumption that in the event of hostilities the French would relentlessly bomb London. To counter this, the British created the Home Defence Air Force. At the same time, the ever-present Churchill, by 1920 colonial secretary, agreed in Cairo to replace the army in colonial occupations with the RAF, exercising air control in Iraq and the Northwest Frontier as a new instrument of policy—and a cheaper one—using war-surplus machines. Nevertheless, the threat of war in Europe and the empire necessitated Chief of the Air Staff Air Marshal Sir Hugh Trenchard's policy of maintaining the ring of aircraft and engine manufacturing firms in case of war.

Equally important to national defense were the paradoxical aims of prestige and pennants. There were not only long-distance flights, but also the search for trophies. The former involved route rationalization and layout for Imperial Airways, KLM, and Air France, but also taking Sir Sefton Brancker, the British director of Civil Aviation, to Rangoon and back, for instance, in 1926, and then the Imperial airship *R101* scheme that killed him in 1930 on his way to India. More successful was the pursuit of the high-speed Schneider trophy, which in 1931 was retired permanently to England.

Across the Channel the same pressures and desires were shaping French airpower. There was also an emphasis on "raids"—long-distance flights—to the Far East, and Joseph Vuillemin's exploration of the Sahara. Less happy was the disbanding of the successful massed airpower of the Duval Division of 1918 and Paris's subjugation of the Arme Aéronautique to the army, ironically at the same time that France was trying to make the Little Entente in the Balkans into the Eastern bloc to oppose Germany. But that depended on Italian acquiescence to French reinforcements' crossing Italy to reach southeastern Europe. The marshals of France

Major General Hugh Trenchard, commanding general of the Royal Flying Corps in France and of the Independent Forces RAF in 1918. (Robin Higham Collection)

in the 1920s dominated Paris's policy making in the name of collective security, but their militaristic plans ran afoul of the Locarno peace initiative, the League of Nations, and the strengthening international impulse for disarmament.

In the later 1920s a number of trends undercut the forces striving for a pacific outcome of international relations. The Soviet Union was developing its own aeronautical technology and by 1934 had the world's largest and best air force. At the same time, Japan, negated as a threat to peace for a time by the Washington treaties of 1922 and its own briefly flowering liberal impulses, began to reemerge as a threat in the Far East. The technological revolution in aviation and Hitler's rise to power in Germany, Mussolini's in Italy, and FDR's in the United States made the world a different place economically and psychologically. In 1934 Britain began to rearm under the impression that the bomber would always get through to London—and, the English hoped, also to Berlin. Neville Chamberlain saw the Royal Air Force as the cheapest form of rearmament. But across the Channel in France, ideology and internal frictions following the creation of the Armée de l'Air in 1933 slowed modernization by spurring nationalization of the aircraft industry (though not of the design offices). In addition, by the 1930s statesmen had added to their fear of the "air menace" and their pessimism about defense the idea that flying could also have a powerful propaganda value to aid their causes, the Germans and Italians in particular exploiting this.

The road to Munich—the pact signed by Nazi Germany, France, Britain, and Italy allowing Germany's annexation of Czechoslovakia—in 1938 sprang from oscillations and ideologies in Paris, including the internal questions of a Soviet alliance (as in 1894 with Russia). By 1935 Hitler had produced the Luftwaffe in a surprise move, just as Mussolini in Italy was finding his country had shot its financial and matériel bolt in imperial ambitions in Ethiopia. Yet Britain, at the time, largely held itself aloof from another Continental commitment. Mixed with all this, in the Western Hemisphere, was the German commercial penetration of Colombia, which caused President Franklin Roosevelt to use Pan American World Airways as a diplomatic foil to curb the Nazis and to preserve the Americas under the Monroe Doctrine and Teddy Roosevelt's

The Hawker Nimrod two-seater light bomber with which London threatened Paris at the end of the 1920s. (Robin Higham Collection)

1904 corollary to it, affirming, "We have acted in our own interest as well as in the interest of humanity at large."

In addition to these political changes, the interwar years also saw an increase in aviation range and power, as it became a more effective and wider instrument of policy. In the Middle East the threat of airpower developed early. In 1920 Kemal Ataturk, the new ruler of Turkey, moved the capital from coastal Constantinople (now Istanbul) to inland Ankara to escape the pernicious Royal Navy influence on the sultan and to be away from the threat of the RAF's De Havilland DH-9 bombers. Ataturk was well aware that the British navy had exercised subtle pressure on the ruler of the former Ottoman Empire by simply anchoring a warship in the Bosphorus Strait, which separated the European and Asian sides of Constantinople. Whenever the British ambassador had an audience, the white ensign was clearly visible out the window behind him. Thus it was that Ataturk moved the capital several hundred miles to Ankara. In the Chanak Crisis of 1922, when Turkish troops challenged British and French troops there, the RAF's DH-9 bombers had too little range to be a menace. And thus it was lack of range and endurance as well as the insufficient armament that made airpower at that time an ineffective instrument of policy.

Some eighty years later, aircraft range had increased to where U.S. Air Force B-52s flew nonstop from the continental United States to bomb Iraq. By the 1940s World War II had spread airfields with concrete runways all around the world, mostly to the benefit of the U.S. Army Air Force (USAAF), and aircraft carriers had become mobile force-projection platforms. The arrival of the Douglas DC-3 Dakota had been necessary for the development of economical air services of the 1930s. This twin-engined, all-metal monoplane enabled passenger and air cargo operators to run regular services in most parts of the world, thus expanding the reach and stimulus of air mail.

The interwar years saw a revolution in various aviation technologies. As the range, speed, ceiling, and carrying capacity of aircraft became greater, the aircraft and engine industries started to flourish. It began to appear that aviation could have a global diplomatic and economic significance, and this possibility could be seen in aviation industry investments and employment. American concerns about being drawn into another international conflict were expressed in the Neutrality Acts of the 1930s, which limited other powers' access to U.S. industry. Yet, at the same time, strictly military aviation was also growing in influence. The U.S. Navy, U.S. Army Air Corps (the USAAF's title at the time), Royal Air Force, Luftwaffe, and Soviet air force began to expand in anticipation of a new war. The French did not enlarge their aviation industry, however, and the Italians could not. Practical experience of war was gained by the Soviets, Germans, and Italians in the Civil War in Spain, while the French and the British stayed neutral. The Japanese also gained invaluable aviation experience in their prolonged operations in China, commencing in July 1937, and against the Soviets in border incidents in 1938 and 1939.

All was not steady progress in the new aeronautical age, however,

The fighter defense of Great Britain relied on the Bristol Bulldog from 1929 to 1937. The planes were sent to the Sudan when Mussolini invaded Ethiopia in 1935. (Robin Higham Collection)

as difficulties were caused by residual Victorian mind-sets. Stolid trends from the Great War were entwined in the French hope for a future long war behind the Maginot Line and their failure to face the reality of the new German air and mechanized blitzkrieg. The Munich agreement bought only limited time by delaying the coming war, enough for the RAF to recover some ground lost to the Luftwaffe, but not enough for the Armée de l'Air to do so, as Hitler dismantled the Eastern bloc and its French support.

The air menace did not strike in Douhetian fashion at the outbreak of war in September 1939, except on Warsaw. Douhetism—the philosophy of a swift, early attack on an enemy's most vital centers—did not strike Paris, which was declared "open" (undefended), nor were the Germans able to subjugate London in 1940. The politicians proved to have been gullible in their belief that the bomber could devastate cities and destroy civilian morale, for not until early 1944 was such a weight of bombs available for a consistent urban assault. And the tremendous cost of the air forces was subsequently masked by the extraordinary devastation of the atomic bomb, which itself proved to be a misleading weapon, impossible to utilize. The Cold War started with a few bombs that could only occasionally be readied for war—the automobile batteries had to be changed frequently at Strategic Air Command, which had only six crews competent to install them.

Technology and Change

The arrival of nuclear weapons and the bipolar reality of only two great powers shifted the focus of statesmanship to diplomacy; still, airpower and aviation remained important as instruments of policy in nonnuclear diplomacy. Specific uses of airpower in international relations after 1945 were shaped not only by strategic necessities (the range of the machines) and national interests (as in the Berlin Blockade of 1948), but also by personalities of the leaders. The technological growth of the instrument of airpower has been characterized by advances in speed and range as well as lifting power, but also by the sophistication and growth of airframes and engines and the miniaturization of electronics; all this progress has caused a revolution in the weapon as a whole.

The single-sideband radio is an example of the technological evolution that enabled British Overseas Airway Corporation (BOAC), starting in the 1960s, to communicate from Heathrow (London) to any aircraft in its worldwide fleet and the maintenance and repair organizations (MROs) that enable aircraft to be sent for overhaul to an international array of shops for inspections and rebuilding. Electronics may be supplied by many international firms, though the consolidation of designs and possibilities means that there will be fewer and fewer aircraft manufacturers—and these mostly multinationals.

The ever-widening pool of technical support personnel has changed the ways in which airlines have had to be managed. In the period before World War II, personnel from an airline or from the country supplying arms were assumed to be a necessary part of the deal, at least to get the new aircraft to fly. After World War II there were indigenous persons who had been trained locally to assist, and whose nationalism demanded they take over, perhaps at first only outwardly. This indigenous workforce soon came to combine anticolonialism in the old empires with a patriotic nationalism. Examples of this were the Indian and Pakistani air forces and the African airlines. World War II gave a great fillip to the New Zealand and other Commonwealth airlines as they flew onto the world stage. Japan built its Home Defense Force and Japan Air Lines out of the Cold War need to resurrect itself after 1952. China has expanded its airlines and manufacturing facilities as a major step on the road not only to independence, but also to rivalry with its former American and Japanese opponents. By the first quarter of the twenty-first century, China has felt strong enough to use airpower as a diplomatic instrument, including the formation of close supply relations with the Pakistani Air Force.

A Wider View

An important use of aviation in the Cold War was in the gathering of intelligence on a global scale. But we should also recognize civil and commercial aviation, including the aircraft industry, as well as tactical, strategic, and grand-strategic airpower as instruments of policy. Note that, for instance, in World War II the blitzkrieg and later tactical air forces had been themselves instruments of policy, and the medium bomber and carrier task force had been strategic instruments. Now, however, carrier task forces have become tactical, strategic, and grand strategic, in part because of the technological improvements in aircraft range, speed, fuel burn, and capacity over the 1945 jet fighters by the current air-refuelable long-range bombers. A nation's airpower consists not only of offensive and defensive capabilities and activities but also in the supply of aircraft and spares, and technicians to assemble and maintain them, as well as instructors at all levels. On the civil side, airpower involves the supply of aircraft, notably airliners, but also overflight rights and air traffic control at airports, communications and navigation assistance, and standardization tests and acceptance criteria. The airliner that became the center of all sorts of diplomatic controversies was the Anglo-French Concorde. Agreed on by the governments in London

and Paris in 1962, and widely at that time assumed to be the successor
to the Boeing 707, the Concorde raised new technological challenges.
The public in various countries raised alarms about the aircraft's potential sonic boom, which would be heard and felt 120 to 180 miles
from takeoff as the Concorde passed 1,340 miles per hour. The public's
reactions meant that the supersonic transport (SST) could not reach the
speed of sound until over the Adriatic on the London-Bahrain route.
Landing rights at Heathrow, had to be granted to Syria in exchange for
supersonic passage over that deserted country.

But the biggest fight over the Concorde came in the United States.
Contentions about airports and residential areas beneath takeoff and
approach paths peaked with the pressure to ban Air France's and British Airways' operating the airliner out of New York's John F. Kennedy
Airport; the conflict ultimately had to be settled by resort to the commercial and foreign-policy powers granted to the federal government by
the U.S. Constitution. American citizens had gone to both Congress and
the courts and had delayed the entry into French and British transatlantic
routes from January to 24 May 1976. BOAC had by then become British Airways, which flew to Bahrain, whereas Air France chose to operate
across the South Atlantic to Rio de Janeiro via Dakar. What broke the
logjam in the United States was the secretary of transportation's being
convinced that foreign commerce was reserved by the Constitution to
the federal government.

Airpower also extends into the fiscal area by way of foreign aid,
import-export arrangements, and resources with which to finance these.
In addition, airpower is about fuel, taxes, facilities, and pipelines, as
well as fuel farms and refueling stations. All these are intimately connected to domestic and foreign policy, prejudices, personalities, and
politics. The use of airpower as an instrument of policy must be seen as
the linking of technology, grand-strategic policy, and tactics, whether
civil or military. Though diplomacy generally is intended to achieve
objectives without fighting, as Stephen J. Harris has shown in *Why Air
Forces Fail: The Anatomy of Defeat* (revised edition, 2013), the British
deterrent policy during appeasement in the later 1930s was not only
a diplomatic failure but also a tactical one, as evidenced by the RAF

bombing raid routed by the Luftwaffe over the Heligoland Bight in December 1939. It took the Royal Air Force until 1944 to rise, phoenixlike, from that failure and become an effective bomber force to help bring Germany to its knees.

Parameters of Airpower to 1945

Early Activity and Barriers

Airpower became an instrument of policy, despite its humble beginnings, because of a number of economic and technological developments. Though lighter-than-air craft had been employed in wartime intermittently since the late eighteenth century, it was not until the advent of powered flight in 1903 that airpower became a factor in policy. Even before World War I, Italian airplanes had been used in the campaign in Libya against the Ottoman Empire in 1911, and Greek aircraft fought in the Balkan Wars in the following years. Admittedly, these were fewer than ten flimsy infant machines, each carrying one or two airmen, sent mainly to gather intelligence from the other side

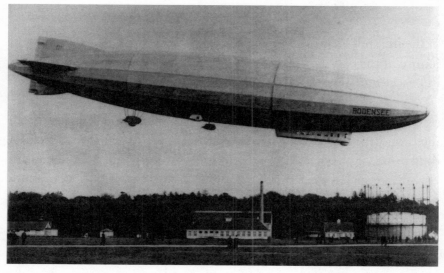

The *Bodensee* was a local tourist zeppelin at Potsdam in 1912, ridden on one occasion by Admiral Sir John Jellicoe. (Robin Higham Collection)

The British R-34, a copy of the Zeppelin L-33, shown here landing on Long Island after its 1919 transatlantic flight. (Robin Higham Collection)

of the hill, but they marked the emergence of airpower as a permanent fixture in the conduct of war. Soon it became an instrument of policy in peacetime as well.

As the Chinese kites and Alexander's mountain climbers demonstrated, airpower has always had both psychological and technical dimensions, the former long overshadowing the latter. The psychological dimension of airpower is related to "rumor, fear, and the madness of crowds." Fear has been a political double-edged sword affecting both perpetrators and victims. The paradox arises from the belief among airmen, especially bomber types, that civilian and even military morale will crack when confronted by unrealistic (until the atomic bomb) concepts of the destruction that can be wrought. And in the early twentieth century the potential victims' beliefs in doomsday were reinforced by the reluctance of governments to discuss and implement countermeasures to attacks from the heavens, a hesitancy abetted by their general ignorance of aviation matters. Thus, from the zeppelin and Gotha raids on London during 1915–1918 there emerged the unbridled anxiety about what was labeled the "air menace," which in turn spawned the deterrent mission of the Royal Air Force's Home Defence Air Force, two-thirds of which was composed of bombers capable of merely a bird-droppings effect on Paris. But by the end of World War I engine and airframe development had enabled bombers to join the great zeppelins in bombing London, with great psychological and fiscal effect. The wartime experience profoundly influenced the course of airpower evolution, for it generated much greater attention to the development of interceptors as well as raiders, which resulted in ever-mounting range, speed, and endurance in the air arm. This made both the reality and the propaganda threat of the airplane of increasing importance from the Treaty of Versailles in 1919 onward.

For British airmen in the 1920s the anticipated target was the former ally's capital; meanwhile, French politicians were in a funk, and for them the "air menace" remained a threat into 1940. But the RAF's near impotence at Douhetist bombing was due to the scrapping of the planned long-range heavy bomber, the Handley-Page V-1500; this forced a reliance on single-engined biplane bombers of the De Havilland DH-4/DH-9 type, which could carry only 240 pounds of bombs to Paris and then return. The offensive was always presumed to get through, and the machine's defensive power of one or two machine guns was considered sufficient. Indeed, RAF maneuvers in the early 1930s apparently proved the validity of these ideas, although the defensive concepts used in 1918 had shown the opposite when employed in maneuvers in 1927. Defending a nation geographically isolated from the other great powers, the U.S. Army Air Corps gradually developed a theory of international grand-strategic bombing that was a lesson in the need to link theory, policy, and means to achieve the end desired. Transatlantic round-trip range with reserves and a significant bomb load, however, was beyond the capacity of the practical designers before and even during World War II.

In the various national colonies between the wars, the threat of airpower—its use as an instrument of policy—was widely hailed as successful against native tribes without antiaircraft (AA) defenses. But, in fact, in Iraq and the Afghanistan–Northwest Frontier areas, stone and mud huts proved resistant to the hundred-pound bombs in use in interwar British attacks, and the residents often decamped to the hillsides to watch the show. Political officers on the ground provided the punch of an added threat that usually settled matters for a while. In Haiti and Nicaragua in the 1930s, the U.S. Marine Corps integrated airpower and ground forces to impose a pacification policy. The French in the 1920s emphasized the Arme Aéronautique in Syria to impress on rebels in their mandate the need to behave—but, again, in conjunction with the army.

Gradually, as airmen and aircraft constructors developed bigger and better bombers of greater range and payload, the radius of action (40 percent of still-air range) extended the reach of the threatening arm. Still, that depended on the imagination of the specifications writers; on the artistry of designers, engine makers, and constructors to achieve those requirements; and on a service determination to enable the aircrew and airplanes to do their job. For example, the instrument of policy was useless if it could not find the target, even assuming one that had been carefully selected within a grand-strategic framework, that the bomb aimer could hit it, and that the bomb would deliver a sufficiently damaging blow. With so many intertwined factors determining its design and performance capabilities, a great many pieces have to be fitted together before a bomber can take off for a sortie against the enemy.

The converse is that enemy defenses have to be known and understood. Here the weakness is often at home. The RAF by the 1930s had developed strategies and policies about bombers penetrating Germany without looking at what its own Air Defence of Great Britain (ADGB—after 1936 Fighter Command) was doing. As it turned out, the Luftwaffe was not able to sustain a 90-mile penetration to London, and the RAF faced a 900-mile flight to Berlin, which could not be accomplished in daylight with the acceptable loss rate of less than 5 percent.

Long-distance record breaking was part of the propaganda of airpower, especially in the 1920s. Here a French crew bids farewell before takeoff on a flight to East Asia in a Breguet 19. (SHAA 85-1507)

Toward the end of the interwar years, the Bristol Bombay served as a troop transport and bomber in the Middle East. (Robin Higham Collection)

Decisions and Developments

As aviation much depended on money, in the 1918–1924 period foreign policy was exercised through subsidies. There was intense competition on those airliner routes from London to the Continent, especially on that to Paris; but the British could not compete in fares with the subsidized French establishments. Thus, with reluctance, because Winston Churchill as air minister had declared that aviation had to fly by itself, the British paid temporary subsidies in order to compete. Finally, in 1923 the Hambling Committee recommended £1 million over ten years to subsidize a company to fly both European and imperial routes. Accordingly, Imperial Airways was chartered in 1924 as "the chosen instrument" of British aviation policy, the four original companies being folded into it. Other nations followed with their chosen instruments: Air France, Lufthansa, Pan American, and Aeroflot.

Paralleling this development was Great Britain's Air Navigation Act

Part of statesmanship was selling abroad. Here a two-seater Hawker is seen in Swiss markings, circa 1935. (Robin Higham Collection)

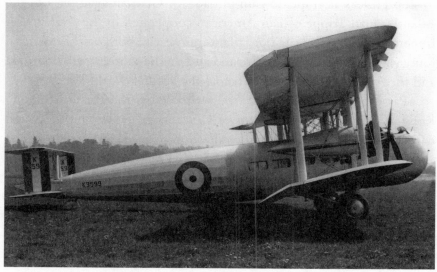

A problem for the disarmament conference at Geneva in 1932–1934 was the capability of converting transports to bombers. Shown is a British Vickers Vimy transport, a type that could be converted. (Vickers)

of 1919, which became the model for air development in other countries, as well as the guide for the growth of international air routes and the bilateral treaties that have ever since governed air traffic between nations, including overflight rules. At the same time, the International Air Traffic Association (IATA) was created as a European business clearinghouse. These two entities were basically European until 1944, when at Chicago the International Civil Aviation Organization (ICAO) was established to recognize the globalization of air transport by the development of airliners with intercontinental range. Within a decade, these airliners would be able to cross the Atlantic nonstop, and the Pacific in three leaps. This meant that Qantas, from Australia, could fly to England not only by the route opened in 1934 via the Middle East, hopping almost all the way from one British territory to another, but also via a new route across North America.

During the Franklin Roosevelt presidency, Pan American was the chosen instrument of international presence for American aviation. In Latin America the airline followed the Teddy Roosevelt doctrine of walking softly but carrying a big stick, as in the intervention in Colombia to stop Hitler's attempts to gain inroads for German aviation. On the Atlantic, Juan Trippe of Pan American cooperated in the rivalry with Imperial Airways to create transatlantic air service both on the northern route via Newfoundland and Ireland and on the southern via Bermuda and the Azores to Portugal just before the Second World War.

Pan American also pushed westward across the Pacific to Hong Kong as part of that third focus of U.S. foreign policy: most favored nation status. The Hong Kong connection opened the gates to China and Japan, while also connecting to Imperial Airways, enabling around-the-world service to begin tentatively.

When war came, after 1941, Pan American sent airfield and staging-post experts to create the landplane routes across the South Atlantic and Africa to India, and from the West Coast to Australia. Though these routes were immediately part of wartime grand strategy, the potential postwar benefits were not lost on Trippe and the other Pan American executives.

The limitations of airpower and the constraints on statesmen in

Air refueling allowed fighters to stretch their endurance from fifty minutes to several hours. Using the probe-and-drogue system, English Electric Lightnings fill up from a Handley Page Victor, circa 1982. (Crown copyright P.R.B: 30574)

employing it were well demonstrated in the British aid to Greece in 1941. In addition to all the difficulties of working with an Allied government that spoke a different language and whose equipment was incompatible, there was the whole question of the adequacy of the supply of matériel and trained personnel, and their maintenance and sustenance. Means did not match ends, and consumption and wastage went beyond the capacity of the supply system. A further constraint was the lack of knowledge of the system by statesmen and their civil servant advisers. In the end, however, it was a matter of balancing ends and means.

During the war the radar-based Gee system of navigation was supplemented by the two-thousand-mile Loran system, which enabled airliners to fly over large bodies of water and make safe, accurate landfalls. And wartime air-traffic control, pioneered in the United States and installed of necessity in RAF Bomber Command in Britain, together with radar sector control, enabled regulation of civilian air traffic. Another diplomatic outcome was the adoption from 1919 on, but particularly from World War II and the Chicago Convention, of English as the language of international aviation, replacing French.

As World War II drew to an end in 1945, bilateral rights became a concern of foreign policy as airlines increased their options. Pan American World Airways, as we have seen, already had established routes into Latin America, Europe, and Asia. The United States, which had developed a large fleet of ocean- and continent-crossing four-engined landplane transports, was also positioned to dominate the sale of such aircraft, including the Douglas DC-4 Skymaster and the Lockheed 049 Constellation. Moreover, as part of the postwar efforts to help Europe recover, the United States made it easy for other countries to acquire these American-built, transoceanic machines. Also, during the war, the U.S. Army had built air bases around the world, which were subsequently donated to the countries in which they existed, but on the condition that they could be used by American aircraft as refueling stops.

Parameters of Airpower since 1945

The Influence of Air Policy and Diplomacy

The technological revolution and World War II altered the playing field of airpower and the aviation industry. Oceans no longer were insuperable barriers that had to be crossed via multiple staging posts, for the new four-engined landplanes enabled these stepping stones gradually to be eliminated. The whole of commercial long-distance aviation was dominated by Boeing, Douglas, and Lockheed until the 1970s and 1980s, when economic realities eliminated first Lockheed and its L-1011 TriStar wide-body, and Douglas (later McDonnell Douglas) and its DC-8 four-engined jet liner and tri-engined DC-10; Boeing, with the 707 large and the 747 jumbo wide-body jets, dominated until challenged by the European Airbus consortium in the 1980s.

The influence of international relations—diplomacy by another name—on designs is epitomized by the Boeing 747SP in the late 1960s. This special performance aircraft was developed to meet the need of apartheid-era South African Airways for a machine that could fly from

The Lockheed C-5A could carry 100,000 pounds of cargo nonstop for 6,225 statute miles at more than five hundred miles per hour, making its humanitarian and military reach effective. (Lockheed RL 8195-2)

Johannesburg to London without a refueling stop in native-ruled black Africa on a "thin" route—that is, one with a low passenger load. The 747SP was also sold to the Iranians to allow them to obtain parts from the United States without the danger of the aircraft's being embargoed in a European airport. At that same time, political pressure, and economic and technical efficiency, enabled maintenance to be withdrawn to airline headquarters cities, and local traffic staff to be hired abroad, a trend accelerated in the 1960s by anticolonialism.

The public's ideological revulsion to war and the military's own intense emphasis on hardware have tended to conceal the importance and relevance of statesmanship backed by armed forces. But the nuclear standoff of the Cold War from 1949 to 1991 required that diplomacy and statecraft be used instead of military force. The nuclear standoff and diplomacy and statecraft also meant—as the Korean and Vietnam wars showed the United States, the Arab-Israeli conflicts showed everyone, and struggles in the Middle East and Afghanistan confirmed—that tactical aviation and logistics would be the practical instruments of policy, especially tactical aircraft rather than bombers. The new machine also emphasized that intelligence would be more critical than ever, whether gathered on the ground, by unmanned PRU aircraft, or by satellites.

The negative side of using airpower as an instrument of policy and a diplomatic tool, however, was demonstrated in Vietnam. There President Lyndon Johnson gradually increased the U.S. presence from 1965 to 1968, but without decisive results. Subsequently, it was President Nixon who believed that an excruciating blow on Hanoi would do the trick, and, following the Linebacker I and II air campaigns in 1972, North Vietnam finally returned to the peace table in Paris. But by 1975 the North had taken over all of Vietnam.

Nevertheless, commercial aviation has been and remains a notable force for the promotion of peace by breaking down barriers and fostering direct and individual communications in aviation's common language of English. But the industry also promotes international accord through commercial pressure, forcing states to upgrade their facilities. These have been subtle diplomatic forces, as have been regulatory practices for the certification of both personnel and machines: accident investigation and safety standards as well have become international. In all these cases, the Federal Aviation Administration as it now is in the United States and the Air Registration Board in Britain—and most recently the Joint Aviation Authority in the new European community—have set global standards in part because they have had the experience, standards, and procedures to do so with international effect. Though the media have tended to focus on the military side, especially during the Cold War, civil aviation has been more influential. Some airlines actually outnumber their military counterparts in numbers of machines and personnel.

The Effect of Technology and Diplomacy

The very rapid growth of air transport (14 percent per annum) and of technical knowledge saw the size of airliners grow from the DC-3 of under 30,000 pounds in 1936 to the Boeing 747-100 of 550,000 pounds of 1968. The range increased from under 1,000 miles to well over 5,000. Moreover, countries along the newer routes had to build new airfields or be bypassed. The DC-3 still operated from grass airfields and remained in airline service in 2000. Of significance in the burgeoning aviation changes have been the economic consequences of the costs of the new jet engines and airframes, which have caused airlines and their financial backers to rethink their orders, schedules, flight plans, and investments. The classic example was Pan American, whose order for twenty-five jumbo 747s was a contributing factor to its road to bankruptcy. To provide funds needed, the United States already had lent foreign companies money from the Export-Import Bank so that they could buy American. When BOAC needed the final 10 percent tranche to be from a foreign source for its Boeings, it borrowed from the Bank of Nova Scotia, since Her Majesty's Treasury would not permit the state's own airline to use pounds sterling.

The effect of technology and diplomacy became more visible again after 1958, as the jet age started, and noise and then later emissions became international concerns. These were also linked not only to bilateral agreements, but to landing slots at busy airports. Both commercial necessity and diplomatic advantage came into play. By the 1960s the concept of a single national chosen aviation instrument had given way to the recognition of several national carriers and a juggling of who would be eligible to use which gateways in each country. Linked to these issues and to the increasing ranges of aircraft, as well as to decolonization, has been the so-called fifth freedom, the cabotage right of a carrier of one nation to pick up passengers or freight in a second or third country and fly them to another destination in the same state or even to a fourth nation. An example of the linkages is the 1978 deregulation of the airlines in the United States, which sent ripples around the world and precipitated mergers, stock swaps, and bankruptcies that have raised questions (especially in the United States and the United Kingdom) about domination of national enterprises by foreigners. The sprawling influence of the aviation industry is not always so obvious, however, as much of aeronautical diplomatic activity is really made public only in the technical and professional press and in reports in connection with the annual fare-setting conference of the IATA.

International aspects of domestic political considerations can be cited from the history of BOAC in the 1950s and early 1960s. The corporation was given directives by the British government to run services to certain destinations, notably South America and Kuwait. In the later 1960s the allocation of certain BOAC routes to its rival, British Caledonian, enabled the latter to survive while still keeping a British presence in South America. Subsequently, the 1962–1976 advent of the supersonic civil transport, the Concorde passenger service, led to both positive and negative aviation diplomacy.

Amid all this aviation evolution, military airpower continued to be a predominant instrument of policy. Beginning in the early days of the Cold War, the surreptitious U.S. balloon reconnaissance of the USSR, followed by the Lockheed U-2 spy/reconnaissance flights and finally by satellites, provided intelligence on which to base foreign policy. The existence of overflights was highlighted in the May 1960 U-2 incident, which caused both the unusual Eisenhower admission of the activity and Khrushchev's cancellation of the coming Paris summit.

Statesmen and Airpower

In 1978, when former President Gerald Ford was conducting my military history seminar, he was asked if, when he had ordered an aircraft carrier to the American merchant ship's rescue in the SS *Mayaguez* incident of 1975, it was because he had been a naval officer. He thought for a moment, then acknowledged he guessed that was correct. Insights into the minds and actions of the statesmen who did or did not employ airpower may be gleaned by dipping into the biographies and memoirs of such practitioners; Henry Kissinger is but one example. Politicians, like other people, tend to rely on instincts acquired in life or that have impressed them in others. It can be argued that both Franklin D. Roosevelt and Winston Churchill, as former naval persons, knew and understood the use of sea power—and by World War II that included

The international supply of aircraft is one aspect of air diplomacy. The RAF acquired McDonnell Douglas F-4 Phantom IIs for the European strike role. (McDonnell Douglas 12-423-3)

naval aviation from carriers. But both understood in a political way the three-dimensional nature of modern war and its substantial industrial lead times.

Churchill had been a pilot in 1912, and it can be presumed that he realized clearly that airpower could be produced quickly and applied over greater distances more rapidly than could land power. Hitler and Mussolini, and Stalin to a lesser extent, were partly aviation-minded. Hitler used aircraft for political campaigning and used the threat of the new Luftwaffe first to help break the restrictions of Versailles and then to press Germany's neighbors with its claims to parity and power. Mussolini employed the Regia Aeronautica to impress the world in the 1930s and to humiliate the Royal Navy in 1936 over Ethiopia; he also used it alongside Germany's Condor Legion in Spain to aid Franco.

Stalin used the Red air force in Spain, but he withdrew his contribution when the Condor Legion received the superior early Me-109 fighters. Concurrently, in May 1939, the Red air force met the Japanese army over Khalkin Gol/Nomonhan in a border incident that escalated into a summerlong battle that destroyed an entire Japanese division. The Soviets, however, wrapped up in the war against Hitler from June 1941 on, did not take on the Japanese again until August 1945, after Germany had surrendered.

In the post-1945 world dictators in the Middle East and South Asia took a considerable interest, of necessity, in airpower. The shah of Iran prided himself on being a Grumman F-14 Tomcat pilot, and he equipped the Iranian air force with modern aircraft, making his country a threat across the Persian Gulf. In Iraq, Saddam Hussein modernized both his air force and his flak with Soviet assistance and brandished the threat, but he succeeded merely in fighting a draining but inconsequential war with Iran (1979–1988) and then taking little Kuwait, only to relinquish it in the disastrous Gulf War of 1990–1991. The Iraqi air force proved to be a chimera. Ironically, in 1991 most of it fled to Iran, as its officers did not trust or were not trusted by Saddam. His airpower weakness had been exposed in 1981 when the Israeli air force in a predawn deterrent strike destroyed his nuclear reactor at Osirak.

Anthony Eden, the much-experienced British foreign secretary, had risen to be prime minister by 1956. He disliked dictators, and that led to the 1956 Suez intervention to reopen the canal and face down the Egyptian autocrat General Gamal Abdul Nasser. The chosen instrument was an Anglo-French naval aviation force supported by long-range bombers from Malta, and by the Israeli seizure of the Sinai peninsula. Such a preemptive act required secrecy and speed. It failed in 1956, however, because neither was available, owing to indecision at the top in London and Paris and to American pressure to desist because of the Cold War. This primarily naval and air operation was carrying out a diplomatic threat, but although the mid-twentieth-century carriers had considerable reach, they also were vulnerable.

Air Vice Marshal Hosni Mubarak, president of Egypt, after yet another Egyptian air force defeat, recognized the need to create a new,

The Anglo-French Sepecat Jaguar of the 1970s was notable for its lethality, in contrast to the Hawkers of the 1930s. (BAC AW 38821)

winning weapon in his nation. He chose to rebuild the air force because of the limited manpower pool available in Egypt, and there were enough well-educated men to form pilot cadres as well as men and women for the ground-support forces. Mubarak rebuilt, with U.S. help, an instrument of policy that proved able to hold its own against the Israelis and thus provided an effective shield against further Israeli aggression from the Sinai.

All these examples bespeak not only the potential uses of airpower but the pressing need for today's statesmen to come to grips with its many facets and dimensions. If properly understood and applied, airpower can be a nation's salvation on the international stage. If mishandled, whether by a great power or a small and emergent state, it can spell doom for national policy.

The Middle East Fishbowl

The modern Near East, to use an old term that covers Libya to Pakistan, swims with examples of airpower used as an instrument of policy. At roughly the same time in the post–World War II world, India and Pakistan were created out of the old British Raj, Iranian nationalism surfaced, Israel carved a home out of the Arab area, Egypt rose as a sovereign state under the new military dictators, and Libya became independent. Colonial rivalries were converted into arms sales contests, the results varying depending in part on domestic policies of the supplying nations. So, for instance, France and Britain supplied both Arab and Israeli forces through the 1956 war, at which point their approaches diverged. The Soviets then came in, as the sides played off each other. The advantage for both arms suppliers and the benevolent air forces was that they gained experience by proxy. By 1973, however, the Soviet welcome in Egypt had worn thin, as their technology and tactics as well as mental rigidity convinced the Egyptians that Arabs could do better with the West. This revolutionary change allowed the Egyptian air force

Controlling the skies and enjoying tactical superiority, the current British Hawk can also be used as a two-seat trainer, especially in Middle East air forces. (BAC 834224)

to obtain parity with the Israelis and brought some peace in that part of the Middle East. The Soviets bolstered Iraq until the 1990–1991 Gulf War showed that the entire approach was bankrupt, just as the USSR itself collapsed.

At the eastern end of the Near East, both north and south of the old Northwest Frontier, the links between statesmanship and airpower were amply demonstrated. Soviet intervention in the Afghan civil war (1979–1988) proved to be a failure, not only mostly because of the former's own clumsy tactics, but also in part because the West supplied arms to the Afghans through its proxy in Pakistan. And the latter was supplied with U.S. F-16s to counter Soviet intrusions into its air space. An unintended consequence of this diplomatic effort was the U.S. Congress's passing the Pressler Amendment, which stopped aid to foreign nuclear powers after India and Pakistan each indicated they had such weapons. Thus, the Pakistanis set up their own parts supply organization.

In all the Near Eastern cases, the situations have been complex. Pakistan faces the larger India, and they both have been and continue

A French-owned Douglas DC-4 enabled post-1945 transatlantic air service and face-to-face meetings among statesmen. (SHAA 382-2716)

to be in conflict over Kashmir. But Hindu India does not wish to have to occupy Muslim Pakistan. At the same time Pakistan still faces tribal unrest in its northwest and the problem of an unstable neighboring Afghanistan. To solve its arms supply dilemma, Pakistan has linked with Chinese aircraft manufacturers, whereas India has bought Soviet products. Both opponents in Southwest Asia still have strong links to their British colonial heritage as well as volatile domestic politics, none of which makes U.S., British, and Russian—as well as Chinese—foreign policy making easier.

In the complexities of the Middle East, the various countries built their own air forces for possible use against colonial and neighboring enemies. The result was a polyglot of bought and donated aircraft types for various purposes, from suppression of rebels and guerrillas to supersonic air defense. In the Middle East airpower has been and continues to be used in numerous ways as an instrument of foreign and domestic policy.

The Present and the Future

An important question for future statesmen to ponder is: Who will have aircraft carriers in, say, 2020? If the answer is no one, then what will replace them, or will the world need only a different sort of policeman?

On the other hand, if aircraft carriers are to remain, how often will they have to be overhauled and rebuilt and their electronic suites replaced entirely? Will their weapons be manned or unmanned?

To judge by the history of the latter twentieth century, statesmen have not done a particularly brilliant or cost-effective grand-strategic job of defense management. Procurement reform has been opposed or diluted by political expediency, vested interests, or unstable funding. By 2010 the British Ministry of Defence was finally working out a ten-year initiative operating agreement with the Treasury that had still to encompass the whole, not just the parts. But how the envisaged deficit will be handled and how that will affect weapons programs was still not clear. Proposed solutions include defense reviews in each Parliament and an executive committee of the Defence Board to be accountable for the equipment program, thus linking short-term budgets to long-term programs, and to obviate the ministerial delays, which cost an average of 0.5 percent per annum—a figure the Ministry of Defence had no rational methodology to counter.

On 21 March 2011 President Barack Obama—after days of what his opponents called hesitation and his supporters termed prudence—on 21 March 2011 committed U.S. airpower to a humanitarian duty to protect the rebels from Colonel Muammar Gaddafi's dictatorial forces, but not to intervene in Libya, as it had in Iraq and Afghanistan. Moreover, on 24 March U.S. planes would be under NATO command, as they had been in Kosovo. As America entered April 2011, it was not clear what the outcome, including the exit strategy, would be. In a return to the roots of U.S. foreign policy, and as in the Iraq case, however, the use of transatlantic airpower was aimed to support rebels and bring down a dictator. In the meantime, both carrier-based U.S. Navy and land-based U.S. Air Force planes and missiles were engaged.

Yet almost immediately President Obama withdrew U.S. aircraft, as belatedly it was discovered that Libya had Russian SA-24 "Grinch" antiaircraft missiles, particularly effective against low-flying machines. Jam-resistant, these missiles had apparently been overlooked by intelligence, harking back to Cold War days when the Soviet jets were thought to be unsophisticated.

On 2 May 2011 U.S. airpower was again called on as U.S. Navy SEALs successfully demonstrated its stiletto tactical use by landing helicopters inside the world terrorist Osama bin Laden's covert compound at Abbottabad, Pakistan. The SEALs avenged bin Laden's 11 September 2001 use of airliners in destroying the Twin Towers of the World Trade Center in New York City, killing nearly three thousand, and the attack on the Pentagon, as well as the nearly simultaneous downing of an aircraft in a Pennsylvania field when an intended attack on the White House went awry.

Bin Laden was killed on 2 May by the SEALs and his body deposited in the Indian Ocean to avoid his body's being buried in a grave that could become a religious shrine. The Abbottabad compound, however, remained intact as a shrine. Whether the embarrassment of the secretive strike sours Pakistani–U.S. relations in the Afghan War remains to be seen. What is certain is that airpower, again, can be a valued tactical tool.

Who was Britain's most effective wartime prime minister or America's best wartime president? What was the real reason behind the successes of Alexander the Great, Tokugawa Ieyasu, George Washington, and Otto von Bismarck: military skill, political skill, or perhaps the subtlest skill of all—the adroit application of military force? The leaders of the past had to understand the complexities—military, diplomatic, psychological—of great armies and of sea power. But in the last century those elements have been superseded by a more far-reaching and powerful military force. The stakes of international conflict are higher, not only for warring belligerent nations, but for all humanity. Crucial to national, and perhaps global, survival and prosperity is the relationship between statesmen and airpower.

Further Reading

The use of airpower against opponents with limited, little, or no airpower is not a new phenomenon. The Italians attacked the Ottoman Empire in Libya in 1911. The British pursued the Mad Mullah in Somalia circa 1919. And the French used aircraft against Abd el-Krim in Morocco in the interwar years, while the British patrolled Iraq and the Northwest Frontier of India. Indeed, earlier, in 1916, the United States had invaded Mexico and later employed aircraft against guerrillas in Central America.

See James S. Corum and Wray R. Johnson, *Air Power in Small Wars: Fighting Insurgents and Terrorists* (Lawrence: University Press of Kansas, 2003); David E. Omissi, *Air Power and Colonial Control: The Royal Air Force, 1919–1939* (Manchester, U.K.: Manchester University Press, 1990); Mark Clodfelter, *The Limits of Air Power: The American Bombing of North Vietnam* (New York: Free Press, 1989); Laurence S. Kuter, *The Great Gamble: The Boeing 747* (Tuscaloosa: University of Alabama Press, 1973); Mario Del Pero, *The Eccentric Realist: Henry Kissinger and the Shaping of American Foreign Policy* (Ithaca: Cornell University Press, 2009); Brian Cull et al., *Wings over Suez* (London: Grub Street, 2006); Robin Higham, introduction to Robin Higham, ed., *Intervention or Abstention—The Dilemma of U.S. Foreign Policy* (Lexington: University Press of Kentucky, 1975); Donald J. Mrozek, "Surrogate Intervention: Alliances and Air Power in the Vietnam War," in Higham, *Intervention or Abstention*, 184–201; Sir Philip Goodhart, *A Stab in the Front: The Suez Conflict—1956* (Windsor, U.K.: Wilton 65, 2006); Sir James

Cable, *Gunboat Diplomacy: Political Applications of Limited Naval Forces* (New York: Praeger, 1971); Peter Cappelli, ed., *Airline Labor Relations in the Global Era: The New Frontier* (Ithaca: Cornell University Press, 1995), a perspective not directly related to the diplomacy of air commerce; Carlo d'Este, *Warlord: A Life of Winston Churchill at War, 1874–1945* (New York: Harper, 2008); Comité de Bibliographie de la Commission International d'Histoire Militaire, *Bibliographie Internationale d'Histoire Militaire,* 33 vols. to 2012; Kenneth Owen, *Concorde and the Americans: International Politics of the Supersonic Transport* (Shrewsbury, U.K.: Airlife, 1997); Arthur Pearcy Jr., *The Dakota: A History of the Douglas Dakota in RAF and RCAF Service* (London: Ian Allan, 1972); Antony Preston and John Major, *Send a Gunboat: The Victorian Navy and Supremacy at Sea, 1854–1904* (London: Longmans, Green, 1967; rev. 2007), and the journal *Foreign Affairs,* 1922–. On Vice Admiral Sir Herbert Richmond, RN, see Barry D. Hunt, *Sailor-Scholar: Admiral Sir Herbert Richmond, 1871–1946* (Waterloo, Ont.: Wilfrid Laurier University Press, 1982).

See also *SSQ: Strategic Studies Quarterly* (2006–); and *Aviation Week,* 18 January 2010, 32–33.

1

States and Strategic Airpower

Continuity and Change, 1906–1939

John H. Morrow Jr.

> No power on earth can protect the man in the street from being bombed. Whatever people may tell him, the bomber will always get through.
>
> —Stanley Baldwin, lord president of the Council,
> before the House of Commons, 10 November 1932

Prime Minister Stanley Baldwin's dire prediction of the future inevitability of the bomber's ability to penetrate aerial defenses epitomized the fears of enemy aerial attacks on capital cities and civilian populations during the years between the world wars. Yet this quote merits contextualization, and not merely within the interwar years, but one that encompasses the history of strategic bombing and political attitudes toward aerial bombardment since the origins of aviation.

Such examination reveals a much more complex and nuanced reception of, as well as certain recurring themes toward, the threat of strategic bombing on the part of European statesmen and soldiers. Studies of the aerial threat also invariably focus on Great Britain, because flight portended an avenue of assault on the island kingdom until then immune to invasion for centuries.

Initial British responses to flight as early as 1906 recognized, in the words of the press magnate Alfred Harmsworth, Lord Northcliffe, that "England was no longer an island" and prompted fears of "aerial chariots of a foe descending upon England."[1] H. G. Wells's fictional account of 1907, *The War in the Air*, portrayed the ultimate destruction of civilization by gigantic airships and airplanes in a future aerial conflict. The flight of the German rigid airship, or zeppelin, in 1908 elicited speculations from Northcliffe's paper, the *Daily Mail*, about Germany's future use of airships to invade England.

International jurists discussed air warfare at peace conferences at The Hague in 1899 and 1907. In 1899 French, German, and Russian representatives would not foreclose the use of new weapons in warfare and imposed a five-year prohibition against bombing undefended towns and cities. In 1907 the conferees agreed only not to bomb undefended towns and villages. Though British aerial jurists would still lament the very existence of flying machines four years later—a reflection of their new fear of aerial invasion—it was clear that the closer flying machines drew to becoming a useful weapon, the closer international jurists edged to acknowledging their legitimacy as weapons.

In 1908 the achievements of zeppelins and airplanes in Germany and France, respectively, launched a popular clamor for aviation, particularly military aviation. In France aviation became a "universal preoccupation" and aviators, popular heroes. National aviation leagues, spurred by a burgeoning aviation press, formed in both countries to promote military aviation, as farsighted civilians envisaged the economic and military potential of aviation. In 1908 the public actively intervened to promote the zeppelin to the Prussian War Ministry, an indication that governments would have to contend with public opinion in their decisions concerning military aviation. By the end of 1908 flight was being drawn into the web of increasingly bellicose popular attitudes encouraging militarization.

By 1909, as Northcliffe's press discussed how air raids could assist a foreign invasion force, the press had launched a campaign for aviation and the Aerial League of the British Empire was emphasizing British aerial unpreparedness. An "airship scare" spread, as speeches and editorials published in the *Times* and aviation press declared London, the nerve center of government, defenseless and open to aerial attack. R. P. Hearne's book *Aerial Warfare* bleated that everything was at the mercy of the zeppelin, whose raids would destroy morale and disable military forces. A few members of Parliament responded to these cries by forming the Parliamentary Aerial Defence Committee to press for military aviation.

Although British politicians lived in fear of an aerial attack on England, the government was the first to understand the implications of the airplane for colonial domination and white imperial supremacy. In 1910 the Committee of Imperial Defence directed the War Office to consider the use of the airplane "in war against uncivilized countries such as the Sudan, Somaliland, and the Northwest Frontier of India." Charles Grey, editor of *The Aeroplane*, suggested in 1913 the use of the airplane "for impressing European superiority on the enormous native population." In March 1914 Winston Churchill endorsed a possible joint project of the Colonial Office and the Royal Navy whereby the white population would employ aircraft to control and threaten the empire's native populations in the face of the "distinct possibility" of black uprisings.[2]

As air arms developed and the performance of both airships and airplanes improved, but not yet sufficiently to pose a realistic threat of strategic air attack, military and civilian expectations ran far ahead of reality. In Germany Chief of the General Staff Helmuth von Moltke informed the War Ministry on 24 December 1912 that "in the newest Z-ships we possess a weapon that is far superior to all similar ones of our opponents and that cannot be imitated in the foreseeable future if we work energetically to perfect it. Its speediest development as a weapon is required to enable us at the beginning of a war to strike a first and telling blow whose practical and moral effect could be quite extraordinary."[3] German aviation journals echoed such sentiments in articles in 1913 that expected pinpoint and unstoppable zeppelin attacks on enemy targets in the dark of night. Prospects of "aerial blackmail" of neighboring powers loomed, but, ironically, zeppelins would perform only one bombing trial before the war.

Only in Italy, where the military aviation industry lagged behind those of the major powers, did the little-known Major Giulio Douhet, commander of the Italian airplane battalion and a staunch advocate of aviation in the Italian press, support the establishment of the aircraft factory of a young friend, the aircraft designer Gianni Caproni, who was convinced of the importance of a fleet of multi-engine bombers for tactical and strategic purposes. War thus began in 1914 as soldiers and politicians dreamed of and feared strategic aerial attacks but possessed no means to execute their grandiose visions.

As early as 2 August 1914, French Minister of War Paul Painlevé and two industrialists, the Michelin brothers, desired to bomb Essen, the German center of industry and home of the Krupp munitions works. Although the French air service had no airplanes capable of the mission, the French high command was planning the strategic bombardment of German industrial centers by November.

German parliamentary deputies, reflecting sentiments in military, diplomatic, and industrial circles, were equally sanguine about "breaking British resistance" through air warfare. The German minister in Stockholm, Franz von Reichenau, hoped "with all his heart" that "Germany would send airships and aircraft cruising regularly over England dropping bombs" until "the vulgar huckster souls" of those "cowardly assassins" would forget "even how to do sums." The industrialist Walther Rathenau advocated "systematically working on the nerves of the English towns through an overwhelming air force."[4] In England, however, "zeppelinmania" reigned, as rumors of zeppelin raids, stories of new types of zeppelins, a report of a zeppelin flying on the surface of the North Sea—which turned out to be a dead whale—abounded, prompting the fad of London insurance agents' selling bomb insurance. In contrast to these rabid aims and morbid fears, zeppelins proved to be perfect targets for antiaircraft gunners on all but the darkest nights; they were thus liabilities rather than threats from the outbreak of war in late July 1914.

By summer 1915 French parliamentary Deputy Pierre Etienne Flandin was demanding the construction of large, long-range bombers to strike German industrial centers. Even the French professor A. Le Châtelier of the Collège de France was advocating an air arm of a thousand

Statesmen confronted with the realities of airpower. David Lloyd George, H. H. Asquith, Arthur Balfour, and Murray Sueter, RN, inspect the wreckage of Zeppelin L-33, 1916. (Robin Higham Collection)

planes, each carrying 600–800 pounds of bombs, to assault the Rhine zone to achieve "victory, by shock, in the rear of the German front."[5] In contrast, the French high command by midyear had renounced its hopes for strategic aviation because of inadequate airplanes, high casualties in bombing raids, and its awareness that the proximity of Paris to the front lines would render it a prime target for German reprisal raids in any strategic air war.

If the French admitted failure, the Germans persevered, although the zeppelins had proved vulnerable to antiaircraft fire during their night raids, given sufficient light conditions. Late in 1914 the German navy had urged Kaiser Wilhelm II to use the zeppelin to carry "the war to the soil of old England," "diminish the enemy's determination to prosecute the war," and thereby "shorten the war."[6] Kaiser Wilhelm II consented to attacks on parts of London at the end of April 1915 to demoralize the population and damage war production. Giant naval zeppelins targeted London for the rest of year and dropped 1,900 bombs totaling just over thirty-six tons, killing 277 and wounding 645 civilians and causing an estimated £870,000 in damage.

The German submarine and aerial assaults on England in 1915 prompted dissatisfaction, hysteria, and ultimately a burning desire for revenge. At a meeting of the War Council on 24 February 1915, Secretary Lieutenant Colonel Maurice Hankey suggested the distribution of a "blight" on Germany's next grain crop by air attack; First Lord of the Admiralty Winston Churchill preferred burning the crop; but the future prime minister David Lloyd George, then minister of munitions, averred that the blight "did not poison, but merely deteriorated the crop." Prime Minister A. J. Balfour deferred such extreme forms of air warfare by advising that they should resort to such measures only under extreme provocation. In June members of Parliament advocated the destruction of Essen and other German cities with daily massed raids. William Joynson-Hicks, an air advocate, demanded the construction of a fleet of ten thousand—even twenty thousand—large, powerful airplanes to stage reprisal raids against Germany. Undersecretary of State for War Harold J. Tennant could only reply that industry had not the resources to build them, nor could the small air service man them.[7]

In Italy Giulio Douhet continued to press for the formation of a large group of heavy airplanes to stage strategic operations against the enemy war machine and military and industrial centers. Douhet's support of Gianni Caproni had started to bear fruit, as giant Caproni trimotored biplanes began to appear at the front in early fall 1915. Douhet, however, paid for his initiative, as his superiors had stripped him of command of the aviation battalion in December 1914 and exiled him to an army division to discipline him for exceeding his authority in ordering the Caproni bomber.

Expectations of bombardment far exceeded the technological and industrial realities of the day into 1917. During 1916 the French bomber squadrons, lacking any satisfactory machines and incurring severe casualties in return for indecisive results during daylight raids, turned to night bombing and planned to restrict their targets dramatically in 1917. Individual French bomber commanders regretted their inability to stage reprisal raids to "strike the morale of the enemy, to intimidate him," "to fling enough German entrails on the pavement of the city [Munich in this case] to give [them] pause for reflection."[8] French builders, lacking powerful engines, were reluctant to commit to the unprofitable and arduous task of strategic bomber development.

The British Royal Naval Air Service desired to combine with the French air service to strike munitions, chemical, and ironworks in the economically important Saar. They wanted to shake German industrial and popular morale and force the Germans to divert resources from the front to home defense, just as the Germans had hoped to do through their zeppelin attacks on England. Once again, however, the British, like the French, lacked a suitable airplane to accomplish the task, and their inexperienced aircrew had difficulty hitting targets smaller than a large town.

Ever-larger German zeppelins continued to raid England during 1916. Naval Airship Commander Peter Strasser was convinced that airships could deprive Britain of the means of existence "through increasingly extensive destruction of cities, factory complexes."[9] In 1916, however, British airplanes armed with machine guns firing incendiary bullets could reach the zeppelins, which had earlier flown at altitudes unattainable by airplanes. By the end of the year the biplanes of the Royal Flying Corps had gained an ascendancy over the zeppelin that they would never relinquish, and the height of the zeppelin raids had passed, Strasser's sanguinity and his successful procurement of even larger airships notwithstanding.

If the zeppelins had passed their prime, the German army air service decided in the fall of 1916 to attack England in a bomber campaign,

A 1917 Sopwith Camel in the RAF Museum in London. The Camel dominated the skies over the Western Front in 1917–1918. (Stuart Howe)

named Turk's Cross, in 1917. The Germans had what the British and French lacked—the airplanes to attempt the task. Gotha bombers and huge R-planes, driven by powerful engines, began to raid England late in May 1917.

In Italy the size and power of the Caproni trimotors steadily rose in 1916 and 1917, as they attacked cities like Trieste at long range and flew tactical raids over the Austrian lines. Yet if Caproni's fortunes were rising, Douhet's plummeted, as he was arrested and sentenced to one year in prison in the fall of 1916 for leaving a memorandum criticizing the Italian war effort on a train. Writing essays, "The Great Aerial Offensive" and "The Resistance of Peoples Facing a Long War," from prison in June and July 1917, Douhet called for an Allied air fleet to bomb enemy cities and urged Italy to build 1,000, France 3,000, England 4,000, and the United States 12,000 planes. He emphasized the necessity of massive force and underlined the effect on morale of the German raids on London.

Yet as of early 1918 the Germans remained the sole combatant on the Western Front to mount strategic air attacks, but their window of opportunity was quickly closing. On 4 May Naval Airship Commander Peter Strasser was shot down and killed over England, which ended the naval airship campaign. German giant bombers continued their raids until May 1918, when the German army high command committed them to tactical air strikes against the advancing Allies on the Western Front. On 16 February a German giant plane dropped the war's largest bomb, a one-ton monster, on England. In the final analysis, though the German bombers had forced the diversion of significant British forces to home air defense, they had failed in their first and most grandiose aim—to drive Britain from the war.

Both the British and the French were determined to strike Germany with heavy bombers in 1918. On 24 May French army Commander in Chief Philippe Pétain included in his proposals of future aircraft types a long-range heavy bomber to attack German industrial centers as far east as the Ruhr. He believed that the bomber would "paralyze the economic life of Germany and its war industries by methodical, massive, and repeated action against principal industrial cities," and "weaken the morale of its population by giving them a feeling of insecurity."[10] Despite Pétain's stipulations, the French aviation industry was never able to deliver such a bomber to the Gallic air service. Deputy Flandin, who remained an advocate of strategic bombing to the end of the war, lamented this failure, as the parliamentary deputies had accorded top priority to the strategic bomber's attack on the German war industry. He pointed out correctly, however, that the French high command, and Prime Minister Georges Clemenceau, emphasized tactical aviation and the defeat of the German army on the Western Front.

Only the British remained, and they resolutely insisted on retaliation. In fact, the development of a strategic bombing force was the primary motivation for the formation of an air ministry and independent air force, the Royal Air Force (RAF), in spring 1918. The South

The ultimate two-seater fighter of World War I, the Bristol "Brisfit," soldiered on in colonial service in the 1920s as an instrument of policy. (Robin Higham Collection)

African soldier-statesman J. C. Smuts's two influential reports of 1917, which advocated the formation of an independent air arm, envisioned that while the Western Front would be advancing at a snail's pace in the summer of 1918, a large, powerful air force attacking German lines of communication and industrial centers, and consequently the morale of their civilian inhabitants, might possibly be the "determining factor" in ending the war. Smuts reflected the prevailing alarm at the apparent panic the German air raids caused, although a dissenting Winston Churchill, minister of munitions, correctly believed that "terror bombing" would "steel the nerve of the public."[11]

William Weir, who had controlled aviation production in the Ministry of Munitions in 1917, became Secretary of State for Air in April 1918. Weir, soon to become a peer, was convinced that the heavy bomber was the weapon of the future, and he had sent the Handley Page factory a rough specification that initiated the development of the giant four-engine V1500. He planned to build an independent force of bombers to conduct a massive aerial offensive against German cities to destroy key German war industries. On 10 September 1918 Weir wrote to Independent Force Commander General Hugh "Boom" Trenchard: "I would very much like it if you could start up a really big fire in one of the German towns. If I were you, I would not be too exacting as regards accuracy in bombing railway stations in the middle of towns. The German is susceptible to bloodiness, and I would not mind a few accidents due to inaccuracy."[12]

Trenchard, however, although he was convinced of the effect of bombing on civilian morale, never launched such a campaign. Neither his aircraft nor his aircrew was capable of the task. Perhaps most ironically, the first two Handley Page V1500 bombers arrived at the front on 11 November 1918—Armistice Day. Had the war lasted into 1919, the RAF planned a full-scale campaign against Germany.

With the end of war and demobilization of the air arms of all countries, air advocates confronted the challenge to justify and preserve an air force amid economic pressures and challenges from the older services. The RAF sent 400 officers and men and 277 aircraft to help the monarchist "white" army in its abortive struggle against the Bolsheviks in southern Russia. More crucially, under Trenchard's leadership the RAF survived the postwar reductions through a policy of "air control," policing the far corners of the British Empire more cheaply and effectively than the army. The successful use of a few RAF bombers to locate, then bomb and strafe, the camp of the "Mad Mullah" in Somaliland in 1919 and 1920 and ultimately drive him into Ethiopia, where he died, convinced the British government to enlarge the RAF's role in policing the Middle East. The RAF further stationed two squadrons in Ireland for population control, "to fly low over the small villages and inspire considerable fear among the ignorant peasantry."[13] Events in Ireland, Africa, and the Middle East demonstrated that the war had perfected the air weapon sufficiently to enable the realization of prewar visions of imperial domination through aviation.

The other colonial powers followed suit. The French, Italian, and Spanish governments all employed airplanes to bomb, strafe, and drop poison gas on rebellious native populations in North Africa during the colonial wars of the 1920s. This practice culminated in Fascist Italy's savage invasion of Ethiopia in 1935, in which the Italian airplanes wantonly bombed, strafed, and gassed Ethiopian soldiers and civilians. The European powers' willingness to use all the weapons in their aerial arsenal, including poison gas, against "inferior" native populations during the 1920s and 1930s provides the backdrop for statesmen's approach to the air weapon in the interwar era.

Aviation staffs and statesmen, however, focused not on the colonies but on the threat that strategic bombing posed to Europe. They recalled the British experience of German bombing and the concerns about the fear that the bombs caused among the poor inhabitants of the East End of London. Often overlooked, but certainly a factor in their concern, loomed the Russian Revolution and the resulting dread of the power of the masses to overthrow established government. The home front consequently appeared more vulnerable than the fighting front. That German strategic bombardment had failed to drive the English from the war, and that British and French bombers had proved incapable of striking the German homeland effectively, paled before convictions that future strategic bombers would vault the front lines and strike at civilian morale in political and industrial centers, thereby causing the enemy populace to "squeal first," in Trenchard's words,[14] and ending the war. Giulio Douhet became the most eminent of these airpower theorists. His book *The Command of the Air,* published in 1921, encapsulated the claims for strategic airpower that its proponents everywhere asserted. He postulated that "merciless pounding from the air" would cause "the complete breakdown of the social structure," and the people "would rise up and demand an end to the war."[15] The willingness to strike at civilian centers with high-explosive, incendiary, and poison-gas bombs rested on the preconception that civilians would be less able to withstand such pounding than soldiers.

The British, in particular, suffered from a profound sense of vulnerability, the conviction that airpower rendered Britain's island security irrelevant. As the historian Barry Powers explains, "England's defensive security was lost with the development of the airplane and . . . England existed . . . in grave jeopardy. The fundamental shift in England from confidence to insecurity about its defensive position was of major consequence during the interwar years."[16] Interwar depression in Britain in general, and the General Strike of 1926 in particular, raised fears that under severe aerial attack, England's industrial society might fracture. As Stanley Baldwin reflected in 1926, "Who does not know that if another great war comes our civilization will fall with as great a crash as that of Rome?"[17] As defense against aerial attack appeared impossible, the only counter, literally speaking, became a good offense—one's own strategic bomber force. In 1923 the Joint Sub-Committee of the War Office and the Air Ministry acknowledged the overriding principle that "offensive action by aircraft in the enemy's country is the best form of defence."[18]

A gap between doctrine and reality, however, appeared immediately in the postwar years. The giant Handley Page V1500 bomber that appeared late in 1918, and other large aircraft, fell to the budgetary axe during demobilization, while the air staff neglected the development of expensive heavy bombers during the 1920s. That group even ignored bomb development, as it had concluded erroneously from superficial surveys that aerial bombing would break enemy morale—the most significant and more easily attainable objective—before the need arose to inflict *extensive* material destruction. Such analysis led to "a theory of strategic air power that was based on supposition and wishful thinking, not on historical experience and sound doctrinal evaluation."[19]

Britain was not alone in its unfounded belief in strategic airpower in the 1920s. The air staffs of some of the other European powers became equally enthusiastic about grand-strategic airpower, whereas others vacillated between strategic and tactical aviation. Although the Versailles Treaty prohibited Germany from even having an air force, it could not stop the German military establishment from planning in secret. In 1926 the German air staff's directives stipulated that its strategic bombing force would attack "the enemy's major cities and industrial centers" in an attempt to "crush the enemy's moral resistance and will to fight."[20] German officers who were sent to train the Soviet air force in the 1920s also noted the enthusiasm of Soviet air force officers, and high military commanders such as General Mikhail Frunze and Marshal Mikhail Tukhachevskii, for Douhet's theories and strategic airpower. In

Italy, ironically, Douhet's theories did not reign supreme; ground assault aviation gained ascendancy as more appropriate to the wars that Italy would wage. The French and Italians fought lengthy colonial wars in the 1920s, and both concentrated on supporting ground operations in North Africa during the decade. By the late 1920s the French air arm was shifting toward a focus on grand-strategic aviation in order to establish its independence from the army, whereas in the Soviet Union theorists shifted toward support of the army as the primary goal of aviation. In the United States official army doctrine emphasized the air arm's support of the army, but U.S. Army Air Corps theorists gravitated toward grand-strategic airpower as the weapon to win a future war quickly and decisively and secure independence for the air arm.

The state of aviation technology in the 1920s through the early 1930s did lend credence to a belief in strategic aviation, but in an ironic manner, as no state pursued the development of large, long-range grand-strategic bombers until the mid-1930s. Commercial aviation transport planes evolved from single- to multi-engine all-metal aircraft, starting with the Junkers F13 in 1919, whose speed exceeded that of both the standard wood-and-fabric biplane and the later early monoplane military pursuit planes with fixed landing gear. The performance of these civilian transport airplanes enabled them to double as military bombers capable of outrunning the fighter planes of the day. The lack of differentiation between military bombers and civilian transports thus aroused fears of the rapid formation of large bomber fleets through the easy modification of civilian into military aircraft.

By the 1930s British statesmen, politicians, and airmen had become obsessed with the danger of aerial attack. The historian Uri Bialer terms interwar Britain's fear of aerial bombardment and an "aerial knock-out blow" by the German air force "unprecedented and unique," even "apocalyptic." It dominated British planning by 1936, and it led to the government's decision to rearm mainly in the air in 1934 and 1935, and in 1937 to limit British ability to intervene on land in a Continental war. He cites the historian Correlli Barnett's judgment that interwar "rearmament in Britain was dominated throughout its course by an obsession with air power."[21]

In the cinema, the most popular form of mass entertainment by the 1930s, British newsreels presented sensational coverage of the air wars in Spain and China, particularly the bombing of Guernica by the German Condor Legion and of Shanghai by the Japanese air force in 1937, with editorial comment on the bombing of Barcelona that it was "only a foretaste of what Britain could expect . . . in a new war." A major feature film of 1936, Alexander Korda's production of H. G. Wells's *Things to Come,* depicted the collapse of civilization in a future war initiated by aerial bombing of major cities. A devastating air attack became a common theme in the popular fiction of the 1930s, particularly in Britain. The great anxiety of the British public about air defense and the danger of air attack led in 1935 and 1936 to parliamentary pressure on such government officials as Neville Chamberlain and Sir William Weir, who, after a fifteen-year hiatus in industry, had returned to the government as an adviser on air rearmament, to give priority to aerial over land rearmament.

This atmosphere provides the context for Stanley Baldwin's famous statement on 10 November 1932 at the end of the debate on disarmament in the House of Commons, with which this essay begins. Baldwin's anxiety reflected that of the Air Ministry—that "devastating air attack was inevitable in any future war"—but no one mentioned a potential enemy, at a time when the German Luftwaffe did not yet exist and war with France was most unlikely. The international movement toward disarmament foundered in 1934, as the Disarmament Conference broke down. In early 1935 British Chancellor of the Exchequer Neville Chamberlain, among other government officials, expressed his concern about an enemy knockout blow from the air, which led the historian John Kyba to observe, "The fear of attack from the air was a prevalent phobia throughout 1934."[22]

By then the British faced a very likely potential enemy, with Adolf Hitler's rise to power in Germany and reports of Germany's initial plans for rapid rearmament, particularly in the air, which would come to fruition in 1936. The reports plunged certain elements in the British government, particularly in the Foreign Office and in Parliament, into an "air panic" about the apparent inadequacy of Britain's aerial defense from November 1934 to May 1935. In April 1935 the permanent Undersecretary of State in the Foreign Office, Sir Robert Vansittart, wrote, "Apart from the visibly growing German menace, any continued inferiority in the air will weaken our influence throughout Europe."[23] As the Nazi regime "cast a lengthening shadow over Europe," Bialer observes, "British anxiety concerning the air menace increased," which led to the government's decision to emphasize aviation over other arms and increased the appeal of appeasement to the Foreign Office.[24]

The years from 1935 to 1937 witnessed the consolidation of the British government's belief that Germany would attempt to launch a knockout blow against Britain. From 1936 to 1939, Bialer suggests, "this fear [of aerial bombardment] exercised a dominant influence over British strategic thought . . . , and supplied a unique (and hitherto neglected) motive in the making of British foreign policy."[25] The German Condor Legion's Spanish Civil War aerial bombardment of Guernica and Barcelona influenced British cabinet discussions of 1937–1938, convincing policy makers that Germany would launch even greater attacks on Britain in a future war.

Such strong British apprehension about the revival of German airpower under the Nazis requires comparison to the actual state of German aerial doctrine and strategic aviation. Robert Knauss, an accomplished aviator for the German airline Lufthansa and a close associate of Erhard Milch, the new Secretary of State for Air, staunchly advocated a force of four hundred powerful, heavy bombers to cripple an opponent's industrial base and government and terrorize the urban population. He noted Italy's formation of a bomber force and the efforts of France's recently appointed air minister, Pierre Cot, to build a bomber fleet.[26] In the event, France and Italy failed to figure in strategic bomber development by 1939: the French aviation production effort never arrived at or executed any coherent plans, whereas Italy, lacking industrial might, exhausted its aerial effort in the Spanish Civil War. After the initial enthusiasm for strategic airpower, the Soviet air fleet, having few targets within range, focused on tactical aviation. That left Germany and Britain alone in the European race to develop strategic aviation.

Milch's advocacy of strategic bombers flew in the face of the Luftwaffe air staff's concentration on tactical airpower in the early 1930s, but Knauss was not the sole advocate of strategic airpower. The new chief of the air staff of the Luftwaffe, Lieutenant General Walther Wever, who served from 1933 until his untimely death in a plane crash in 1936, and his subordinates considered strategic bombing the primary mission of the air force. In 1934 Wever commissioned his staff, under the leadership of Major General Helmuth Wilberg, to establish a comprehensive air doctrine for the new Luftwaffe. At the center of LDv 16, "Conduct of Aerial Warfare," published in 1935, lay an "attack on the sources of enemy power" by a strategic bombing force of "Ural Bombers."[27] Unlike his British and American counterparts, Wever and his staff "regarded strategic bombers as part of an integrated force to support the Army and the Navy."[28]

In 1934 the Luftwaffe began to develop a four-engine heavy bomber and the air staff granted the program top priority. As the historian James Corum notes, "For military airmen of all powers, the heavy bomber was the ultimate symbol of air power in the 1930s."[29] Russia built the lumbering Tupolev TB-3 in 1931 and had 250 of them by 1934, when it began development of a new heavy bomber. In August 1934 the U.S. Army Air Corps issued the specifications for a fast, long-range, four-engine heavy bomber; the result became the immortal B-17, whose prototype would fly in 1935. The British and the Italians began heavy bomber programs, and in the case of the former, among the ultimate results would be the equally immortal Avro Lancaster. The powers initiated their development of the generation of heavy bombers that would serve in the Second World War in the mid-1930s. In fact, the same William Weir who as Secretary of State for Air in 1918 had ardently desired to set the torch to German towns became industrial adviser to the Secretary of State for Air in 1935. Weir and Arthur Harris, RAF, deputy director of plans as of late 1935 and wartime chief of Bomber Command, would press the sustained development and production of a fleet of heavy bombers that would burn so many German cities to the ground in the Second World War. Such heavy bombers would give Britain grand-strategic rather than numerical superiority over the German air fleet. Yet only Britain and the United States would pursue, produce, and deploy strategic airpower to devastating effect during the war. What happened to Nazi Germany?

The German aircraft engine industry of the 1930s "lagged behind both Britain and the United States in the design and production of powerful aircraft engines" necessary to power these giants.[30] During the First World War the British and Germans had evolved sufficiently powerful engines to equip bombers, but in the 1930s it would take the German engine industry until the outbreak of the Second World War to evolve excellent engines. As a consequence, the first four-engine bomber prototypes, the Dornier DO 19 and the Junkers Ju 89, which both flew in 1936, possessed grossly inadequate speed, range, and bomb load. The Luftwaffe air staff terminated these initial heavy bomber projects in 1936 and decided to skip the first-generation development and initiate a second-generation "Ural Bomber" produced by Heinkel that would appear when the German engine industry could produce a suitable power plant. In the meantime, the Heinkel He 111 and Dornier Do 17 twin-engine medium bombers would suffice to carry the war to the enemy.

No one could have predicted that a German heavy bomber would never appear. The Heinkel He 177 would fall prey first to a unique design combining two engines in one nacelle of each wing, which resulted in constant fires and the nickname *Luftwaffenfeuerzeug* (Luft-waffe's cigarette lighter), and then to the absurd stipulation that it had to be able to dive-bomb. Walther Wever crashed to his death in 1936, the same year that the Luftwaffe's strategic bomber program essentially died, although German air planners continued their interest in a heavy bomber. In fact, the pressure to develop a large air force quickly within the industrial and raw material limitations of Nazi Germany implied that a larger air force of smaller airplanes would receive preference over a smaller air arm that included heavy bombers.

For the time being, at least, it seemed that the Luftwaffe, whatever its limitations, sufficed to frighten potential opponents into submission. The German occupation of the Rhineland in 1936, accompanied by the aerial bluff of flying the same airplanes over the territory repeatedly with different identification insignia, convinced the French and British, and the American observer Charles Lindbergh, that the Luftwaffe was too strong to challenge. The *Anschluss,* Nazi Germany's incorporation of Austria, was accompanied by a substantial display of airpower, which, flawed as it was, met no opposition. Both the British and French air staff chiefs believed that their bomber forces would be useless against German aerial defenses. Hitler was already planning for the Luftwaffe to destroy the Czech air force and support the German army in an invasion, but he did not intend to attack industrial centers or the civilian population unless necessary. Just as it had been before the First World War, aerial blackmail had become an important component of German foreign policy under the Nazi regime, the debatable condition of the Luftwaffe notwithstanding, because contemporary observers overestimated the capabilities of the German air force.

Of course, a major factor in this overestimation was the Condor Legion's role in support of Francisco Franco's nationalist forces in the Spanish Civil War. The air attack on the Basque town of Guernica on 26 April 1937 came to epitomize in the popular mind an atrocious example of "terror bombing" intended to crush the morale of the Basques. Yet James Corum cogently explains that the Legion bombed Guernica because it contained a key bridge and crossroads, and German bombers had enjoyed more success "carpet bombing" the villages than hitting the pinpoint targets within them. The myth of terror bombing that seized the popular imagination resulted from the press's sensationalized reporting of the bombing, Pablo Picasso's famous mural, and the illogical conclusion that if the Luftwaffe could destroy a small town, it must be capable of obliterating major cities.[31] The destruction of Guernica actually stiffened Basque resistance, in the opinion of the historian E. R. Hooton, who also considers Guernica a legitimate military target, but he believes that the German aerial experience of the entire war allowed no clear lessons about the effectiveness of strategic bombing.

Though senior Luftwaffe officers continued to believe in the importance of a heavy bomber, Corum concludes, officers in Spain understood the limitations of strategic bombing in a civil war and departed the war with "considerably more skepticism about the claims made for strategic bombing."[32] The historian Edward Homze has further determined that by 1938 the "Spanish war welded the Luftwaffe to a tactical concept of operations" and reaffirmed the conviction of the General Staff and the Air Ministry that "Germany needed a tactical air force suitable for limited continental wars."[33] While German strategic air war theorists continued to address the subject, the Luftwaffe General Staff focused more on fighter development and air defense doctrine.

The RAF actually had concrete indications of the tactical focus of the Luftwaffe. The air staff analysis of Luftwaffe maneuvers in September 1936 indicated a concentration on air support for the army, and the British Secretary of State for Air received confirmation of this focus from Colonel General Hans-Jürgen Stumpf late in 1937. The Luftwaffe was rearming to support the army, and in 1939 Hitler in private asserted, "A country cannot be brought to defeat by an air force," a clear indication that he did not consider the possibility of a knockout blow. Regardless of the evidence, the British air staff believed that the Germans would conduct their air war the same way that the British would, what Bialer refers to as the "mirror image" of the Luftwaffe.[34]

Fortunately for Great Britain, the air staff began to change perspective by 1937. RAF observers in Spain noted that the fighter "seemed to have an edge over the bomber," which required fighter escort for protection.[35] This perception, in fact, proved true, and it stemmed from the technological evolution of aviation in the mid-1930s. Not only were the powers launching the development of four-engine bombers, but the fighter plane took a definitive leap forward with the development of fast, maneuverable, primarily metal low-wing cantilever monoplane fighters with retractable landing gear and the capability to mount more powerful weapons, including twenty-millimeter cannons. The German Messerschmitt Bf 109 and the British Hurricane and Spitfire exemplified this new generation of fighter aircraft and would become the primary contenders in the Battle of Britain in 1940. These aircraft tipped the balance between bomber and fighter to the latter.

The British also first tested radar in 1935 and then moved to employ it as an early warning system within the superb fighter-control system for Fighter Command. If the RAF was to assume the primary role in the defense of Britain against the German threat, this role would rest not only on the counterstrike capacity of the bomber, but also on the ability of British interceptors to counter German bombers. The Inskip Report of December 1937 indicated that the Luftwaffe was no longer a "purely diplomatic problem" but now "a war threat" to Britain, which the RAF would counter in two phases. The first would entail Fighter Command's parrying of the knockout blow; the second would involve Bomber Command's sustained attack on the German economy, which threatened Germany with a long war.

In conclusion, an overview of governmental response to the rise of airpower indicates that the British, certainly because of their prior invulnerability to invasion, became particularly anxious about the potential for aerial attack on the island kingdom. Before both world wars the British public and press, and consequently members of Parliament and the government, dreaded the possibility of invasion from the air and later of an aerial knockout blow, although no power could possibly have achieved such feats.

Before and during the First World War, the German public and civilian and military leaders, on the other hand, believed that Germany's possession of the zeppelin, and later giant multi-engine bombers, would enable them to drive Britain from the war. Such inflated expectations were dashed on the rocks of experience: although the German air service did bomb London during 1917 and 1918, these attacks did not force the British out of the war. In fact, despite some public panic and the transfer of some fighter units from the Western Front, the German attacks spurred the British to retaliate with reprisal raids. Secretary of State for Air William Weir ardently desired to set the torch to German towns in 1918, but aviation technology set a limit to the burning aspirations of Germans and British in those early years of military aviation. The drives for and expectations of strategic bombing that endured through the Second World War had all appeared by the end of the war of 1914–1918.

British public panic about aerial attack loomed large again in the 1930s, conditioning the government's perception of its German opponent, its approach to rearmament, and even its conduct of foreign policy. Such apprehensions drove the British government, like its German, American, French, and Italian counterparts, to concentrate on the development of four-engine strategic bombers. The French and Italian efforts foundered, and the lack of suitable engines thwarted German designs, just as the lack of sufficiently powerful engines had frustrated French strategic aims in the First World War. The German Luftwaffe, whose mere existence terrorized the rest of Europe in the mid-1930s, proved later in combat to be a superb tactical air arm, but its unescorted medium twin-engine bombers lacked the strategic punch to inflict crippling destruction on a major adversary. These circumstances left only Great Britain and the United States in pursuit of the steady development and production of four-engine strategic bombers. Their success enabled their statesmen to employ airpower to pummel Germany from the air starting in 1942–1943, a pounding to which the German air force had no comparable riposte.

Notes

1. Alfred Gollin, *No Longer an Island: Britain and the Wright Brothers, 1902–1909* (Stanford: Stanford University Press, 1984), p. 193.

2. Thomas A. Keaney, "Aircraft and Air Doctrinal Development in Great Britain, 1912–1914," (Ph.D. diss., University of Michigan, 1975), pp. 147–148.

3. Kriegswissenschaftliche Abteilung der Luftwaffe, *Die Militaerluftfahrt bis zum Beginn des Weltkrieges 1914*, ed. Militaergeschichtliches Forschungsamt, 2nd ed., 3 vols. (Frankfurt: Mittler und Sohn, 1965–1966), 2:86.

4. Fritz Fischer, *Germany's Aims in the First World War* (New York: W. W. Norton, 1967), pp. 280–282.

5. Philippe Bernard, "A Propos de la stratégie aérienne pendant la Première Guerre Mondiale: Mythes et Réalités," *Revue d'histoire moderne et contemporaine* 16 (1969): 360.

6. Douglas H. Robinson, *The Zeppelin in Combat: The History of the German Naval Airship Division, 1912–1918* (London: Foulis, 1962), p. 64.

7. AIR 1/2319/223/29/1–18, Public Record Office (London). *Flight* 7, no. 26 (25 June 1915): 446–448, 455; no. 30 (23 July 1915): 525–526, 539–542; no. 43 (22 December 1915): 798, 802.

8. Bernard, "A propos de la stratégie aérienne," p. 363.

9. Douglas H. Robinson, *Giants in the Sky: A History of the Rigid Airship* (Seattle: University of Washington Press, 1973), p. 122.

10. Pétain to Dumesnil, 24 May 1918, no. 30605, 130AP7, Dorand Papers, Musée de l'Air.

11. Scott Robertson, *The Development of RAF Strategic Bombing Doctrine, 1919–1939* (Westport, Conn.: Praeger, 1995), p. 20.

12. Weir to Trenchard, 10 September 1918, MFC76/1/94, Trenchard Papers, Royal Air Force Museum Hendon.

13. *United States Military Intelligence, 1917–1922,* 20 vols. (New York: Garland, 1978), 11:2, 626.

14. Malcolm Smith, *British Air Strategy between the Wars* (Oxford: Clarendon Press, 1984), p. 61.

15. James S. Corum, *The Luftwaffe: Creating the Operational Air War, 1918–1940* (Lawrence: University Press of Kansas, 1997), p. 91.

16. Robertson, *The Development of RAF Strategic Bombing Doctrine,* p. 42.

17. Smith, *British Air Strategy between the Wars,* p. 47.

18. Robertson, *The Development of RAF Strategic Bombing Doctrine,* p. 48.

19. Ibid., p. 135; emphasis added.

20. Corum, *The Luftwaffe,* p. 82.

21. Uri Bialer, *The Shadow of the Bomber: The Fear of Air Attack and British Politics, 1932–1939* (London: Royal Historical Society, 1980), pp. 2–4.

22. Ibid., pp. 44–46.

23. Ibid., p. 53.

24. Ibid., p. 126.

25. Ibid., p. 125.

26. Corum, *The Luftwaffe,* pp. 130–133.

27. Ibid., pp. 129, 135–144.

28. E. R. Hooten, *Phoenix Triumphant: The Rise and Rise of the Luftwaffe* (London: Arms and Armour, 1994), p. 99.

29. Corum, *The Luftwaffe,* p. 171.

30. Smith, *British Air Strategy between the Wars,* p. 143.

31. Corum, *The Luftwaffe,* pp. 198–200.

32. Ibid., pp. 209–212, 222.

33. Edward L. Homze, *Arming the Luftwaffe: The Reich Air Ministry and the German Aircraft Industry, 1919–39* (Lincoln: University of Nebraska Press, 1976), p. 174.

34. Bialer, *The Shadow of the Bomber,* pp. 132–133.

35. Smith, *British Air Strategy between the Wars,* p. 71.

Further Reading

The place to start for the story to 1919 is John H. Morrow Jr., *The Great War in the Air: Military Aviation from 1909 to 1921.* Follow that with Scott Robertson, *The Development of RAF Strategic Bombing Doctrine, 1919–1939;* Malcolm Smith, *British Air Strategy between the Wars;* James S. Corum, *The Luftwaffe: Creating the Operational Air War, 1918–1940;* Uri Bialer, *The Shadow of the Bomber: The Fear of Air Attack and British Politics, 1932–1939;* E. R. Hooten, *Phoenix Triumphant: The Rise and Rise of the Luftwaffe;* and Edward L. Homze, *Arming the Luftwaffe: The Reich Air Ministry and the German Aircraft Industry, 1919–39.* These may be supplemented by Robin Higham and Stephen J. Harris, eds., *Why Air Forces Fail: The Anatomy of Defeat,* 2nd ed. (Lexington: University Press of Kentucky, 2012), and Douglas H. Robinson, *The Zeppelin in Combat: A History of the German Naval Airship Division, 1912–1918* (London: Foulis, 1962).

2

Politics and French Aviators

A Prism on the International European Crises of the 1930s

Patrick Facon

The international crises of the 1930s are an interesting and pertinent lens through which to understand and analyze the role of airpower in the creation of policy. The crises allow close observation of the complex dialogue between military aviators and the political leadership in the early stages of airpower's rise to prominence in decision making. In contrast to the pre–World War I period, by the 1930s aviation had in effect become a problematic factor in the highest-level government discussions of the international crises of the decade.

Airpower had become truly important for the armed forces, a very profound element in military reality. The possibility existed—because of the air force's special abilities to fly over national frontiers and to overcome the particulars of geography—that any great power could surprise a foe by a lightning strike well before a ground attack could ever materialize. Above all, an air force could be a strategic instrument, though in that role it ultimately proved to be less than decisive.

The spread of the radical ideas of the Italian airpower prophet Giulio Douhet has to be taken into account. At the heart of the military mind-set was the fear that the air weapon was capable of destroying a state, or at least its principal population centers. Conventional or chemi-

French aircraft factory workers on strike in 1936. Such labor actions weakened air policy. (SHAA)

cal bombardments (using combat gases such as yperite, or mustard gas) could be part of the next major conflict in Europe. This fear of the air menace surfaced in some of the proposals at the Geneva Disarmament Conference in the early 1930s, in particular those from some European representatives who wished to outlaw bombing. There is no better example than the delegates from France, a country chilled and traumatized by the casualties of the Great War.

French aeronautical weakness, at least up to 1939, helps explain the reticence of the French government to oppose Hitler's pretensions. This weakness was still critical in the Munich crisis and, again, when France and Britain went to war in September 1939, regardless of the expected cost.

In the 1920s France felt insecure because the Treaty of Versailles had not been ratified by the United States, nor was Britain wholeheartedly supportive of it. Thus, France sought to surround the disarmed Germany with a cordon of small treaty states—the Eastern bloc—from Poland

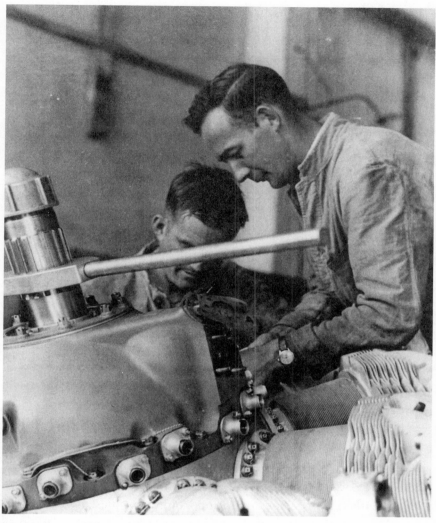

Mechanics assembling a radial aircraft engine, circa 1938. Their activities affected air strength and thus policy. (SHAA 88-3368)

in the north (1920) to Romania (1926) and Yugoslavia (1927) in the south. Each one of these agreements promised a supply of French war matériel, including aircraft. In the cases of Yugoslavia and Romania, the deals even provided for the establishment of factories that turned out aircraft built under license, such as the Breguet, Potez, and other makes. Foreign Secretary Louis Barthou was seeking more allies when he was assassinated in 1934. The Franco-Italian Pact of 1935 was focused against Germany, as was an alliance with the USSR.

Hitler's rise to power in 1933 began a shift, however, as Germany moved rapidly to dismantle the French Eastern bloc. In March 1936 Hitler challenged the old powers by remilitarizing the Rhineland. The Gallic walls of the League of Nations collapsed, and the Belgians reverted to neutrality, making France's northeastern frontier vulnerable. Meanwhile, Italy had moved into Ethiopia. Secret Italian arms shipments to Hungary and the failure of the Franco-Czech plan for a Danubian federation vitiated French defenses further, helping bring about the Rome-Berlin Axis. In March 1938 Germany annexed Austria, thus also flanking Czechoslovakia.

The effect of all these shifts was to negate French plans to help its Eastern bloc by aerial reinforcements, as Italy was now neither neutral nor friendly. The realities of geography and the state of technology had negated Parisian policy.

The Need for a System of Alliances

How is the paradox of the brusque about-face explained? It is necessary to start by analyzing the state of French aviation, the additional problems that beset the nation, and the blows suffered during the interwar years of troubles and agitation.

In countries with an independent air force before the Second World War, such as Britain and Italy, there were bitter debates regarding a third service, marked by virulent opposition from the armies and the navies. France had not escaped this evolving controversy, in which the traditional services, as partisans of the status quo and guarantors of a certain conservatism, clashed with the flyers, who thought that their arm was likely to overturn the rules of conflict that had existed before the advent of aviation. The struggle for institutional autonomy raged from the end of the Great War through the second half of the 1920s. The Air Ministry was not created in France until September 1928, and it was nearly another five years, in April 1933, before the airmen got their own service.[1]

Aircraft being assembled in the Breguet factory, 1938. (SHAA)

Less than three months after Hitler came to power, this new Armée de l'Air was in limbo. It also suffered the considerable loss in 1933–1934 of its new ministers (Pierre Cot, and then General Victor Denain), as the government started rearmament with Plan I, the main impetus for which was the threat of Nazi aggrandizement. When the Nazis took the reins of government in Germany in early 1933, the weight of French aviation in the balance of forces in Europe did not conform in the slightest to the image of the great military power France thought itself to be. "French aviation was mediocre in 1933," explained Denain. "Its matériel was obsolete, resting on excellent maintenance but absolutely incapable of facing a modern air force. Worse was the fact that the matériel being tested, evolved for the most part from the 1928 program, was already out of date before it even entered service."[2] While the Luftwaffe (the German air force) was already an agile, adaptable force, the Armée de l'Air, even with superior numbers, was an instrument of doubtful military worth.

Two views of the Breguet factory assembly floor. (SHAA)

Three years later, on the occasion of the remilitarization of the Rhineland, the "iron arm" confronted the Nazis and survived its first major test of force. The air had become a military sphere with which governments had to reckon.[3] The French put up 110 strong escadrilles, totaling 1,000 machines, whereas the Luftwaffe could put up only 72, composed of 860 mostly obsolete aircraft. (The Luftwaffe, a recent creation, had not yet had the time to develop suitable designs.)

The influence of Gallic airpower on the attitude adopted by Hitler and on an eventual armed confrontation with the Germans remained nevertheless measured. The chief of the General Staff Air Force, at the time General Bertrand Pujo, wanted to run the risk of a general embarrassment no more than his two colleagues of the army and the navy wanted to use force. Thus, Pujo advised the politicians, in what proved to be a very cautious manner, that in spite of a French superiority of three to one, a mass engagement of the air force could not be subordinated to general mobilization: "That which represented 412,000 men and that which would then require the calling up of all the mobilizable men of this *armée* [that is, the air force]. . . . At the start in the present conditions we will have the preponderance, but in a long war, the balance of numbers and the industrial potential will be with our adversaries."[4]

To alleviate the fears of French inferiority, air ministers and military airmen asked to buy foreign aircraft (aircraft, engines, and accessories in the United States, in the Low Countries, and even in Italy) as an exception to the foreign policy of seeking alliances.[5] Each one of these procurements reflected an impermanent reality; without partners and without accords with other states, the Armée de l'Air was incapable of deploying sufficient numbers of fighters and bombers to be effective in any type of mission, so it was virtually powerless.

In 1936, when he was again air minister, Pierre Cot promoted an alliance with the Soviet Union, the greatest airpower on the planet in his eyes. The system that he envisioned, outside Stalin's Russia, would include Czechoslovakia, the principal ally of France in central Europe, and Great Britain. Of this the minister wrote:

General Vuillemin (*left*), General Maurice Gamelin (*center*), and Henri d'Astier de la Vigerie (*right*) walking on the tarmac before making a flight, circa 1936. (SHAA)

Pierre Cot, air minister, Armée de l'Air, on and off from 1933 to 1938. (SHAA 90-587)

It is necessary, immediately, to organize an interallied air command. The organization will be simple. This command will be charged with the role of coordination and general direction, sufficient to run a coalition war. It would leave to each state . . . an important part of its air force; in France this air force would be subordinate to the command of the army general in-chief, the same in Czechoslovakia. The remainder of aviation, in particular all of the Soviet air force engaged in the European war, would constitute the interallied force. This air force . . . will have three main missions. For one part, reinforcing the defense of politically essential centers, the destruction of which would seriously injure the war effort. . . . Another part, to rein in the too rapid reinforcement of the Czech bastion to permit the arrival of Russians to fight the Germans . . . and finally, above all, the interallied force will lead to major reprisals and bombing.[6]

Convinced that the union of the air forces of France, Russia, and Britain would overcome the German Luftwaffe and the Italian Regia Aeronautica, Cot began a very close approach to Moscow. While in Russia, he gave the Red Army a license for the French twenty-millimeter cannon and borrowed from the Soviets the idea of creating a parachute force in the French air force, the Air Companies.

The policies engaged in by the Popular Front air minister underwent an abrupt reversal when in early 1938 Guy La Chambre and General Joseph Vuillemin arrived at the Boulevard Victor, the seat of the Ministry and of the General Staff Air Force. Without a doubt anticommunist and leery of Poland's sentiments—fundamentally anti-Russian—in any system of alliance opposed to what they wished to build, the two men changed France's direction.

Aside from alliances with the Poles and the Czechs, the French awarded Great Britain pride of place in their strategic dispositions. The head of the French air force estimated that Germany, faced by a bloc of these three countries, would hesitate to pursue a policy of aggression.

If Plan V, launched in March 1938, had in mind the acceleration of aerial rearmament, with the emphasis on fighters and little to do with bombers, that was because the French counted on the Royal Air Force to play this latter role. In fact, the British alliance was at the heart of Vuillemin's preoccupations, and he undoubtedly nourished great hope in this respect. It was in 1936, under the press of international threats, that General Staff contacts with the Royal Air Force were realized, but the negotiations were laborious.[7] The British reserved their fighters, now assembled in Fighter Command, for the defense of their homeland. This attitude evidently generated friction with the French, who desired the massive intervention of their partners on the Continent.

It was only under the pressure of the major crises of 1938, the *Anschluss* between Austria and Germany and, above all, the dismantling of Czechoslovakia, that the two Allies at last came to some fundamental decisions. An accord was signed in London in March 1938; the parties agreed that in the event of war, the British would deploy two air elements to France: about twenty bomber squadrons under Bomber Command designated the Advance Air Striking Force and some observation units organized as the Air Component attached to the British Expeditionary Force (BEF). The British air staff, preoccupied with the defense of its national airspace, however, would not guarantee to dispatch a fighter force to the side of the Armée de l'Air. It was not until after the 1938 Munich crisis that relations warmed enough to foster other agreements between the two allies. These staff talks, held in London in the early weeks of 1939, resulted in a much more positive arrangement when the Royal Air Force pledged to increase the Expeditionary Force in France to 160 Battle and Blenheim bombers for the Advance Air Striking Force (AASF). The British air staff went even further, promising several dozen fighters (80 Gladiators and Hurricanes), as well as observation machines added to the Air Component of the BEF.

These arrangements were balm to the heart of Vuillemin, who, visibly relieved, insisted on the "great change that came over the air forces on the side of the allies with the major addition of the British air forces. Defensively our neighbors' fighters were capable of breaking the daily spirit of the enemy bombers." Offensively, operating from either their own bases or French airfields, these modern British bombers could hit targets day or night and could substantially influence the land battle. The AASF's efforts in France in the first months of the war were more valuable, in Vuillemin's eyes, than those of France's own bomber force.[8]

Perhaps the chief of the General Staff Air Force deluded himself with too many illusions about the willing engagement of Britain. Perhaps he hoped secretly that by the time war broke out, the RAF would not be able to do other than what the accords forecast. Certainly, his staff thought, however, that the arrangements of March 1938 were not absolutely obligatory and that national self-interest would, without doubt, take precedence in an acute crisis. Nevertheless, the Armée de l'Air had, at least, the assurance that it would not have to fight alone.

The Munich Crisis

Vuillemin's concerns about the abilities of his forces to act alone against the German and Italian air menace were increased by the international crises of the second half of the 1930s, which presented a grave warning. The Armée de l'Air General Staff was paralyzed not only by the Sudeten crisis, resulting in the limitations of the Munich accords (September 1938), but also because the revealed weakness of French airpower influenced the attitudes of statesmen and the military. Certainly, never had the national air force descended to such a low or powerless level as it did in that summer, nor had the crisis with Nazi Germany struck such consternation, itself a menace to peace.

It was not that paralytic nadir that stopped the plan, however; rather, the tragedy that restrained the leaders of the Armée de l'Air—including Vuillemin—was the simple inferiority of the aircraft. The chief of the General Staff Air Force, involved in the Plan V expansion in matériel and personnel, was above all convinced that nothing could be available before the 1941 completion of his program. Besides, both Vuillemin and La Chambre were pacifists, burdened by the recollection of the Great War, so they envisioned the possibility that a new war might devastate Europe again. Vuillemin said much later in regard to his minister, "M. Guy La Chambre, on leaving the Council of Ministers, often called me into his office, and I left with tears in my eyes thinking that certain ministers wished us to go to war." It was thus that La Chambre and Vuillemin sided with those in the Daladier government and in the high command opposed to any acts of provocation vis-à-vis Germany, a stance that was shortly to include tolerance of an understanding with Hitler.

Between the new minister and his chief of the General Staff Air Force there developed a mutual esteem, dictated more by the sentiment to pursue a common end—a desire to avoid going to war prematurely, before the Armée de l'Air was ready—than by a simple personal affinity. The rapport between the two persons in charge seems even to have been molded by a candid faith that France was not in a position to make war against Germany and Italy with such a weak air force. Guy La Chambre was part of the busy faction, including Georges Bonnet, Paul Marchandeau, and Charles Pomaret, who were firmly pacifist and lobbied for a diplomatic solution. Throughout 1938 La Chambre, supported by Vuillemin, kept the French political leadership informed not only of the weakness of the Armée de l'Air, but also of the catastrophic situation in which the country would find itself if it opposed Hitler by arms.

The chief of the General Staff Air Force, as he had since the first of the crises with which he had been faced (Austria in March 1938), expressed himself with clarity and precision. Having already sounded the alarm about the lamentable state of the air force (notably the bombers) in January 1938, a little before the departure of Pierre Cot as air minister, he predicted, two months later, that in a fortnight of war the Armée de l'Air would be swept from the skies. In August he was invited by the highest authorities in the Luftwaffe to visit air bases and the German aircraft industry. Impressed both by the military demonstrations he witnessed and by the energy of German rearmament, he met the French ambassador in Berlin and confided to him his fear of seeing the French air force founder in a fortnight in the face of the intensive, powerful Luftwaffe.

Upon his return to France, his mind was made up, and he affirmed his conviction that the power of German industry was

Generaloberst Erhard Milch (*left*) escorts General Joseph Vuillemin on his inspection visit to Germany in August 1938, just a month before the Munich Conference. (SHAA 90-587)

truly impressive. . . . Power is obtained from the cadence of production which, already, actually surpasses the needs created by the renovation of matériel by consumption and waste and even by exports that we know to be limited, production which, in case of war, helped by the perfection of tooling and installations, could be doubled or even tripled at once. Power is obtained by the quality of the materials fabricated, which denote undeniably advanced techniques. Both fighters and bombers have the performances, armament, and flying characteristics that grant them primacy in international aeronautical prowess, and the presence of the Heinkel 100, holder of the speed record . . . ready to be launched into series production when necessary requires us to prove we are equally prepared for the future.[9]

At the height of his despair, perhaps too little conscious of having been tricked and seemingly intoxicated by the flyers of a nation with which war seemed inevitable, he spoke to empty benches.

Alas, if we go to war the Armée de l'Air will be annihilated in two weeks. We have only old aircraft whose top speed is just 300–350 kph [186–217 mph]. Our air force is not only outclassed by the German, which is assumed to have a speed of 500 kph [311 mph], 200 kph [124 mph] faster than ours. So if war breaks out and I must take to the air in obsolete machines, I shall be obligated to order up my mediocre pilots because they will, alas, certainly be sacrificed. I must conserve my good pilots for the moment when we will have modern aircraft and when they will be able to fight the enemy on equal terms. . . . I will have only one recourse, that is to climb into an aeroplane and drop a bomb on an enemy town and then descend.[10]

What had impressed Vuillemin certainly influenced the leadership of the army, such as General Maurice Gamelin, generalissimo-designate in case of war, but also the diplomats and the statesmen of France, such as Guy La Chambre and Edouard Daladier. The head of the French army, General Gamelin, in his memoirs noted: "On 24 August [1938] I received General Vuillemin on his return from Germany. He had been invited to assist in the celebration of aviation and the government had guessed that he was proper in accepting for another reason, he would be interested to see the aircraft and air formations of our adversaries. He returned enormously impressed by what he had been able to verify."[11]

On 8 September, while on a visit to Neville Chamberlain, newly back from an interview with Hitler at Berchtesgaden, Daladier received just as he boarded the airplane a very pessimistic letter from Vuillemin. A week later, in a report for which he had been asked in the middle of

On 5 February 1938 Air Minister Guy La Chambre (*center*) greets General Joseph Vuillemin, chief of the General Staff Air Force. General d'Astier de la Vigerie, in the background, still wears a formal sword. (SHAA 892-4020)

the Munich crisis, the chief of the General Staff Air Force summarized that France faced a Luftwaffe of growing power with only 250 fighters, 320 bombers, and 130 strategic reconnaissance machines of notably insufficient performance. In short, if war followed, the French air force, owing to the notorious insufficiency of its reserves, had not the capacity to last. Vuillemin's conclusions not only were disturbing, but also truly foretold disaster. He predicted the crushing of the Armée de l'Air in a few hours on the ground and in the sky (40 percent of the effectives would be lost in the first month of war and 64 percent in the second).

Observation and reconnaissance missions for the French army and the engagement of the Luftwaffe in its massive bombing of cities, which would inflict considerable loss of life among civilians, were beyond the French air force. Industry would fare only slightly better, and the damage it would suffer would lead to the decline of production to an unsupportable level. Vuillemin concluded with some explanations of the incapacity for war in which France would find itself in response to enemy attacks, including a lack of assistance from the bomber force, which could barely operate at night. Never, he repeated, had the Armée de l'Air been so feeble as in the last trimester of 1938. This Guy La Chambre confirmed: "The situation of the French air force was so deficient that it raised the question of freedom of choice in international matters, and its restoration was a precondition for all future decisions."[12]

For his part Vuillemin advanced: "What machines do we have to oppose the 5,000 modern, first-line aircraft of the Germans and Italians? Nothing for the present: on 1 April 1939 probably fewer than 500 aircraft manned by personnel who will not have had the time to familiarize themselves with them and obtain the best out of them."[13] When he went to Munich with Prime Minister Chamberlain to negotiate with Hitler, Premier Daladier was obsessed with the views of the chief of the General Staff of the Armée de l'Air.

A Basic Evolution

A most fundamental evolution of the Allies' diplomatic stance took place in the first months of 1939. Hitler's seizure of Bohemia-Moravia in March convinced France and Britain they could no longer tolerate new diplomatic initiatives by Nazi Germany. They themselves decided to risk war if needed without worrying about other factors, such as their own military power. This consistent policy was launched in the spring with the guarantees to Poland by the two Western democracies following further Nazi ventures. In the minds of the two Allies, there was no question of backing down.

At first Paris promised Warsaw, without much thought, to speed up the stationing of French bomber and fighter groups in Poland, the very machines that the French air force itself lacked. General Jules Armengaud, charged with deploying this expeditionary air force, arrived on Polish soil in August, but the aircraft never followed him.

The gulf that opened between the military and civilians was never

The Morane-Saulnier 406 was the frontline Armée de l'Air fighter in 1939, but it was technically two years behind the German Me 109. It was out of production by the time of the German attack on France on 10 May 1940. (SHAA 83-4024)

more obvious than in this same month, when on 23 August came the surprising announcement of the German-Soviet Pact. Daladier, as minister of war, called a special meeting of the Council of National Defense. Present were all the ministers concerned, as well as the chiefs of staff of each branch—General Gamelin for the army, Admiral Jean-François Darlan for the navy, and General Vuillemin for the air force. When Foreign Minister Georges Bonnet asked everyone about potential problems caused by the accords concluded with Poland and the influence of rearmament on military readiness to go to war, Gamelin declared the army ready and predicted that the Poles could undoubtedly hold out until spring 1940. Darlan spoke in the same vein. But when Vuillemin's turn came to follow his two colleagues, in the normal council fashion, it was Guy La Chambre who spoke to all those present. The air minister, in front of his somewhat stupefied chief of the Air Staff, put forth a reassuring view of the air force. After having outlined the progress that had been made since Munich, he emphasized, "From the standpoint of fighters, we now have modern machines rolling out in large series and confidence in the Franco-British ability to combat the Italo-Germans on an equal basis. However, our bombers are not yet in serial production, not until early 1940. But in that respect, Britain is taking charge of the massive bombing of northern Germany. Cooperation with the ground forces can be assumed to be acceptable. In spite of what we know of the German forces, the situation of our air force should not weigh on the government's decisions, as it did in 1938."[14] The line adopted by the governmental authorities for this is clear: nothing must contradict the blind faith in the Allies' aerial strength, clearly affirmed from now until the entrance into the war. The self-appraisal of the military was thus reinforced—the dominant word was once more that of the statesmen.

The silence on the true state of the air arm was pervasive and prevented the raising of a number of basic questions. Thus, when Gamelin and Darlan were interviewed, each representing his branch of the military, the chief of the General Staff Air Force was unable to say a word. Why did he not say anything in this forum? Why had not La Chambre, and with him Daladier, put a stop to the pronouncements that had astonished the council of 23 August or rendered them worthless with their more or less fictitious unanimity? This meeting assuredly marked the start of a gulf between the air minister and his chief of staff, a division that became very obvious several months later, in the first quarter of 1940. Vuillemin, upon his return to the office at Boulevard Victor, impressed on his staff the need to write a letter as a record for posterity of his renunciation of responsibility for the events that would follow. He said a little bit later, "If I had never said a word at the session of 23 August 1939, it was because at that moment my views had not been solicited."[15] This was naïve on the part of a man who did not lack character but was shown without doubt to be too timorous or obeisant because of his rapport with his minister, so much so that he would not shoulder his responsibilities. The views he embedded in his report of 26

The Amiot 143, of which the Armée de l'Air had fifty in frontline service in metropolitan France on 10 May 1940, were limited to night missions because of its slow speed and inadequate armament. (SHAA)

August, three days after his weak showing at the meeting, were far from those of La Chambre, even if the two men's statements meshed from time to time. The chief painted a pessimistic picture of the situation, even while conceding that the state of the fighters was better than it had been at the time of the Munich crisis. But in his view, the state of the bombers was catastrophic. "The capacity of our bombers," Vuillemin averred, "had not improved even slightly since Munich. As they were almost nonexistent then, the French bombers were 'cantoned' [segregated], limited to prudent actions at short ranges."[16] This did not lessen the belief in the decisive importance of the aid announced by the RAF in this respect and the confidence that it would balance the forces: "In the next six months the Allies would nearly be able to equal the German and Italian air forces if there was no interference by massive bombings and if the USSR did not help the Germans. . . . The major air effort followed in the past year by Britain and France at the same time had allowed making up the lag acknowledged last September in the report on the available forces."[17]

La Chambre's claims were a great distance from the truth about the status of the Armée de l'Air in August 1939. Thus, when the mobilization of the French air force took place, there were 1,355 first-line aircraft based in metropolitan France—530 fighters, 415 bombers, and 410 reconnaissance (intelligence-gathering) planes—the least effective models, which reflected the weak state declared by those who found themselves in the Armée de l'Air. Four of the twenty-three *groupes* of fighters and nine regional escadrilles continued to fly totally obsolete machines whose technology dated to the early 1930s (notably the Dewoitine D-510). This situation led to an important transformation beginning at the end of 1939. In the meantime, however, it spawned the events of September, the coming of war, and even the later changes did not see the disposal of transitional aircraft such as the Morane-Saulnier MS-406. The state of the bombers was disastrous; twenty-seven of thirty-three *groupes* in the first line were equipped with marginal matériel (Amiot 143 or Bloch 200 and 210), two were supplied with the slightly more advanced Farman F-221, and four were in the course of conversion to the Breguet 690 and 691 attackers. Only five modern aircraft were available—some LeO-451 still in testing. Four *groupes* of strategic reconnaissance aircraft were transitioning to the Potez 637; ten others were equipped with the out-of-date Bloch MB-131 and the antique Potez 540 or Potez 39. The observation units had at their disposal forty-seven *groupes,* plus eight police escadrilles, which had no combat value.

The reality is now undeniable. Daladier and his ministers went to war completely ignoring the great weakness of the air force. The extreme gravity of the Bohemian-Moravian crisis of March 1939, France and Britain admitted, had required "a change forcing their priorities."[18]

In the interwar years French statesmen had started by constructing the Eastern bloc to surround its late enemy Germany. As France was until the early 1930s one of the two dominant air powers (the USSR would become the other by 1934), its statesmen's only policy options were to supply France's clients with air matériel. But in the 1930s the rise of Hitlerian Germany, with its modern air force based on a supporting aircraft industry, suddenly made the Armée de l'Air obsolete and impotent, as was made plain by the 1936 remilitarization of the

Symbolic of the failed alliance, these RAF Hurricanes were abandoned on a French airfield, as there were no pilots to fly them home. (SHAA)

General Vuillemin at his retirement ceremony, December 1940. (SHAA)

Rhineland. French generals then began to warn their statesmen of this weakness. Though they were aware of it at Munich in September 1938, there was a volte-face in August 1939 when Air Minister La Chambre took the floor at the 23 August council meeting and declared the French air force almost ready for war, not wishing to appear more backward than his confreres of the army and navy. General Vuillemin at once wrote the truth to him. But it was too late; the statesmen had opted for war.

Notes

1. See Patrick Facon, "Le projet avorté d'Armée de l'Air de 1929," *Revue Historique des Armées* 233 (2003): 65–76. Translated by Robin Higham.

2. Deposition of General Denain before the Cour Suprême de Justice, 21 April 1941, Service Historique de la Défense/Département de l'Armée de l'Air, Z12975.

3. General Charles Christienne and Patrice Buffotot, "L'Armée de l'Air et la crise du 7 mars 1936," *Colloque International: La France et l'Allemagne (1932–1936)* (Paris: Editions du CNRS), pp. 313–331.

4. Ibid.

5. John McVickar Haight, "Les négociations françaises pour la fourniture d'avions américains, avant Munich (1)," *Forces Aériennes Françaises* 198 (December 1963).

6. Pierre Cot, *L'Armée de l'Air, 1936–1939* (Paris: Grasset, 1939), pp. 118–119.

7. See Jean Lecuir and Patrick Fridenson, *La France et la Grande-Bretagne face aux problèmes aériens, 1935–mai 1940* (Vincennes: Service Historique de l'Armée de l'Air, 1976).

8. General Vuillemin to General Gamelin, 28 October 1938, Service Historique de la Défense/Département de l'Armée de l'Air, Z12964.

9. See Patrick Facon, "La visite du general Vuillemin en Allemagne, 19–21 août 1938," in *Recueil d'articles et d'études (1981–1983)* (Vincennes: Service Historique de l'Armée de l'Air, 1987), pp. 241–262.

10. Paul Stehlin, *Témoignage pour l'histoire* (Paris: Robert Laffont, 1964), p. 92.

11. General Maurice Gamelin, *Servir: Le prologue du drame, 1930–août 1939* (Paris: Plon, 1964), pp. 340–341.

12. Declaration of Guy La Chambre before the Commission de l'Aéronautique de la Chambre des Deputés, 12 January 1940, Service Historique de la Défense/Département de l'Armée de l'Air, Z12947.

13. General Vuillemin to Ministre de l'Air, 26 September 1938, Service Historique de la Défense/Département de l'Armée de l'Air, Z12964.

14. Minutes of the meeting held at the War Ministry, 23 August 1939, Service Historique de la Défense/Département de l'Armée de l'Air, Z12907.

15. Deposition of General Vuillemin before the Cour Suprême de Justice, copy, Service Historique de la Défense/Département de l'Armée de l'Air, Z12975.

16. General Vuillemin to Ministre de l'Air, 26 August 1939, Service Historique de la Défense/Département de l'Armée de l'Air, Z11275.

17. Ibid.

18. Peter Jackson, "La perception de la menace aérienne allemande et son influence sur la politique extérieure français, pendant les crises internationales de 1938 à 1939," *Revue Historique des Armées* 4 (1994): 82.

Further Reading

The place to start is with Charles Christienne, Pierre Lissarague, et al., *Histoire de l'aviation militaire française* (Paris: Charles-Lavauzelle, 1980), English edition, *A History of French Military Aviation* (Washington, D.C.: Smithsonian Institution Press, 1986); Patrick Facon, *L'Armée de l'Air dans la tourmente, la bataille de 1940* (Paris: Economica, 1997); Patrick Facon, *Histoire de l'Armée de l'Air* (Paris: La Documentation Française, 2009); Patrick Facon, *Batailles dans le ciel de France, mai–juin 1940* (Saint-Malo: Editions Pascal Galodé, 2010); Thierry Vivier, *La politique aéronautique militaire de France: Janvier 1933–Septembre 1939* (Paris: Editions L'Harmattan, 1997); and Martin S. Alexander, *The Republic in Danger: General Maurice Gamelin and the Politics of French Defence, 1933–1940* (New York: Cambridge University Press, 1992). See also Piotr S. Wandycz's two volumes on the Eastern bloc, *France and Her Eastern Allies, 1919–1925: French-Czechoslovak-Polish Relations from the Paris Peace Conference to Locarno* (Minneapolis: University of Minnesota Press, 1962) and *The Twilight of French Eastern Alliances, 1926–1936: French-Czechoslovak-Polish Relations from Locarno to the Remilitarization of the Rhineland* (Princeton: Princeton University Press, 1988).

Also helpful are Pierre Guillen, "Franco-Italian Relations in Flux, 1918–1940," in *French Foreign and Defence Policy, 1918–1940: The Decline and Fall of a Great Power,* ed. Robert Boyce (London: LSE/Routledge, 1998), pp. 149–163; Robert Boyce, "Business as Usual: The Limits of French Economic Diplomacy, 1926–1933," ibid., pp. 107–131; Talbot Imlay, "France and the Phoney War, 1939–1940," ibid., pp. 261–282; Robert J. Young, "The Use and Abuse of Fear: France and the Air Menace in the 1930s," *Intelligence and National Security* 2, no. 4 (October 1987): 88–109; Thierry Sormant, "Les plans d'operations français en Europe centrale (1938–1939)," *Revue Historique des Armées* 4 (December 1999): 13–22; François Pernot, "L'Armée de l'Air et les projets périphériques 1939–1940," *Revue Historique des Armées* 4 (December 1999): 77–88.

Suggestions for Further Research

Investigation of France's greatness in the 1930s and 1940s is still a sensitive topic. One result is that outside the Service Historique de l'Armée de l'Air little scholarly work has been done. We badly need studies of the organization, command, and workings of the French air arms between the wars. Thierry Vivier's work on pre-1939 logistics, procurement, and airfields, for instance, has never been exploited as a resource for producing a definitive organizational history of the interwar French air force.

3

Hitler, Airpower, and Statecraft

Richard R. Muller

As war clouds gathered over Europe in the summer of 1939, Nazi leaders and propagandists pointed to the German air force, the Luftwaffe (barely four years old at the time), as the embodiment of German power and technological superiority. They argued that the air arm was almost entirely a creation of Adolf Hitler's Third Reich, that it was the most powerful in the world, and that it stood, in the words of the Luftwaffe commander in chief Hermann Göring, "ready to carry out every command of the Führer with lightning speed and undreamed-of might."[1]

Subsequent events would reveal the hollowness (or at best, partial truth) of these claims. Yet during the 1930s, and to a declining extent after war broke out in September 1939, the Nazi air arm served as an effective tool of Hitler's statecraft. Aviation achievements provided a source of German domestic pride and lent credibility and prestige to the new regime. The latent power of German air fleets provided a secure umbrella under which German rearmament could proceed apace. Fear of German aerial might cowed the small states of Europe and affected the senior decision makers of even the major powers as they sought to contain German expansion in central Europe. Some commentators have gone so far as to suggest that what the Luftwaffe accomplished by the mere threat of its use at the time of the Munich agreement exceeded anything it later achieved in battle. This is a difficult claim to sustain;

Ready for war, pilots of a German Henschel Hs 123–equipped ground attack unit are briefed by their squadron commander. Photos such as this, showcasing the new Luftwaffe's striking power, were widely distributed in books and periodicals in the late 1930s. (Smithsonian Institution Archives)

the campaigns in Poland and the West in 1939–1940 and the virtual annihilation of the Red air force in the first week of Operation Barbarossa in June 1941 provide the most obvious counterarguments. Still, the diplomatic and coercive power of the Luftwaffe was undeniable. In peace and war, it was a flexible instrument of "policy by other means" until Germany's opponents took its measure.

Hitler and Aviation

Adolf Hitler, führer and Reichs chancellor of Germany, was one of the first world leaders to come of age in the era of aviation. Hitler's worldview was shaped by the nationalism and anti-Semitism rampant in late nineteenth-century Europe, the searing experience of the First World War, and a megalomaniacal sense of Germany's destiny and future status as a world power. The former frontline soldier of World War I recognized that the powerful emerging technologies of that conflict—motorization, modern artillery, armored vehicles, submarines, and aircraft—would be essential tools for the realization of his vision. Even before attaining power, he recognized the value of air travel. For his 1932 election campaign he chartered a Junkers Ju 52 trimotor from the state airline, Deutsche Lufthansa. Employing the catchy slogan "Hitler over Germany!" Hitler barnstormed across the country, making dozens of speeches and seeming to be everywhere at once. After 1933 he became the first head of state to have a personal aircraft.[2] Most accounts of Hitler's stagecraft mention the impressive opening scene of the Leni Riefenstahl film *Triumph of the Will*, in which Hitler descends from the clouds in a silver trimotor to attend the 1934 party congress at Nuremberg.

Ironically, Hitler did not like flying—his first flight, like those of many novice air travelers, turned out poorly. Rushing to Berlin from Bavaria in bad weather during the abortive Kapp Putsch in 1920, Hitler became airsick, and his pilot had to make a forced landing before reaching the capital. Though he later flew regularly, Hitler was never really comfortable in the air. He was reportedly white-knuckled when his fellow dictator Benito Mussolini, an amateur pilot, took the controls of a huge Condor transport plane and maneuvered it enthusiastically during an inspection tour of the Eastern Front in August 1941.

Hitler's grasp of aviation, especially its operational application and technology, remained superficial. His closest collaborators frequently commented on his good memory for technical details and statistics, but he gravitated toward army armament and naval gunnery. Field Marshal Erhard Milch, Göring's deputy and the Luftwaffe's chief of technical air armament, recalled that Hitler was keenly aware of aviation's benefits, but that "the technical as well as tactical principles of aviation were foreign to him. . . . He compared flying with the movement of tanks or motor vehicles and therefore could not understand the greater possibilities or the difficulties of aviation." Milch believed that Hitler viewed the airmen he decorated as merely "skilled workers."[3]

Despite rare affinities for individuals such as the aircraft designer Willy Messerschmitt and the rocket engineer Wernher von Braun, Hitler tended to distrust "experts" and "mathematicians." His understanding of technical innovations such as jet propulsion and rocketry was sketchy, and he tended to support developments, such as super-heavy artillery mounted on fighter aircraft, that were at best impractical. He tended to get much of his aeronautical information from his personal pilot, Hans Baur, and from young combat pilots who visited his headquarters and gave Hitler their enthusiastic but often narrow recommendations.

Yet it would be a mistake to dismiss Hitler's grasp of airpower in its most basic form. Often wrong about specifics, Hitler had an intuitive sense of airpower's geopolitical utility as a tool of coercion. His air minister, Göring, assisted in his education. Ruthless and energetic in the early years of the Third Reich, the World War I ace and old fighter pilot from the early days of the Nazi Party enjoyed a privileged position as Hitler's designated successor. In some ways, his technical grasp of modern airpower was as deficient as Hitler's (developments such as radar were especially alien to him). His many roles, to include command of the Luftwaffe and chief of the economic Four-Year Plan, coupled with his shrewd diplomatic and political instincts, enabled him to make broad connections between statecraft and aviation. As the historian Edward L. Homze explains:

> It was Göring who educated Hitler to the potentialities of air power. Göring had no clear idea of strategic air power, for he was not a methodical or profound military thinker. He was, however, an excellent assimilator and promoter. He thought about air power along Douhetian lines, as an independently organized weapon capable of inflicting a decisive blow on an enemy. Air power was a type of third-dimensional extension of Schlieffen's annihilation battle, a concept embedded in the Prussian military tradition. Göring and Hitler, with their sharp political sense and intuitive grasp of mass psychology, appreciated its uniqueness for their immediate purposes.[4]

Later in the war this amateurishness and dilettantism would have severe consequences. But at that time the collaboration between Hitler and his senior airman helped shape the nascent Luftwaffe into an instrument of coercive diplomacy.

Above all, Hitler's ambitions set the strategic and diplomatic stage for the employment of German airpower. His plan, laid out clearly in his 1925 testament, *Mein Kampf*, called for the dismantling of the Versailles security system, the aggrandizement of Germany at the expense of the weak states to the east, the humbling of France, and ultimately the conquest of vast living space (*Lebensraum*) to the east—the USSR.

Germany—An Air Nation

Despite Nazi boasts of having created the Luftwaffe out of whole cloth after 1933, the air weapon wielded so effectively in the late 1930s was firmly rooted in the soil of Weimar, rather than Nazi, Germany. The strategic and diplomatic aspirations of the Weimar Republic (1918–1933) included a desire to redress the situation of the Polish Corridor, to regain Upper Silesia, to counter French power, and eventually to achieve *Anschluss* (union) with Austria. This was to be accomplished through patient revisionism, international agreements, and occasionally clandestine measures, such as a secret military collaboration with the USSR initiated after the Treaty of Rapallo in 1922.

Germans, with some justice, considered theirs one of the leading aeronautical nations in the world. Count Ferdinand von Zeppelin's airships inaugurated safe passenger flights in pre–World War I Germany, in the process sparking an "airship craze" and an outpouring of national pride that cut across traditional class barriers. The German air service had given a good account of itself in the 1914–1918 war. Its noteworthy accomplishments included the employment of massed airpower over the battlefront in order to gain air superiority and the development of modern fighter tactics and close air-support procedures. The Germans also pioneered the strategic bombing of economic and population centers, first with zeppelins and later with multi-engine bombers.

The Treaty of Versailles of 1919 outlawed German military aviation and for a time severely limited the development and production of even civilian aircraft. As the latter restrictions were gradually relaxed,

German commercial aviation soon became a force to be reckoned with. German airlines blazed new air routes through Africa and South America. Numerous small regional carriers gave way to form the state airline, Deutsche Luft Hansa, in 1925. Glider and sport flying clubs proliferated, helping instill "airmindedness" in a whole generation of Germans. And the globe-circling flight of the dirigible *Graf Zeppelin* in 1929 was a powerful—if seemingly peaceful—symbol of Germany's renewed aviation prowess.

Yet all this activity should not obscure the fact that Germany was completely disarmed in the air. The few paramilitary police squadrons hardly constituted an air arm, and though Lufthansa's long-range navigation and bad-weather flying experience and gliding club zeal were important, neither translated directly into military capability. Aviation was conspicuously absent from the 100,000-man Reichswehr (defense force) permitted Germany under the terms of the treaty. General Hans von Seeckt, the head of the Troop Office, essentially a camouflaged General Staff, retained a number of airmen within the Reichswehr's officer corps. These officers conducted rigorous analysis of the airpower experiences in the 1914–1918 war. By 1926 the Reichswehr possessed one of the most comprehensive and realistic airpower doctrines of any nation. Very limited training of aviators took place inside the Soviet Union, in exchange for industrial assistance provide to the Soviets. The German aircraft industry was on a solid footing, but it suffered from the developmental lag during the lost Weimar years. High-performance aircraft engines and very long-range aircraft were particularly lacking. German military aviation in the Weimar years possessed a foundation of study, theory, planning, and organization, even if actual capability was deficient. It represented considerable latent power ready to be channeled.

The Nazi seizure of power in January 1933 removed many of the constraints on the development of German military aviation. A separate Reich air ministry, the RLM, was created in April 1933, laying the groundwork for an independent service led by the second man in the Reich. Göring's power and prestige gave it unique political, economic, and diplomatic clout. Nazism, a vigorous movement that looked to the future and emphasized modernity, embraced aviation in much the same manner as had Mussolini's Italy and Stalin's USSR. The slogan "Germany must become a nation of fliers" became a staple of Göring's speeches. Just as every aspect of German society underwent a process of *Gleichschaltung* (literally, harmonizing or bringing into line), the aviation institutions and organizations of Germany were "brought into line." The sport flying and gliding clubs were merged into the Deutscher Luftsport Verband (German Air Sports League, or DLV), which in turn gave way to the National Socialist Flying Corps (NSFK). The party also hijacked the zeppelins, symbols of German reach and power, and used them for political campaigning and other propaganda, most visibly at the 1936 Berlin Olympic Games. Enormous swastikas were painted on their vertical stabilizers. The airship pioneer Hugo Eckener, no friend of the Nazis, responded tersely to American journalists' questions about the paint job, "Because it's the law!"[5]

Hitler's regime had successfully established itself as a child of the air age. But how was the Luftwaffe actually to be employed in attaining German foreign policy objectives? The early Reichswehr studies concluded that airpower was most effectively employed as an offensive weapon, and the prevailing currents of international airpower thought, most clearly espoused by Giulio Douhet in his *Command of the Air*, concurred. A memo sent to Milch by Lufthansa's director, Dr. Robert Knauss, catalyzed German airpower thinking. Knauss was an airpower theorist of some note. He had written (under a pseudonym) a dramatic "death from the skies" book titled *Luftkrieg 1938: Der Zertrümmerung der Paris* (Air War 1938: The Demolition of Paris) and was also a trained economist.[6]

Knauss's May 1933 memo, "Die deutsche Luftflotte" (The German Air Fleet), proposed the swift creation of a powerful force of four hundred four-engine bombers. This bomber fleet would serve two purposes. It would function as a "risk" or "deterrent" force, shielding Germany from attack while the rest of its rearmament programs gathered momentum during the vulnerable early years of the regime. If war should break out, the "air fleet" would have a powerful war-fighting capability against Germany's putative enemies France and Poland. Knauss borrowed freely from airpower thinkers such as Douhet and explicitly invoked Admiral

Alfred von Tirpitz's pre–World War I "risk fleet" battleship-building program. He also echoed some of the ideas of an American airpower prophet, General Billy Mitchell, in arguing that such a bomber fleet could be built for the cost of two pocket battleships and would be far more effective. Yet the proposal had original, as well as derivative, elements. As Homze notes, "Knauss' memo was new in the emphasis it placed on the political, diplomatic, and psychological impact that an air force would have. He clearly anticipated much of the deterrent strategy used in game theory analysis in the nuclear weapons age."[7]

The specifics of Knauss's "Risiko-Luftwaffe" vision were not realized as the Luftwaffe rearmed throughout the 1930s. Industrial and technological limitations precluded the immediate manufacture of such large aircraft. Indeed, Germany never succeeded in developing a satisfactory long-range bomber. But in an important sense, Knauss's central idea survived. A numerically large Luftwaffe, even one lacking the long-range strategic "reach" Knauss envisioned, might serve well enough as Germany's rearmament pace quickened. If the initial antagonists were seen to be Czechoslovakia, Poland, and even France, a medium-range air force, capable of operating effectively with the army and against neighboring capitals, might serve Germany's immediate needs. Göring later recalled, "At that time we possessed only limited means, but we did have enough to build a risk fleet which could ensure further rearmament and prepare the way for the Führer to proclaim the resumption of the universal draft."[8]

The years 1934–1938 were a dramatic time of technological, doctrinal, industrial, and personnel expansion for the new service. An infusion of top-quality officers from the army, including the first chief of the air staff, General Walther Wever, added the needed professional expertise and general staff training. Under Wever's guidance, the Luftwaffe issued its capstone doctrine manual, LDv 16, "Conduct of Aerial Warfare," in 1935. The manual stressed the need for a modern air force to be able to gain and maintain air superiority, cooperate effectively with the army and navy, and attack enemy "centers of national resistance."[9] Air defense was not neglected, but Wever's doctrine writers emphasized the offensive character of an air force. Later writings elaborated on these basic premises. Major Hans-Detlef Herhudt von Rohden emphasized not only the psychological character of air warfare, but also Germany's unfavorable geopolitical position in central Europe, and he argued that the German air force could best protect the Reich by helping the army seize neighboring territory and acquiring the necessary "depth" from which to conduct more far-reaching air warfare.[10] German industry provided the Luftwaffe with a generation of superior aircraft types. Its medium bombers, interceptors, and dive bombers were state-of-the-art. For a time these new types served alongside obsolete earlier models, but the German modernization program was moving faster than those of its potential adversaries.

German Airpower and the Bloodless Conquests

Between the Rhineland remilitarization in March 1936 and the "Rape of Prague" three years later, Nazi Germany managed to upend the post–World War I European balance of power. In Winston Churchill's memorable words, "The whole equilibrium of Europe has been deranged."[11] Many factors contributed to this German diplomatic triumph. Western statesmen misjudged Hitler's true character and intentions. Some truly believed that almost anything was preferable to a repetition of the slaughter of the First World War. Still others felt that some German revisionism of the punitive Versailles peace was acceptable and legitimate. Revived German military power played a central role in this geopolitical transformation. And the new Luftwaffe came to symbolize this resurgent Germany. One observer noted, "As an agent of the foreign policy of Nazi Germany the Luftwaffe became a diplomatic instrument of supreme coercion, for it posed a direct and omnipotent menace to the cities and peoples of the nations opposing the creation of the New Order in Europe."[12]

The formal unveiling of the Luftwaffe took place on 10 March 1935. Göring claimed that the Luftwaffe was already as large as the Royal Air Force (a claim that had the unintended effect of galvanizing British aerial rearmament). In sheer number of airframes, this was not far from the truth, but, then as later, there was considerable bluff involved. The numbering of its flying units was designed to generate confusion and obscure the real numerical strength of the new service; supply, training, and research establishments were transformed overnight into fighter and bomber wings.[13] One Luftwaffe commander recalled that foreign visitors were amazed by the enormous hangars springing up on new Luftwaffe bases, but they failed to realize that these structures were either empty or filled with obsolete "furniture vans." He compared the display to a circus strongman who is actually juggling dummy weights.[14] Göring himself admitted that his intent was "to impress Hitler and to enable Hitler, in turn, to impress the world."[15]

The Luftwaffe played only a minor supporting role in Hitler's first major international success, the Rhineland remilitarization in March 1936. The movement of German forces into the demilitarized zone took many in the Luftwaffe's top leadership by surprise. The few fighter squadrons committed to the operation—with armament that was not even properly installed—flew from airfield to airfield, and ground crewmen changed the registration numbers and insignia on the aircraft at each stop.[16] It is not clear what, if any, effect this charade had on the Western powers, who in any case did nothing beyond making diplomatic protests. Despite operating from a position of weakness, Hitler gained a real diplomatic success, undermining the possibility for collective action against his designs.

Some of Hitler's diplomatic moves were the product of calculation; others were more opportunistic. So it was with the decision in 1936 to intervene in the civil war in Spain on the side of the rebel General Francisco Franco. Hitler's rationale for assisting Franco included a desire to check the power of France, to shore up his relations with Mussolini, who was also aiding the rebels, to gain access to raw materials, and to distract attention from events in central Europe.[17] Additionally, the war in Spain would serve as a "military and ideological proving ground,"[18] benefiting both the German military and the regime.

From the outset the Luftwaffe proved to be the most visible and powerful form of German assistance. Shortly after Franco appealed to Hitler for assistance, Luftwaffe Ju 52 transports ferried Franco's colonial troops from Morocco to northern Spain in one of the first mass troop airlifts in history. Throughout the conflict the German air component, known as the Condor Legion, provided powerful air support for Franco's forces. Wolfram von Richthofen, who would become the Luftwaffe's top tactical airman during the Second World War, refined the tactics and procedures soon to dominate the battlefields of Poland, western Europe, and Russia. The latest types of German aircraft, including the Messerschmitt Bf 109 fighter and the Junkers Ju 87 "Stuka" dive bomber, received their baptism of fire in Spain.

The Spanish Civil War's value to the Luftwaffe was real enough in terms of the tactical lessons and experience gained by the Condor Legion's "volunteer" aviators. Yet Hitler and Göring reaped some additional psychological and propaganda benefits. Strategic bombing of population centers in Spain did not seem to pay large dividends—the lack of genuine "strategic" targets and the relatively small scale of the raids seemed to preclude drawing many conclusions for war between the great powers. Yet events such as the destructive April 1937 Condor Legion raid on the Basque town of Guernica seemed to endow the Luftwaffe with a genuine "city-busting" capability.

The dramatic unveiling of the Luftwaffe, its use in the Rhineland remilitarization, and its combat debut in Spain all served to draw international attention to the new player on the world's airpower stage. Other "atmospheric" events in the mid- to late 1930s also combined to increase awareness of the power of aviation in general and German airpower in particular. News reports of Italian bombings in Ethiopia and Japanese air attacks on Chinese cities combined with reports from Spain to underscore the effect of terror bombing on defenseless civilian populations. Military observers at the annual German army maneuvers reported increasingly elaborate participation by the expanding Luftwaffe bomber and fighter squadrons. German aircraft took home many honors at international air events; at the Zurich meet in July 1937, a prototype Dornier 17 medium bomber won the Alpine race and displayed a performance that outstripped contemporary fighter aircraft. German fighter planes (actually specially modified prototypes) from Heinkel and Messerschmitt captured several speed records. Collectively, these events served to increase perceptions of airpower's importance and Germany's leading role.

Particularly significant were the activities of a well-known foreign visitor to Germany. This was Colonel Charles A. Lindbergh, the "Lone Eagle," hero of the epic 1927 transatlantic flight. In July 1936, at the request of Major Truman Smith, U.S. military attaché in Berlin, Lindbergh made the first of five inspection trips to German aviation facilities. Although a reservist in the U.S. Army Air Corps, Lindbergh traveled as a private citizen and guest of the German government; as a result he was granted access to places even the attachés could not tread. His second visit to Germany in October 1937 was probably the most important. Lindbergh inspected the latest German types, including the Bf 109 fighter, the Heinkel 111 and Dornier 17 bombers, and other first-line hardware. The trip resulted in a concise four-page report (signed by Smith but ghosted by Lindbergh) that told of the great strides made by German aviation. It observed: "Germany is once more a world power in the air. . . . The astounding growth of German air power from a zero level to its present status in a brief four years must be accounted one of the most important world events of our time."[19] Lindbergh concluded that Germany had already surpassed France in overall air strength and threatened to overtake Britain and the United States.

Though some dismissed Lindbergh as a complete dupe, or even a Nazi sympathizer (and his evident chumminess with top Nazi leaders and acceptance of a medal from Hitler angered many of his countrymen), Lindbergh correctly assessed much of what he saw. His technical appraisal of the quality of the German frontline types was accurate, as was his evaluation of German aircraft production potential. He rightly noted weaknesses in German pilot training (something that in fact would plague the Luftwaffe throughout the coming war). Yet some of his more measured judgments were lost in the transmission. His reports, their details often embellished and inflated in the retelling, fanned fears in Britain and France regarding their extreme vulnerability to German aerial might, and he spoke with seeming credibility as an air expert. His findings on a later visit to Germany pushed French Minister of Finance Georges Bonnet into a state of near panic. "Colonel Lindbergh has returned from his tour horrified at the overwhelming strength of Germany in the air and the terrible weakness of all other powers. . . . French and

British towns would be wiped out and little or no retaliation would be possible."[20] Lindbergh would later be immersed in controversy; his anti-Semitic utterances, isolationist agitation, and involvement with the America First movement earned him FDR's undying enmity. Though his precise influence on the course of events in the late 1930s is hard to quantify, there is no doubt that his prognostications shaped Western perceptions of the capabilities of the Luftwaffe at a critical juncture.

In late 1937 Hitler began to accelerate the pace of his geopolitical program. At a secret conference with his top advisers on 5 November (the so-called Hossbach Meeting, after the army adjutant whose hand-written minutes provide the only surviving record of the discussion), Hitler spoke of the need to achieve the required *Lebensraum* through force by 1943–1945 at the latest, by which time Luftwaffe and naval rearmament would be complete. Hitler left the door open for an earlier move against Austria and Czechoslovakia if the situation warranted. Field Marshal Werner von Blomberg, the war minister, and Foreign Minister Konstantin von Neurath expressed concerns at the conference, and a few days later Hitler received a memo from the army commander, General Werner von Fritsch, warning of the danger of precipitating a war before Germany was fully ready. Within months, these conservative "obstructionists" were removed.[21] Hitler took over Blomberg's duties himself; the more pliant Joachim von Ribbentrop and Walther von Brauchitsch replaced Neurath and Fritsch.

With the decks thus cleared, Hitler moved ahead with his plans to bring Austrians and the Sudeten Germans "home to the Reich." Austria had already been weakened through internal subversion by a very active Austrian Nazi party, which had launched a failed coup in 1934. A visit to Berchtesgaden by Austria's Chancellor Kurt von Schuschnigg on 12 February 1938 to address the problem of Austrian Nazi agitation provided the opportunity for Hitler to coerce Schuschnigg with threats of force. To turn up the pressure on the Austrian chancellor, Hitler arranged for the presence of senior military leaders at the meeting. Luftwaffe General Hugo Sperrle's fierce, scowling visage was intended to cow Schuschnigg. Those who knew Sperrle claimed that he was "in reality a good-hearted man despite the brutality and harshness of his features,"[22] yet he was better known to the world for his role in Spain as the commander of the Condor Legion. Hitler's threats compelled Schuschnigg to agree to a list of demands that would have effectively ended Austria's existence as an independent state.

Some indication of the temperature of the times may be gleaned from Göring's bellicose speech on Luftwaffe Day, 1 March 1938: "We shall become the terror of our enemies, nothing shall stop us. . . . I want in this army iron men with a will to deeds. . . . And when the Führer in his Reichstag speech . . . uttered the proud words that we would no longer tolerate that ten million German national comrades should be oppressed beyond our borders, then you know as soldiers of the Air Force that, if it must be, you must back these words of the Führer to the limit. . . . We are burning with eagerness to prove our invincibility."[23] Throughout February and March 1938, the Luftwaffe and German army conducted ominous maneuvers along the German-Austrian border, providing a backdrop to the emerging crisis.

Schuschnigg appeared to accept German demands, but then surprised and angered Hitler by announcing a plebiscite to decide Austria's fate. Hitler redoubled his diplomatic pressure while ordering invasion preparations to commence. The Austrians folded, but the invasion order had already been given. On 12 March 1938 German army units rolled unopposed across the border into Austria. The Luftwaffe played a significant part in the swift occupation. Four hundred combat aircraft participated, including impressive numbers of Heinkel He 111 and Junkers Ju 86 bombers. A fleet of 160 Junkers Ju 52 transport planes flew two thousand troops into Vienna and scattered leaflets over the capital: "National Socialist Germany greets its possession National Socialist Austria and its new government in true indivisible union."[24] Three days later Hitler and Milch took the salute as a massed flyby of German aircraft thundered overhead.

What went down in Nazi lore as the *Blumenkrieg* (flower war) was actually a calculated application of force and statecraft. Hitler pulled off his coup by isolating Austria, weakening it from within, and threatening the use of force—especially airpower. As Schuschnigg himself concluded, "We yield only to superior force." The Luftwaffe reaped significant benefits from the occupation. Despite German propaganda showcasing the transfer of Austrian air force units into the Luftwaffe ("the high point for the Luftwaffe in Austria was the absorption of the first unit to come under the banner of the Third Reich . . . a fighter squadron in Wiener-Neustadt"),[25] most Austrian aviators were simply absorbed piecemeal into the German air arm. Perhaps most significantly, one of these transfers was General Alexander Löhr, who became one of Hitler's most able air fleet commanders. Raw materials and foreign exchange eased the Luftwaffe's economic position; the Messerschmitt plant at Wiener Neustadt eventually became one of the Third Reich's largest factories. In the meantime, Dr. Josef Goebbels's Propaganda Ministry turned up the heat. The period between the *Anschluss* and the outbreak of the Second World War saw a virtual flood of books, graphic maps, cigarette cards, and press articles portraying the might of the Luftwaffe. "Victory in Peacetime!" trumpeted one Luftwaffe publication.[26]

It was in the crisis over the Sudetenland in 1938 that the Luftwaffe played its most significant role in the prewar period. Hitler took up the cause of the German Sudeten minority in Czechoslovakia. Things almost came to a boiling point that spring, when aggressive German moves prompted Czech reaction and international attention. Hitler told his intimates of his "unalterable decision to smash Czechoslovakia by military action in the near future." Without a doubt, Hitler wanted war. It was the task of the German military—which soon set to work on planning for the invasion, code-named "Green"—to wage it. The Luftwaffe had a double task. It was to assist in the quick conquest of Czechoslovakia and keep Britain and France on the sidelines. By September war over Czechoslovakia seemed imminent, and the Allied leaders, Prime Minister Neville Chamberlain of Britain and Premier Edouard Daladier of France, sought to avert war through diplomacy and concessions.

Of the Western powers, it was France that was most thoroughly shaken by the presumed superiority of the Luftwaffe. The French Armée de l'Air, the premier air force of World War I, had fallen embarrassingly far behind after years of budgetary shortfalls, doctrinal confusion, and political volatility. When faced with displays of German air strength, French airmen, cognizant of their own service's numerical, technological,

French air force leaders, including Chief of Staff General Joseph Vuillemin (*center row, second from left*), are hosted by Luftwaffe Inspector General Erhard Milch (*center row, third from left*) on a carefully orchestrated tour of Luftwaffe bases in August 1938. Vuillemin came away convinced that the French air force would not last two weeks against the Luftwaffe. (Smithsonian Institution Archives)

and manpower weaknesses, reacted with pessimism. The culminating point was a 26 August 1938 inspection tour of Germany by General Joseph Vuillemin, chief of the French air staff. The Luftwaffe leadership had prepared carefully for Vuillemin's tour. He was plied with beer and bonhomie, especially by the bluff stunt pilot Ernst Udet, the Luftwaffe's technical development chief. The Frenchman saw airfields filled with brand-new German bombers and fighters, unaware that the rest of Germany had been virtually stripped of aircraft to manufacture this display. Tours of the Messerschmitt, Junkers, and Heinkel factories indicated mass production of the very latest types. A record-setting prototype fighter plane, the Heinkel 100, roared past Vuillemin, and he learned that the aircraft was apparently already in full production. Udet told Milch, in a carefully scripted exchange within the French general's earshot: "The second production line is just starting up, and the third in two weeks' time."[27] In reality, only a handful of He 100s were ever manufactured.

Yet the bluff was successful. As the historian D. C. Watt sums it up, "General Vuillemin . . . gulled and swindled by a series of Potemkin villages—or rather airfields—returned from Germany in 1938 convinced that war would mean the ruin of Paris."[28] He told the French ambassador, "If war breaks out at the end of September as you think it will, there won't be a single French aircraft left after 14 days."[29] Some have argued that this dire report was "the main reason why France refrained from intervening in the Czech crisis."[30] Certainly, his judgment combined with

Luftwaffe personnel taking the oath of allegiance to Adolf Hitler as the standard of yet another new flying unit is unveiled. The Nazi propaganda machine magnified the growth of the air service in the years after its 1935 unveiling, creating the illusion that the Luftwaffe was larger and far more combat-ready than it in fact was. (Smithsonian Institution Archives)

Lindbergh's in a potent one-two punch. Senior French military and civilian leaders were powerfully influenced. The French army commander General Maurice Gamelin told the British that "all the principal cities in northern France, including Paris, would have to be evacuated prior to a French offensive," owing to a fear of German air reprisals. There is little doubt that Vuillemin's pessimistic prognostications affected Daladier as he left to confer with Hitler.

Chamberlain's famous comment after Bad Godesberg seems to suggest that German airpower was also a major factor in the British decision to abandon Czechoslovakia. A witness recalled: "That morning he [Chamberlain] had flown up the river over London. He had imagined a German bomber flying the same course. He had asked himself what degree of protection we could afford to the thousands of homes he had seen stretched out below him, and he had felt that we were in no position to justify waging a war today in order to prevent a war hereafter."[31] Certainly there was an outpouring of British popular relief that war had been averted. Yet on balance British calculations that led to the policy of appeasement were probably based more on a general desire to avoid war than on a specific fear of the Luftwaffe's capabilities. Although Lindbergh's dire predictions found a ready audience in Britain (and were in some cases further inflated in the telling), on the whole the British did not fall for the Luftwaffe's propaganda as thoroughly as the French. One British military journal noted, "Despite statements made by their manufacturers, [the production Heinkel and Messerschmitt fighters] are *not* identical with the machines used to break the world's speed record."[32] Superior intelligence, an ongoing aircraft modernization program, and favorable geography all bolstered the RAF.

Nazi Germany was not content to rest on the laurels of Munich. In November 1938 Hitler ordered a quintupling of the Luftwaffe's frontline strength, a version of the "Risk Air Force" concept carried to extremes. Even though most German thinking stressed airpower's offensive nature, one equally grandiose defensive development played a role in the last year of peace. In June 1938 construction had begun on the *Luftverteidigungszone West* (Western Air Defense Zone). In an attempt to extend the frontier defenses of the West Wall into the third dimension, a costly (400 million RM) program overseen by the creator of the Autobahn, Fritz Todt, constructed what was intended to be an "impenetrable barrier." Consisting of flak positions (light and heavy), searchlights, and sound detectors and augmented by four to five fighter groups, the zone included 245 permanent concrete emplacements and extended for a total length of 375 miles. It was intended to protect not only German industrial and population centers but also army assembly areas on Germany's western border. German contemporary sources credit the zone, and the flak guns and barrage balloons temporarily deployed as it was being completed, with deterring Germany's enemies during the crises of 1938–1939.

The Luftwaffe again played its part in Reich diplomacy as the defenseless remnant of Czechoslovakia was overrun. Hitler threatened President Emil Hacha on 14 March 1939 with the destruction of Prague from the air. Five hundred Luftwaffe planes participated in the resulting occupation; troops were air-landed at Prague in an eerie replay of the Austrian annexation. And the Luftwaffe's influence extended into the last days of peace. Chamberlain noted, "The efforts of France to postpone an official declaration of war as long as possible until the French women and children could be evacuated played an important role in the final, time-consuming agonies preceding the declaration of war."[33]

How much of the Luftwaffe's influence stemmed from the reality, and how much from the carefully crafted image? In one of the earliest postwar histories of the Luftwaffe, *Trumpf oder Bluff?* (Trump Card or Bluff?), the former bomber commander General H. J. Rieckhoff claimed that though the German air force was "no phantom," it was still a "bluff." "The 'Eagle' was illuminated by searchlights," he wrote, "and frightened the world by its gigantic shadow!"[34] Certainly the real numbers and capability were far less than the pessimistic French estimates of more than eight thousand frontline planes. On 1 September 1938 the total establishment strength of the Luftwaffe was 3,714 combat aircraft, of which 2,928 were actually on hand, and 1,669 (582 bombers) operationally ready. Even more significantly, of 2,577 available crews, 1,145 were judged only "partially" ready for operations.[35] Such a force may well have been sufficient to deal with Czechoslovakia in a limited war, but the Luftwaffe was quite unready to extend the war against France and Britain simultaneously in September 1938. There was in any event no real way for the Luftwaffe, with its arsenal of twin-engine medium bombers, to reach Great Britain from its bases in western Germany. Even after Munich, the war games and studies conducted by Luftflotte 2 revealed the Luftwaffe's unreadiness for a general war against the British.[36] As one historian noted, the Luftwaffe of 1938 was *Mehr Schein als Sein*—more image than reality.[37]

Yet in international relations, perception has a way of becoming reality. Even as astute an observer as the historian and strategic thinker Edward Mead Earle, writing an influential *Yale Review* article in 1946, concluded, "It is hard to recapture the mood of 1938, but one who has lived through the Munich crisis and who has read and reread the historical record is justified in concluding that the victory for Germany was primarily victory for the Luftwaffe and perhaps the greatest victory of its entire existence. . . . [The Luftwaffe's] bloodless victory of 1938 came perilously close to deciding the fate of the world."[38] In the words of the French air minister Guy La Chambre, at the time of the Munich crisis "our aviation was so deficient that we were not free agents."

Working with Allies, Keeping Friendly Neutrals Friendly: Aviation Diplomacy in Peace and War

One of the striking things about the history of the Second World War is the stark contrast between the powerful coalition of the "united nations," especially the United States, Great Britain, and the Soviet Union, and the feeble cooperation among the Axis and its satellites. This distinction extended to the air war as well. American Lend-Lease aircraft patrolled the Atlantic sea-lanes and the Western Desert and pummeled German forces in the depths of the Soviet Union. German efforts to assist its coalition partners with aviation technology and training, despite rare successes, were generally thwarted.

Despite producing export versions of some of its combat types, the Luftwaffe during the 1930s had little interest in supplying potential coalition partners with first-line aircraft. Overtures from Romania and Hungary were largely snubbed; they were offered only obsolescent

An early-model German He 111, designed as a mail plane but a major threat to peace in the late 1930s under Hitler's aggression. (SHAA 83-2162)

aircraft that the Luftwaffe did not want. As a result, they took their business to France, Italy, and Britain or (in the case of the Romanians) began developing their own aircraft industries. As was true of so much of the Third Reich's war effort, wartime scrambling was unable to reverse the effects of years of neglect.

Once war broke out, the Luftwaffe leadership saw the need to pay belated attention to building up the air arms of its allies and to help foster self-sufficient aircraft industries. Its major coalition partners, Fascist Italy and Imperial Japan, presented very different strategic and technical problems. Italy was determined to wage a "parallel war" in the Mediterranean. This understandable national impulse also undermined the creation of any kind of meaningful combined command or operational planning structure. Since the First World War, the Italian air force (Regia Aeronautica), once one of the world's most advanced, had gone the way of the French Armée de l'Air. It was saddled in 1940 with obsolescent aircraft designs and an aircraft industry totally unsuited to the mass production of modern combat types—a sad state of affairs in the homeland of Douhet. Some success resulted from combining aerodynamic Italian designs with powerful German engines, but the fall of Mussolini's government in 1943 nipped these promising developments in the bud.

Any cooperation with Germany's Pacific ally, Japan, was hamstrung by distance. Despite an energetic attaché program, strategic and technical cooperation between the two powers remained limited, although some exchanges of aviation technology and equipment took place. A perusal of Allied aircraft recognition manuals circa 1942–1944 would lead one to conclude that the Japanese were operating German aircraft designs. Most prominent was an aircraft code-named "Mike," a Japanese Messerschmitt 109E. (Allied intelligence, bypassing the confusing Japanese nomenclature, designated fighters with boys' names, bombers with girls'.) Three Bf 109s had been sent to Japan in 1941 for testing, but the Japanese elected not to mass-produce them. This did not prevent erroneous reports of "German" aircraft in the Pacific throughout the war. Other exchanges of technology occurred sporadically under the terms of the Nippon-German Technical Exchange Agreement. In most cases, German technology was exchanged for raw materials from Japan, but some Japanese aircraft technology went to Germany, although no production resulted. Japan benefited by receiving examples and engineering drawings of Daimler-Benz high-performance aircraft engines. These were occasionally bartered for strategic materials such as tungsten, which the Germans needed for aircraft cannon shells, and other key raw materials. Some of these exchanges were brokered at the highest levels of the Luftwaffe command. As the B-29 offensive against Japan's home islands began, Japan requested the latest German air defense technology. Radar sets, antiaircraft weapons, turbojets, and even rocket-propelled interceptors (and the associated technical drawings) made it to Japan via submarine, but none of these was ready for action when Japan surrendered.

The protracted struggle on the Eastern Front led to the most sustained opportunity for the Luftwaffe to engage in coalition air operations. At one time or another, German units flew alongside Romanian, Hungarian, Slovak, Finnish, Bulgarian, Croat, and even (briefly) turncoat Russian air arms. Of these, the Romanian collaboration was the most sustained and substantial of all the Luftwaffe's coalition-building efforts. In September 1940 the German Air Force Mission to Romania (DLM) was dispatched as part of a comprehensive Wehrmacht assistance mission. Its ostensible duty was to "defend the Romanian oil fields against air attack" and "to train and reorganize the Romanian air force, both flying and antiaircraft units." In reality, these functions were a cover for the DLM's real purpose:

The German Junkers Ju 88 World War II bomber–night fighter, very much a part of Hitler's threats. This captured model was photographed at the USAAF's Wright-Patterson Air Force Base. (USAF 167940)

to build up Romanian bases as jumping-off points for the upcoming invasion of the USSR. A preliminary investigation of the Romanian aircraft industry revealed that it was "so inferior, that it is unable to cover even the present requirements of the Romanian Air Force."

Once the war against the USSR began, the Luftwaffe began to reexamine its policy. More energetic efforts to equip and train the Romanian air force were implemented. It was believed that well-equipped and well-trained satellite formations might free up first-line German units for more demanding tasks. The Romanian air arm gave a good account of itself in some engagements, but cooperation with German headquarters was generally poor. One defecting Romanian Junkers Ju 88 pilot told his Allied interrogators that the Romanians were treated with condescension by their German comrades, and they suffered the indignity of having their reconnaissance reports verified by German aircraft.[39] License production of modern German types by the Romanians came to naught.

Condescension seemed to be a hallmark of German dealings with coalition partners. The Luftwaffe Mission to Bulgaria was established according to the DLM model as a means of implementing training and organizational reforms. A senior member of the mission noted that the Bulgarians were known as the "Prussians of the Balkans." He was quick to add, "Of course, the slogan 'Prussians of the Balkans' does not mean that the Bulgarian soldier, with his present training, which remains scant despite all training measures, and with his characteristic slowness of mind and body, is adapted to the conditions of modern warfare." Sure enough, despite training, he reported that Bulgarian antiaircraft crews were hopeless, "and after five shots their barrels pointed to all points of the compass."[40] The historian James Corum sums up the German coalition warfare effort as "a case of arrogance and ideology that overrode common sense."[41]

Some brief mention should be made of German efforts to maintain good relations with desirable "friendly neutrals" during the war years. Like the more sustained coalition warfare efforts, these were a decidedly mixed bag. Technical and industrial collaboration with the Soviet Union that had existed during the Weimar Republic was briefly revived under the terms of the Soviet-German nonaggression pact, August 1939–June 1941; there are many examples of German aviation technology being sent to the USSR in exchange for raw materials. The Luftwaffe exported some Dornier reconnaissance bombers to the friendly government of Yugoslavia in 1940, only to destroy those same planes on the ground in the blitzkrieg that followed the anti-German coup in Belgrade in April 1941. Franco's Spain continued its amicable aeronautical relations with the Reich after the civil war, taking delivery of German designs and eventually license-producing them. In what was perhaps the longest-lasting vestige of German aviation diplomacy, Spanish-built Heinkel 111s and Messerschmitt 109s remained in service until the late 1960s.

Switzerland, given its unique diplomatic position, geographic location, and ability to supply scarce raw materials and manufactured goods, was considered sufficiently important to justify the sale of numbers of modern fighter aircraft to that Alpine nation. In 1938–1940, over one hundred of the latest models of the Messerschmitt 109 were made available. These were used for neutrality airspace defense (in the process forcing down a number of German and Allied aircraft that had

A Deuxième Bureau–annotated file photo of a pre–World War II German Me 109B fighter. (SHAA 92-3614)

strayed over Swiss territory). One of the more bizarre episodes of aviation diplomacy took place after a Messerschmitt 110 night fighter landed in error at Dubendorf (near Zurich, in the north of the country) in May 1944. The aircraft carried the newest radar equipment, and the Germans were desperate that the aircraft's secrets not fall into Allied hands. They agreed to sell the Swiss twelve of the latest model Bf 109Gs. The transaction went through; the Swiss received their 109s, and the night fighter mysteriously exploded and was completely consumed by fire.[42]

On the whole, the German experience with "airpower diplomacy" must be given low marks. Coalition warfare was never a priority for the Third Reich; it did little to prepare for it, and the results were predictably dismal. The problems of coordinating international aviation activity, with its complex technology, long developmental lead times, and extended periods of training, only exacerbated the difficulties.

Like any military organization, the Luftwaffe was intended to serve as a tool of statecraft as well as a combat service. From its inception as the

Risk Air Force as outlined by Robert Knauss, through the period of rearmament and the diplomatic crises of the 1930s, it fulfilled the former
role. Once the war broke out, the air arm won tremendous battlefield
victories. After the fall of France, Hitler and his airmen hoped the Luftwaffe might achieve one last diplomatic success, and indeed the British
were perilously close to reaching an accommodation with Germany
in May 1940. British airpower in the form of a superior integrated air
defense system checked German airpower for the first time, and as the
war lengthened, the Luftwaffe's weaknesses became more apparent. Its
failure at Stalingrad hastened the decline of both the service and its chief,
Hermann Göring. The inability of the Luftwaffe to defend home airspace
completed its disgrace; Göring had to field angry complaints from the
Gauleiters that Allied bombers were soaring, seemingly unopposed, over
their cities in "Reich Party Day" formations. By 1944 Hitler was openly
suggesting that the fighter arm be dissolved and the defense of Germany
entrusted solely to antiaircraft artillery. In one of his final rants in the
Berlin bunker in 1945, Hitler expressed a desire to string up the entire
Luftwaffe high command. That Berlin bunker was quite a distance from
the victory parade in Vienna on 15 August 1938.

Yet the Luftwaffe's eventual failure should not obscure the very
real success it had during the early years of the Nazi march of conquest.
It exerted powerful deterrent and compellent effects on the European
powers, both small and great, during some of the most important
diplomatic confrontations of the twentieth century. Certainly some of
its mystique was a creation of Nazi propaganda, which reinforced the
appeasement and pacifistic tendencies of European statesmen. Yet there
was substance as well: Luftwaffe doctrine, technology, and training made
it a formidable opponent. One must agree with the diplomatic historian
Gerhard Weinberg that General Rieckhoff might well have titled his
book *Trump Card and Bluff.* [43]

This success did not come without cost. The course of Hitler's foreign
policy and the demands it placed on the Luftwaffe scuttled the orderly
development plans of the air force. Hitler's need for a demonstration air
force impeded the evolutionary technical development and maturation
process so essential for success in modern aerial warfare. Göring spoke the

truth when he claimed, "The Führer will not ask me how big my bombers are, but how many there are." And the Luftwaffe's image proved to be a double-edged sword. The Reich's leaders also fell prey to the deception and overestimated the power of their air force, a malady not, it should be remembered, entirely unique to Germany in the 1930s. The story of the Luftwaffe and diplomacy remains a powerful cautionary tale. Modern-day observers should consider how a state can get what it wants through high-technology blackmail and intimidation, perhaps coming through the medium of space or cyberspace, rather than the air.

Notes

1. Air Ministry, *The Rise and Fall of the German Air Force, 1933–1945* (London: HMSO, 1948), p. xix.

2. C. G. Sweeting, *Hitler's Squadron* (Washington, D.C.: Brassey's, 2001), p. 1.

3. Erhard Milch, "Apologia," Von Rohden Collection, Library of Congress, microfilm 1750, reel 22, p. 1.

4. Edward L. Homze, *Arming the Luftwaffe: The Reich Air Ministry and the German Aircraft Industry, 1919–39* (Lincoln: University of Nebraska Press, 1976), p. 54.

5. J. Gordon Vaeth, *Graf Zeppelin: The Adventures of an Aerial Globetrotter* (New York: Harper and Brothers, 1958), p. 161.

6. On Knauss, see James Corum, *The Luftwaffe: Creating the Operational Air War, 1918–1940* (Lawrence: University Press of Kansas, 1997), pp. 130–134; Homze, *Arming the Luftwaffe*, chap. 3; Wilhelm Deist et al., *Germany and the Second World War*, vol. 1, *The Build-up of German Aggression* (Oxford: Clarendon Press, 1990), pp. 481–494.

7. Homze, *Arming the Luftwaffe*, p. 56.

8. Ibid.

9. A translation of the manual may be found in James S. Corum and Richard R. Muller, *The Luftwaffe's Way of War: German Air Force Doctrine, 1911–1945* (Baltimore: Nautical and Aviation, 1998), pp. 118–157.

10. Hans-Detlef Herhudt von Rohden, *Vom Luftkriege: Gedanken über Führung und Einsatz moderner Luftwaffen* (Berlin: E. S. Mittler & Sohn, 1938), p. 7.

11. Winston S. Churchill, *Blood, Sweat, and Tears* (New York: G. P. Putnam's Sons, 1941), p. 66.

12. Eugene M. Emme, "German Air Power, 1919–1939" (Ph.D. diss., University of Iowa, 1949), p. 358.

13. Richard Suchenwirth, *The Development of the German Air Force, 1919–1939*, USAF Historical Studies no. 160 (Maxwell Air Force Base, Ala.: USAF Historical Division, 1968), p. 189.

14. Herbert Joachim Rieckhoff, *Trumpf oder Bluff? 12 Jahre deutsche Luftwaffe* (Geneva: Inter Avia, 1946), pp. 60, 157.

15. Homze, *Arming the Luftwaffe,* p. 106.

16. Karl-Heinz Völker, *Die deutsche Luftwaffe, 1933–1939* (Stuttgart: DVA, 1969), pp. 147–148.

17. Gerhard Weinberg, *Hitler's Foreign Policy, 1933–1939: The Road to World War II* (New York: Enigma, 2005), pp. 486–487.

18. Emme, "German Air Power," p. 380.

19. Telford Taylor, *Munich: The Price of Peace* (Garden City, N.Y.: Doubleday, 1979), p. 761.

20. Ibid., p. 765.

21. Jeremy Noakes and Geoffrey Pridham, eds., *Documents on Nazism* (New York: Viking, 1975), pp. 521–531.

22. Suchenwirth, *Development of the German Air Force,* p. 193.

23. Emme, "German Air Power," p. 386.

24. Ibid., p. 389.

25. Hermann Adler, *Ein Buch von der neuen Luftwaffe* (Stuttgart: Franckh'sche Verlagshandlung, 1938), p. 138.

26. Heinz Bongartz, *Luftmacht Deutschland* (Essen: Essener Verlagsanstalt, 1939), p. 88.

27. David Irving, *The Rise and Fall of the Luftwaffe: The Life of Field Marshal Erhard Milch* (Boston: Little, Brown, 1973), p. 63.

28. Donald Cameron Watt, *Too Serious a Business: European Armed Forces and the Approach to the Second World War* (Berkeley: University of California Press, 1975), p. 10.

29. Suchenwirth, *Development of the German Air Force,* p. 192.

30. Ibid., p. 194.

31. Taylor, *Munich,* p. 822.

32. "The German Air Force," *Journal of the Royal United Services Institution* 84 (November 1939): 730.

33. Suchenwirth, *Development of the German Air Force,* pp. 194–195.

34. Rieckhoff, *Trumpf oder Bluff?* p. 148.

35. Air Ministry, *Rise and Fall of the German Air Force* (London: HMSO, 1948), pp. 19–20.

36. Williamson Murray, "German Air Power and the Munich Crisis," in *War and Society: A Yearbook of Military History,* ed. Brian Bond and Ian Roy (New York: Holmes and Meier, 1977), pp. 110–114.

37. Peter Fritzsche, *A Nation of Fliers: German Aviation and the Popular Imagination* (Cambridge: Harvard University Press, 1992), p. 190.

38. Edward Mead Earle, "The Influence of Air Power upon History," *Yale Review* 35, no. 4 (June 1946): 587.

39. Combined Services Detailed Interrogation Centre (CSDIC) File no. (A) 314 (M.E.), 8 August 1943, "First Detailed Interrogation Report on Pilot of Ju 88D1 of the Rumanian Air Force Landed Voluntarily on Cyprus on 22 August 1943 at 1415 hrs," U.S. Air Force Historical Research Agency (USAFHRA) 512.619C-12A.

40. Supreme Headquarters Allied Expeditionary Force (SHAEF) Intelligence Par-

ty (OKL [German air force high command]), Intelligence Report no. 35, "The GAF Mission to Bulgaria: Its Development and Its Activities," USAFHRA 506.6314A-42.

41. James Corum, "The Luftwaffe and Its Allied Air Forces in World War II: Parallel War and the Failure of Strategic and Economic Cooperation," *Air Power History* 51, no. 2 (Summer 2004): 18.

42. Thomas Hitchcock, *Messerschmitt "0-Nine" Gallery* (Boylston, Mass.: Monogram, 1973), p. 109.

43. Weinberg, *Hitler's Foreign Policy,* p. 377.

Further Reading

The use of the Luftwaffe as a diplomatic tool is touched on in most of the better general histories of the Nazi air arm. Especially valuable for this study were Great Britain Air Ministry, *The Rise and Fall of the German Air Force* (London: HMSO, 1948); Karl-Heinz Völker, *Die deutsche Luftwaffe, 1933–1939* (Stuttgart: DVA, 1967); Williamson Murray, *Luftwaffe* (Baltimore: Nautical and Aviation, 1985); James Corum, *The Luftwaffe: Creating the Operational Air War, 1918–1940* (Lawrence: University Press of Kansas, 1997); Matthew Cooper, *The German Air Force, 1933–1945: An Anatomy of Failure* (London: Jane's, 1981); and E. R. Hooton, *Phoenix Triumphant: The Rise and Rise of the Luftwaffe* (London: Arms and Armour, 1994). Early postwar studies by Richard Suchenwirth, such as *The Development of the German Air Force, 1919–1939,* USAF Historical Studies no. 160 (Maxwell Air Force Base, Ala.: USAF Historical Division, 1968), and especially Herbert Joachim Rieckhoff's *Trumpf oder Bluff? 12 Jahre deutsche Luftwaffe* (Geneva: Inter Avia, 1946), offer important insights from the German perspective. Edward L. Homze's *Arming the Luftwaffe: The Reich Air Ministry and the German Aircraft Industry, 1910–39* (Lincoln: University of Nebraska Press, 1976) is in a class by itself. On the Condor Legion in Spain, see Raymond Proctor, *Hitler's Luftwaffe in the Spanish Civil War* (Westport, Conn.: Greenwood, 1983). Peter Fritzsche's *A Nation of Fliers: German Aviation and the Popular Imagination* (Cambridge: Harvard University Press, 1992) contains a thoughtful and original discussion of the social and cultural dimensions of German air-mindedness. One older work deserves mention: a dissertation by Eugene M. Emme, "German Air Power, 1919–1939" (Ph.D. diss., University of Iowa, 1949). Although Emme perhaps exaggerates the Luftwaffe's influence at key junctures, his study is a thoughtful analysis based on a wide range of primary sources.

The best survey of German foreign policy remains Gerhard Weinberg's masterful 1970 two-volume *Foreign Policy of Hitler's Germany,* reprinted and revised as *Hitler's Foreign Policy, 1933–1939: The Road to World War II* (New York: Enigma, 2005). Wilhelm Deist et al., *Germany and the Second World War,* vol. 1, *The Buildup of German Aggression* (Oxford: Clarendon Press, 1990), contains an excellent treatment of the political, military, and diplomatic origins of German conquest.

Williamson Murray, *The Change in the European Balance of Power, 1938–1939: The Path to Ruin* (Princeton: Princeton University Press, 1984), covers the Austrian and Czech crises with emphasis on the military confrontation. Telford Taylor, *Munich: The Price of Peace* (Garden City, N.Y.: Doubleday, 1979), is the most thorough treatment of the Czech crisis and contains the best account of Lindbergh's role. Donald Cameron Watt, *How War Came: The Immediate Origins of the Second World War* (New York: Pantheon, 1989), covers the last year of peace in rich detail.

R. J. Overy's important article, "Hitler and Air Strategy," *Journal of Contemporary History* 15, no. 2 (July 1980): 405–421, is the best starting point for a consideration of Hitler's aviation outlook and role. Many of the better biographies of Hitler, from Alan Bullock's classic *Hitler: A Study in Tyranny* (New York: Harper & Row, 1962) to the recent two-volume work by Ian Kershaw, *Hitler, 1889–1936: Hubris* and *Hitler, 1936–1945: Nemesis* (New York: Norton, 1999 and 2000), contain important perspectives about the German dictator's conception and use of airpower. C. G. Sweeting, *Hitler's Squadron: The Fuehrer's Personal Aircraft and Transport Unit, 1933–1945* (Washington, D.C.: Brassey's, 2001), offers interesting insights into Hitler the flyer. On Hitler's chief airman, R. J. Overy's *Göring: The "Iron Man"* (London: Routledge, 1984), remains the best biography. David Irving's *The Rise and Fall of the Luftwaffe: The Life of Field Marshal Erhard Milch* (Boston: Little, Brown, 1973), remains useful on Milch's role in the Luftwaffe's genesis.

The study of the Luftwaffe as a coalition partner is still in its infancy. An important trailblazing effort in this regard is James Corum, "The Luftwaffe and Its Allied Air Forces in World War II: Parallel War and the Failure of Strategic and Economic Cooperation," *Air Power History* 51, no. 2 (Summer 2004): 4–19. On the more general question of German coalition warfare, see Richard DiNardo, *Germany and the Axis Powers: From Coalition to Collapse* (Lawrence: University Press of Kansas, 2005); Mark Axworthy, *Third Axis, Fourth Ally: Romanian Armed Forces in the European War, 1941–1945* (London: Arms and Armour, 1995); McGregor Knox, *Hitler's Italian Allies* (Cambridge: Cambridge University Press, 2000); and Hans-Joachim Krug et al., *Reluctant Allies: German-Japanese Naval Relations in World War II* (Annapolis: Naval Institute Press, 2001).

Suggestions for Further Research

An in-depth study of German airpower diplomacy and statecraft in 1933–1939 would be a worthwhile project, updating Emme's venerable though still useful work. An economic-military-diplomatic study of the German aviation industry (including Lufthansa) and its dealings abroad would be most welcome. As noted above, historians have only begun to delve into the coalition aspects of the Axis air war. Detailed studies of the German air force's efforts to work with Romania, Hungary, and Bulgaria have yet to be undertaken. A full-scale study of German-Japanese aviation technology cooperation and exchange would be particularly valuable.

4

The Emperor and the Despot

Statesmen, Patronage, and the Strategic Bomber in Imperial and Soviet Russia, 1909–1959

David R. Jones

The vastness of Russia and its remoteness made it immune to grand-strategic attacks against its few targets while making its enemies' vulnerabilities equally distant. These conditions were gradually changed by technology and in the Great Patriotic War (1941–1945) by the advances of the Soviet armies.

The development of Russian airpower was controlled by the small coteries of politicians at the top and supported by the enthusiasm of the masses. Russian and Soviet statesmen dealt with issues of defense, including aviation, within very similar institutional frameworks because the Soviets modeled their bodies charged with strategic decision making and military administration on those of Imperial Russia. This was especially true of those bodies that raised, equipped, trained, maintained, and directed the state's armed forces.

Soviet theorists distinguished between the institutions that led the country's defenses and those responsible for the "building" and leadership of the armed forces. The first were the ministers of the central administration, whereas practical leadership came from the General Staff. From 1917, of course, the Communist Party (CPSU) made all the decisions, supplemented by the new third hierarchy—the Main Political Administration—which maintained the commissars at every level of command, who reported to the Central Committee of the CPSU.

In pre-1917 Imperial Russia the czar, Nicholas II, was the joint commander and administrator in chief. He took his joint role very seriously, not only making decisions in discussions with his top advisers but also even going on a route march to test his soldiers' new boots and uniforms. At the same time, he protected his prerogatives from the Duma after 1905 and in 1915, when he became supreme commander in chief, he recognized his own limitations and left military decisions to his generals. But when he personally inspected Igor Sikorsky's giant *Il'ia Muromets* in June 1914, he joined other "Imperials" in helping legitimize aviation in Russia.

Nicholas II's cultivation of a military image also reflected his understanding that the image of *vozhd* (supreme military leader) was an essential aspect of the Russian ruler's "power myth." When Vladimir Lenin ignored this tradition, the role of *vodzh* fell to Commissar of War Leon Trotsky as he dashed from front to front in his famous armored train. But if he assumed it somewhat unwillingly, his archenemy Joseph Stalin began appropriating the image immediately on emerging as Lenin's unquestioned successor in 1928. Although his Civil War record was dubious at best, Stalin (not Trotsky) was soon hailed as the true architect of the Red victory of 1918–1921. As the military historian Dmitri Volkogonov observes, Stalin now "loved everything about the army," and the "armed forces were his special concern." Like Nicholas II before him, he knew personally almost all the officers above the level of corps commander, interviewed candidates for promotion, and quizzed them on their "personal experience, knowledge of the battlefield, [and] views on restructuring the army in the light of technical progress." He also, Volkogonov adds, spent "many hours with commissars, designers, scientists, and constructors . . . connected with military hardware," and "usually inspected new models himself and was present at tests." The memoirs of the designer A. S. Yakovlev and others make clear that this was especially true for aviation, and Stalin frequently worked personally with the designers to obtain an aircraft he desired.

Despite his unquestioned power Stalin, unlike Nicholas II, long lacked any official position in the state. Rather, he exercised power as the CPSU's general secretary and became head of the Sovnarkom only in May 1941. Even so, during the 1930s he meddled in every aspect of the military-naval establishment, purged the high command after 1937 of all possible opponents, and even oversaw the design of the Red Army's new dress and field uniforms. The dictator finally assumed a post directly involving the armed forces with the outbreak of war on 22 June 1941. On 30 June he concentrated the "absolute power of the state" in the State Committee of Defense (GKO), which, under his personal supervision as chairman, organized the war effort. His direction of the Red Army's actual battles was formalized when he also took direct charge of the new General Headquarters (*Stavka*) on 10 July, became commissar of Defense on 19 July, and finally, again like Nicholas II before him, supreme commander in chief of the armed forces of the USSR on 8 August. So despite M. I. Kalinin's (d. 1946) formal presidency during the war, this post was purely ceremonial, and Stalin's powers fully justified his unofficial title of generalissimo.

Stalin's supreme authority meant that his changing views of aviation necessarily did much to shape the missions and equipment assigned to the Red Air Forces (VVS) . Unfortunately, he lacked the last czar's modesty and fancied himself the leading expert in every aspect of military affairs. In reality, as the near-fatal disasters of 1941 demonstrate, he was at best an amateur, if at times an inspired one, in matters of military technology as well as strategy. Many of his decisions were sensible enough, but others were tragic, and some verged on the comic. Even so, Stalin promoted himself to marshal, unlike Nicholas II, who retained the rank of colonel that he had held at his father's death.

Nonetheless, between 1909 and 1953 two powerful Russian rulers—an emperor and a general secretary of the CPSU—actively united and controlled their defense establishments and intervened to promote aviation in general and, in the event, long-range bombers in particular. Indeed, the influence of their personal patronage of airpower was as profound as that of any external threats from the aviation of likely opponents. Later, although Stalin's wartime concentration of the two leaderships (of defense and of the military) in his person ended with his death in March 1953, subsequent general secretaries of the CPSU also polished up their own wartime military credentials. When Nikita Khrushchev emerged as first among equals in the post-Stalin collective leadership, he suddenly became an essential player in the Stalingrad victory of 1942–1943, and the self-proclaimed nuclear strategist who gave us the Cuban Missile Crisis of 1962. His successor, Leonid Brezhnev, later promoted himself to marshal and retained considerable, although not unlimited, authority in all major decisions on strategy and "military building," strategic aviation included. And finally, if Mikhail Gorbachev dissolved the CPSU after the failed coup of August 1991, the earlier military-administrative framework remained substantially intact within the Russian Federation.

Imperial Origins

In light of its conservative reputation, Imperial Russia's ruling elite was surprisingly open to new technologies. From 1869 the War Ministry looked into using balloons and purchased foreign aircraft for evaluation without Treasury support. Having witnessed Blériot's cross-Channel flight in 1909, Grand Duke Alexander Mikhailovich, who headed the Voluntary Society for Support of the Naval (later Aerial) Fleet, used its funds to help purchase French aircraft and send officers to France for training in 1910. With the czar's blessing, he also headed the Imperial Russian Air Club. Navy and army officers worked in tandem with support from the war and naval ministers, all of whom soon realized that Russia could not depend on aerial imports. They also insisted that aviation would be of "*very serious significance in future wars,*" and saw it, as did others, as operating in the "ocean of the air." This view was further supported by the predictions of novelists such as Russia's Vladimir Semenov and England's H. G. Wells.

   In practical terms, in Russia the airship was eclipsed by Igor Sikorsky's 7,000-pound (2,500-kilogram) transport *Grand,* which became the prototype of the *Il'ia Muromets* (IM) bomber, built at the Russo-Baltic Railway Wagon Works in 1913. Two IMs were immediately begun for the army, which otherwise went to war with some 250 aircraft.

To their credit, then, Imperial Russia's military-political elite had successfully promoted the new arm. Their success reflects the extent to which the "leaderships" of defense and of the armed forces were effectively unified under their joint chief, the emperor. Furthermore, Sikorsky's bomber and "S" series of single-engine fighters justified War Minister Vladimir Sukhomlinov's policy of promoting a Russian aircraft industry, which had given Russia a long-range bomber unlike any other in the world. More important, the IM was a viable alternative to large military dirigibles in that it was cheaper to build, base, and maintain in the field, but it could still fulfill all the airship's operational and strategic missions. Thus, the *Il'ia Muromets* in fact sounded the death knell for military dirigibles in Russia. So work on those in production in 1914 continued; but as resources rapidly became scarcer, the construction of even these dirigibles slowed, and in time most were abandoned.

Despite their support for bombers, Russia's leaders had gone to war with little idea of how to use their new weapons. On the basis of widespread discussions of aeronautics in the military and general press, Von Hardesty argues that Russia's soldiers had, very slowly, begun "to define a rudimentary air theory to shape air operations in a future conflict." Perhaps—but only to the extent that most agreed that aircraft were useful for scouting, artillery spotting, communications, and, just possibly, attacks on ground targets with various devices, metal darts or *fléchettes* included! Here the story of Sikorsky's IMs is instructive. When the first two entered service in September 1914, opinions differed widely on their proper missions. Long-range reconnaissance aside, some suggested they serve as gun platforms to destroy enemy airships, others that they bomb enemy fortresses. In fact, existing orders for further bombers were briefly canceled when the flights of the first two proved disappointing. This decision was reversed thanks to the vigorous lobbying of the aircraft's powerful supporters led by M. V. Shidlovskii, a former naval officer and the president of the Russo-Baltic Wagon Plant (RBVZ), builder of the

IMs. With the rank of major general, he took command of the IM-III and IM-IV at Yablonna, near Warsaw, in December 1914. These became the core of the famous *Eskadra vozdushnykh korablei* (Squadron of Flying Ships), which began combat missions in February 1915 and which received the appropriate bombs thanks to a special Ministry of War task force comprising Russia's leading technical specialists and scholars. Although the squadron's active strength varied from twenty-five to forty, the RBVZ completed seventy-two bombers in all, and only three were lost to direct enemy action. These IMs are credited with dropping a total of two thousand bombs during 442 raids, and those of 1915 against East Prussia, which preceded the German zeppelin attacks on Britain, may be the first examples of the "strategic" bombing of an enemy homeland. But in general, the IMs flew reconnaissance missions of up to 150 miles (240 kilometers) behind enemy lines, and these resulted in over seven thousand photographs of enemy positions.

What was true for the IM was the case for aviation in general, and to conclude that a "theory" of aerial combat or airpower existed in 1914 is to put the cart before the horse. Whatever they thought about the air weapon's future, few senior officers or theorists expected much, either tactically or operationally, of the handful of simple aircraft and airships at their disposal. Indeed, these still lacked effective bombs (usually regarded simply as air-dropped artillery shells), as well as other forms of aerial armament and reliable air-to-ground communications. Consequently, Europe's (and Russia's) military could study "lessons learned" from aerial combat, and develop theories accordingly, only after improved weaponry appeared to remedy the initial deficiencies. At the strategic level, as the case of the IM demonstrates, in 1914 there were no serious doctrinal or theoretical ideas beyond the horrendous fictional visions of future possibilities that sometimes terrified publics and sparked debates over possible air defense. Yet given the costs and the vulnerability of dirigibles, and the limited range and capabilities of the day's aircraft, the *Il'ia Muromets* excepted, Europe's statesmen and generals found predictions like those of Alexander Mikhailovich or the flyer Nikolai Popov as fantastic as H. G. Wells's *The World Set Free* (1914), with its prescient prophecy of an atomic war in 1939.

Early Soviet Concepts of Airpower

When World War I ended, matters were very different. That nearly four-year conflict had provided a mix of practical lessons on which to develop theories about the role of aviation in modern warfare. On both the Western and Eastern Fronts, aircraft had been invaluable for reconnaissance in preparing offensives and, with improved bombs, machine guns, and sighting devices, for directly supporting ground troops. Aerial battles of increasing ferocity occurred when fighter pilots sought to hinder the enemy's missions, and by 1917 massed aircraft fought for local control of the air over the battlefield. But whatever their strategic implications, these missions remained practically tactical and operational, and the only examples of strategic air warfare were the German zeppelin and Gotha raids on London and the British counterstrikes. In the East, despite the capabilities of Sikorsky's IM bombers and their early raids on East Prussia, Russia's leaders had not used them strategically. Instead, critics continually complained that each IM entering service deprived the Aerial Fleet of engines for four single-engine reconnaissance or fighter machines.

If by 1920 aircraft were an accepted component of any armed forces, a theoretical consensus on their future wartime roles proved elusive. Even so, the German and British raids were sufficient to lay the basis for the theory of strategic airpower advanced by the Italian flyer General Giulio Douhet. Like most military men, Douhet believed the recent war demonstrated the technological superiority of the defense, but he saw in aviation the means of avoiding another trench stalemate. In 1921 he published *The Command of the Air,* a title echoing the early "navalist" call for "command of the sea." This argued that air forces must exist as independent services, be equipped with special general-purpose "battle planes" that, with the outbreak of hostilities, would be ready to launch preemptive bombing campaigns against the enemy's cities, industry, and transport system. These strategic raids, he predicted, would be so devastating as to break an enemy's will and destroy its capabilities for combat, and thus be decisive. Since additional battles on land and sea would be unnecessary, an air force could win a war by itself. Given the lack of effective air defenses, it could achieve this decisive result by bombers alone, without any fighter escorts, and the bomber was now advanced as the ultimate offensive system.

Douhet wrote mainly for his fellow Italians, but his theory inspired aviators in all the major powers and eventually became part of the general interwar strategic debate. Opinions differ, however, about its immediate effect on the Soviet military, whose own recent experiences, material situation, and likely opponents differed considerably from those of western Europeans. From the Red Aerial Fleet's creation in 1918, its pilots focused on supporting their ground forces in battles of maneuver along extensive and fluid fronts very different from the trenches of 1914–1918. And when the Civil War ground to an end in 1920, the Reds' air services had practically vanished. According to a survey carried out in 1923 by M. V. Frunze, the army's aircraft inventory then was short by 72 percent and the navy's was nonexistent; in 1924 all air units still accounted for a mere 2 percent of the total military manpower.

Fortunately for the future, the new Communist regime was fully committed to the cause of aviation. Indeed, the enthusiasm shown by leading Bolsheviks paralleled the air-mindedness of the "Futurists" of Mussolini's Fascist Italy, and the later heroic image of the Luftwaffe in Hitler's Germany. Though the pilot seemed a fitting virile and youthful symbol of all these "new worlds," the Soviet leadership still understood full well that the country's weak industrial base constrained the growth of aviation, both civil and military. To remedy their shortage of technical cadres and mobilize supporters for the cause, in March 1923 they sought to harness the air-mindedness of Russia's youth by creating the new "voluntary" Society of Friends of the Aerial Fleet (ODVF). Although still limited by shortages of equipment and instructors, in 1926 it merged with similar societies for chemical warfare and paramilitary training to form the Society of Friends of Defense and the Aviation-Chemical Industry of the USSR, or *Osoaviakhim*. Expanding exponentially during the 1930s, it proved its strategic value during 1941–1945 by providing cadres for rebuilding the badly mauled Red air forces.

Similarly, the Young Communist League, or *Komsomol*, early became the Red Aerial Fleet's official patron, while Soviet leaders, like their Imperial predecessors, publicly demonstrated their personal support for aviation. As early as Moscow's May Day parade in 1918, a Red Nieuport fighter dropped leaflets to spectators, after which Lenin personally attended an air show at the nearby Khodinka Flying School. More important, he became the active patron of Nicholas E. Zhukovsky, a leading specialist in aerodynamics, whose laboratory in December 1918 became the famous Central Aero- and Hydrodynamics Institute, or TsAGI. Here were trained many of Soviet Russia's most prominent designers, A. N. Tupolev, A. S. Yakovlev, and I. V. Iliushin included. Before his death in 1921, Zhukovsky also helped found the Moscow Air Technical College (1919), which was renamed the Institute of Engineers of the Red Aerial Fleet in 1920 and later the Zhukovsky Air Academy. These contributions won Zhukovsky the title "father of Soviet aviation."

The leadership's support for both military and civilian aviation was of considerable significance given the severely limited resources of that time. As the Communists launched their state's material recovery through the New Economic Policy (NEP) of early 1921, they valued aircraft as instruments of agitation and propaganda—and of economic development through creation of a "civil aerial fleet," or GVF. The powerful Council of Labor and Defense (STO) rapidly adopted a ten-year program for aviation that initiated serious work on replenishing aircraft stocks and, in 1922, on creating a network of domestic and foreign airline routes. Yet despite the conversion of three IMs for a Moscow-Kharkov route, the GVF was as starved of aircraft as its military counterpart. Meanwhile, the products of those aircraft and engine factories that had maintained low levels of production after 1917 were now outmoded and incapable of meeting the new demands. To jump-start their program, the Soviet government first sought foreign assistance by purchasing new aircraft from Holland and Weimar Germany, and in April 1922 by entering a marriage of convenience with the latter, the era's other isolated European bad boy. This allowed Germany to escape restrictions imposed by the Versailles Treaty of 1919 by opening a Junkers aircraft plant at Fili, near Moscow, in 1923 and by operating training facilities for flying personnel. For their part, the Russians gained experienced instructors for their own fledgling air services, access to advanced aerial technologies, and a new, domestic source of modern aircraft. In addition, Moscow now had found a partner that shared its hostility for resurrected Poland, Red Russia's most probable immediate enemy in a future conflict.

Equally important, the Red Army's leaders, who were studying their own accumulated lessons learned during the "imperialist" and civil conflicts, gained access to German military theory on the likely nature of a future mechanized industrial war. By 1923–1924 the result was a renewed debate over military doctrine, but this time on one that would be ideologically, as well technically and professionally, acceptable to ruling Communist leadership. With Lenin sick and finally dying in early 1924, the debate's real issue became the future of Commissar of War Trotsky. His political enemies, Stalin included, sought to undermine him by supporting the doctrinal positions of his deputy and rival Frunze. Nonetheless, the resulting debates had real importance for future military building as well, and aviation received considerable prominence in the rivals' public pronouncements. But if all agreed that aviation would be important in modern battle for conducting reconnaissance, providing close support for ground troops, and fighting for air control, no one addressed the issue of strategic bombing. Indeed, the only possible signs of Douhet's influence were Frunze's suggestion that air strikes might be tactically "decisive," and a mention of "the moral suppression of the enemy" in regulations of 1924.

In the end, Trotsky surrendered his post, Frunze briefly became commissar of war, and his views formed the basis for the Red Army's formal military doctrine. Since this merged the views of the army's professionals with the imperatives of the Communist political elite, both the leaderships of defense and of the armed forces now were committed to the same goals in military building. With regard to the air services, this meant eventually developing an expanded and modernized tactical aerial fleet, which in 1925 became the Military Air Forces of the Workers' and Peasants' Red Army (VVS-RKKA) under the command of Frunze's long-term associate P. I. Baranov. The Provisional Field Regulations of that year did designate some units as strategic, but these actually were intended for concentrated mass strikes in support of frontline offensives. Meanwhile, the VVS commander Baranov also became head of *Glavkoa-*

via (the Main Administration of the Unified Aviation Industries of the Council of the Defense Industry), and so was responsible for equipping his forces with domestically produced aircraft. Although Frunze himself died within the year, he nonetheless left realization of both elements of his air force policy united in the capable hands of a single powerful figure. By the time Baranov himself perished in a crash in 1933, he had made considerable progress in restoring Russian airpower.

Strategic Bombing before Stalin

In large part the absence of strategic bombing from the doctrinal debates simply reflected continuing shortages in matériel and personnel, a stunted industrial base's inability to make good these deficiencies, and the limited capabilities of even the most advanced aircraft and bombs of that day. Yet it also reflected a widespread and long-lasting prejudice that bombing was merely an extension of the artillery. In 1928, for instance, the initial study by a leading VVS theorist, E. V. Agokas, was entitled *Aerial Artillery*, and in 1932 the *Soviet Military Encyclopedia* still defined an "aviation bomb" simply as "an artillery shell that is released from a flying machine." Not surprisingly, the Main Artillery Administration retained responsibility throughout this era for developing and designing aircraft bombs, and a VVS study of 1927 on ground attacks in effect equated the role of bombs with that of machine guns. Whatever the theory, this study concluded that given the equipment and weaponry available, flyers might act independently as direct participants on the battlefield, but they still could do so only as one major element in a complex of means, and in themselves they remained incapable of delivering the decisive blow (à la Frunze) at the tactical-operational, let alone at the strategic, level.

Added to the scarcity of urban industrial targets in eastern Europe, these factors seemingly combined to push any Soviet hopes of realizing Douhet's vision to the distant future. Even so, he was not without influence among Soviet airmen, and as the decade progressed, so too did explicit interest in strategic bombing. In particular, another major theorist, A. N. Lapchinsky, who after 1925 taught aerial tactics at the

Frunze Military Academy, discussed strategic strikes as early as 1926. He was soon echoed by V. V. Khripin's articles in the official *Vestnik vozdushnogo flota* (Herald of the Aerial Fleet), and when a Russian translation of Douhet appeared in 1935, Khirpin provided the introduction. Yet both he and Lapchinsky still envisaged that an independent long-range bomber force would supplement the tactical VVS in supporting the ground forces, and denied it any "decisive" influence. But with Trotsky gone, Frunze dead, and the Communist leaders' struggle for primacy now focused on economic issues, the VVS lacked a powerful statesman-patron; it had considerable latitude, within the accepted ideological precepts, to build its service in accord with changing technological and international conditions.

This relatively relaxed environment allowed proponents of bombers to obtain approval for the formation of the VVS's first Heavy Bomber Brigade in 1926–1927. This comprised two squadrons, to be equipped with Junkers-Gorbunov JuG-1 (K 30) trimotor bombers until a new all-metal Soviet-designed replacement became available, and independent bomber operations were included in the 1928 maneuvers. Attention focused as well on defending industrial targets within the USSR. But although the principles for air defense (PVO) reportedly were outlined as early as 1925, a statute embodying them was not enacted until 1928. In accord with this law, both interceptor and antiaircraft artillery units were to be assigned to possible targets of strategic significance, and instructions were issued for organizing local systems of civil defense (GO). Such threats were taken more seriously with the industrialization initiated by the Five-Year Plan in 1928, and M. N. Tukhachevsky proposed that new defense industries, aviation plants included, be dispersed so as to reduce their vulnerability to hostile air strikes.

This growing interest in independent strategic bomber operations paralleled the increasing availability of suitable aircraft. This last occurred despite opposition both within and outside the military. In the absence of a controlling patron, the design and development of a heavy or strategic bomber occurred thanks to the efforts and good fortune of a loose coalition of individual designers like Zukhovsky's pupil Tupolev and compliant air force leaders like Baranov. Working with TsAGI's

Aviation, Hydroaviation, and Special Design (AGOS) section, Tupolev was eager to practice techniques he'd learned from imported machines and foreign engineers by building larger aircraft. The military's lack of interest initially blocked his proposals, but his chance came in 1923. Then the Commissariat of War's Special Design Bureau for Military Inventions (*Ostekhburo*) required a heavy aircraft for testing experimental air-launched weapons. When its British choice proved too expensive, the bureau gave the contract to AGOS in autumn 1924 and by December Tupolev was at work on what became the ANT-4 or, as the TB-1 (for *tyazhelyi bombardirovshchik,* or heavy bomber 1), the replacement for the three-motor K 30. His twin-engine, all-metal cantilever monoplane first flew in November 1925, began its state trials in June 1926, and on 10 July made a twelve-hour flight carrying a simulated bomb load of 2,365 pounds (1,075 kilograms) over a distance of 1,242 miles (2,000 kilometers). Air force Chief Baranov reportedly was eager to receive this machine, which had a capability unlike anything in the existing VVS inventory. Despite this, suitable facilities for the TB-1's serial production became available only in mid-1928, and suitable engines in July 1929, after which some 160 bombers were finally produced (by 1932). But in the interim, the TB-1's initial success of November 1925 had brought Tupolev an *Ostekhburo* contract to design the still larger four-engine ANT-6 or TB-3.

Besides suitable aircraft, VVS bombing squadrons also needed modern munitions with reliable fuses and accurate aiming devices or bombsights. Although the Main Artillery Administration's commission in charge of bomb design had made some incremental improvements during this period, by the early 1930s Soviet and other theorists of airpower still lacked explosive projectiles capable of producing truly devastating battlefield strikes, let alone of achieving Douhet's strategic strikes. This deficiency probably explains the persistent interest in chemical bombs and dispensers of all types. For whatever the real limitations on launching effective gas or other chemical strikes, some theorists clearly hoped that in time these projectiles would provide them with an alternative "silver bullet" with which to replace conventional high-explosive, fragmentation, and incendiary free-fall munitions. Despite numerous "future war" scenarios of annihilating chemical strikes against both military and civilian targets, however, in the end the technical problems involved in using such weapons remained insurmountable.

Rise of the Strategic Bomber, 1928–1941

The successful completion of Tupolev's TB-1 and TB-3 demonstrates that attitudes toward heavy bombers changed after Stalin emerged as leader of the Communist Party in 1927–1928. Having launched the First Five-Year Plan to achieve "Socialism in One Country," he assumed personal responsibility for guiding the state's overall defense policies, the details of military building included. He justified his program of forced industrialization by warning of the continuing threat from "capitalist encirclement" by nations thirsting for a war to crush the world's only socialist state. Though this assessment remains debatable at best, the VVS was nonetheless unprepared for war: in 1929 it still classified 85 percent of its aircraft as reconnaissance machines, and in 1930 it reportedly fielded only 50 bombers, as compared to 630 fighters and 1,800 reconnaissance planes. Clearly, the air services were incapable of supporting the mechanized, mobile blitzkrieg warfare envisaged by Tukhachevsky and his colleagues, which required a continuous round of close, ground-support missions. Even so, Stalin made the creation of a strategic bomber force a priority. He became its most prominent patron and ordered its potential demonstrated by numerous long-distance "prestige" flights both within and beyond the frontiers of the USSR. As early as 1929 the veteran pilot S. A. Shestakov therefore flew a new ANT-4 (TB-1), christened *Strana Sovetov* (Land of the Soviets), across Siberia to Khabarovsk. There it exchanged wheels for floats, then crossed the Pacific to San Francisco, and finally flew to New York to meet an air industry delegation headed by its chief, Baranov.

Stalin's motives remain uncertain. Yet it seems that like other amateurs at other times, he often relied on intuition, favored radical proposals dismissed by most professionals, and preferred quantity and mass over quality. He was therefore easily won over by the visions of offensive mechanized and armored warfare advanced by J. F. C. Fuller and his Russian disciples (Tukhachevsky and company), and of Douhet's doctrine of strategic bombing as moderated by Lapchinsky, Khripin, and, less aggressively, by other leading airmen, Baranov included. If nothing else, Stalin clearly recognized the political value of powerful aircraft as symbols of his newly modernized "Socialist Motherland," and of *Osoaviakhim* as a means of mass mobilization. Under the slogan of "Higher! Faster! Further!" the Komsomol now actively promoted aviation while he himself recognized Red pilots as his personal "falcons." With his tightening grip on power and determination to personally exert "leadership of the armed forces," Stalin soon intervened in any and every major decision concerning the acquisition and use of the array of weaponry becoming available owing to industrialization. Consequently, after 1928–1929 his support for long-range bombing proved decisive in the creation of an independent strategic arm.

Stalin's early support of heavy bombers, and his love of the gigantic, is evident from demands he made on Tupolev in early 1930. Although the four-motor TB-3 still had yet to fly, the designer was summoned to the Kremlin and informed that the VVS wanted a colossal bomber with a wingspan of 328 feet (100 meters), and a bomb load of some 55,000 pounds (25 metric tons). Tupolev objected, successfully arguing that he first had to design a transitional model, "halfway" between the prototype TB-3 and the proposed giant. In April 1930 he received orders for his halfway six-engine bomber, designated the ANT-16 (TB-4), which was to have twice the weight and wing area of his TB-3, on which work meanwhile went ahead. The latter bomber's prototype finally flew in December 1930, but it did not pass its state trials until January 1932. Stalin, who followed these developments closely, immediately ordered eight more completed for the May Day flyover of that year. On that occasion the test pilot A. B. Yumashev led a formation of nine of the new TB-3s, along with seventy TB-1s, fifty-nine reconnaissance bombers, and twenty-nine fighters.

Under Stalin such displays of airpower became commonplace. All major holidays—May Day, November 7 celebrations, Air Forces Day, and so on—were occasions for flyovers demonstrating the creativity of Soviet designers, the destructive capabilities of their aircraft, and the abilities of the USSR's expanding aviation industry to support the air services. A high point came when the giant, eight-engine ANT-20 *Maksim Gorkii* flew over Red Square on 19 June 1933 during celebrations of the aerial rescue of the crew of the trapped icebreaker *Cheliuskin,* a feat that prompted creation of the order Hero of the Soviet Union. This and other feats, which included setting of numerous aerial records, permitted Stalin to present his once backward state as an airpower with a strategic reach that its foes would wisely recognize. By the time the *Maksim Gorkii* perished in May 1935, it had won renown as the centerpiece of a civil aviation propaganda squadron of the same name. This unit also included the five-engine ANT-14 *Pravda,* which then became the flagship. Although a new, updated ANT-20bis (PS-124) finally entered service from late 1939 and flew to the end of 1940, by that date Stalin had lost his enthusiasm for large, multi-engine aircraft. Consequently, neither a suggested bomber version of the ANT-20 nor a proposed fleet of sixteen *Maksim Gorkiis* ever appeared.

Additional proof of Stalin's interest in strategic airpower was his order making Douhet required reading for VVS officers when a translation of *The Command of the Air* became available in 1935, and he undoubtedly supervised the creation of a separate force of such bombers. Its mainstay was Tupolev's TB-3 (ANT-6), with its range of some 1,375 miles (2,200 kilometers). Production reached a rate of some 50 a month during 1933–1934, and thereafter continued on a smaller scale for a total of 818 various models by 1937. Beginning in 1933, these heavy bombers were assigned to 36 *eskadrilii,* and then to 10 special *aviabrigady,* each with three to four squadrons. Three such brigades, totaling 150 TB-3s, immediately went to the Far East, where Japan's occupation of Manchuria threatened Soviet Siberia. There the preparation of their bases and servicing facilities had begun in summer 1932, and Japanese appreciation of the threat was evident in their heightened air defenses. In Europe, meanwhile, Stalin demonstrated the TB-3s' strategic reach through a series of goodwill flights by nine specially modified ANT-6s during 1933–1934. Under the civil designation M-34RD, these visited Rome, Vienna, Prague, Warsaw, Paris, and elsewhere in France (an ally of the USSR after 1934) and Poland. More spectacular still, in June and

July 1937, after two years of preparation, Valery Chkalov and Mikhail Gromov made their celebrated transpolar flights to the United States in two ANT-25s (RD-1 and RD-2) prototypes.

Such displays of airpower were diplomatically deterrent in nature. "Like any leader," writes Volkogonov, "Stalin knew that a country's place in the world, its political regime and its international authority, depend to a great extent not only on its economic power, but also on its military might." Needing peace in order to realize both his rapid industrialization and forced collectivization of agriculture, the dictator doubtless hoped that demonstrations of military might would make "adventurist" leaders of the capitalist nations, then gripped by the Great Depression, hesitate before beginning a diversionary war against the USSR. This consideration gained point after 1933, when Nazi Germany joined militaristic Japan to replace the more distant imperialists of France, Britain, and America as likely possible aggressors. Since Germany and Japan were heavily industrialized, and air-defense technologies were still primitive, both offered tempting targets for long-range Soviet bombers.

More important still, Soviet claims of airpower were backed by real progress in almost every field. Thanks to the Five-Year Plans, the aviation industry's output rose from 2,509 machines in 1932 to 10,342 in 1939 and totaled 45,499 during 1929–1939. Expanded VVS schools aside, by 1941 *Osoaviakhim* reportedly maintained a total of 180 aeroclubs and 46 glider schools that, since 1928, had trained 121,000 aircraft and 27,000 glider pilots, as well as a multitude of technicians. Meanwhile, by 1940 the civilian air routes had grown from 5,810 miles (9,350 kilometers) in 1928 to a total network of 89,925 miles (144,880 kilometers) in 1940. The VVS combat aircraft inventory had been transformed as well: the proportion of reconnaissance machines declined from 82 percent in 1929 to 26 percent in 1934 to only 9.5 percent in 1938. That of fighters rose accordingly, from 25 percent to 39 percent during 1934 and 1938, and bombers made up roughly half throughout and apparently peaked at 60 percent in 1936. Then, as Deputy Chief Khripin of the VVS told the Eighth Congress of Soviets, his service had the world's strongest bomber force.

The missions assigned this force were suggested by the Red Army's

Draft Field Service Regulation of 1936. This defined the basic purpose of war as "the annihilation of the enemy" and assigned tactical VVS units the offensive mission of launching air strikes "on a mass scale" to destroy "those targets that cannot be neutralized by infantry or artillery fire, or that of other arms." Since Stalin simultaneously had reorganized the VVS and concentrated its long-range resources in a new Special Purpose Air Arm (AON), this presumably had a similar strategic mission. Headed by Khripin, the AON operated directly under the high command (not the VVS) and maintained an independent force of long-range bombers to parallel the tactical assets of the VVS-RKKA, but it also supported the army's "deep battle" by transporting paratroops and undertaking airborne operations.

Whereas other early bomber projects had ended in failure, by 1932 it already was clear that despite its merits and records, the TB-3 was too slow and clumsy to deal with the new generation of faster fighters then under development. The VVS therefore issued a requirement for a new long-range bomber, capable of speeds of 235 miles per hour (375 kilometers per hour), and assigned its design to the new Central Design Bureau, headed by S. V. Iliushin. He responded with his twin-engine TsKB-26, or DB-3, later developed into the TskB-30, or Il-4, medium bomber. In all, at this time Soviet designers were working on some fifty bomber projects, and Stalin, for whom bigger usually seemed to mean better, obviously remained impressed by the carrying abilities of Tupolev's bureau's series of gigantic, all-metal multi-engine aircraft such as the ANT-20 *Maksim Gorkii*. His unwillingness to abandon such aircraft seems evident from the stream of proposals he elicited from Tupolev, the most significant being the ANT-42 (TB-7), commonly designated as the Pe-8. Work began on this more streamlined, four-engine replacement for the TB-3 in July 1934, and it first flew in 1936.

Fall of the Strategic Bomber, 1936–1945

As the AON's creation indicates, Stalin's enthusiasm for a long-range air arm continued unabated until 1937, and as a result of his patronage, it had flourished. But in that year this patronage abruptly ended as a result of lessons learned elsewhere. Having sought a strategic advantage by assigning tactical aircraft to Republican Spain in 1936, Stalin monitored events there and noted the failure of General Franco's Italian and German bombers to pound Madrid and other Spanish cities into submission. Stalin's faith in Douhet was shaken accordingly, and he ended by agreeing with Luftwaffe observers that the Spanish experience demonstrated not the value of strategic bombing but the enhanced role of medium, ground attack, and dive bombers, along with air-superiority fighters, over a modern mechanized battlefield. In addition, by 1937–1938 the VVS aircraft were obviously obsolete when compared to German machines. He therefore focused on reequipping his air forces with modern aircraft and on increasing the proportion of frontal (battlefield) aviation. Work on the TB-7/Pe-8 did continue at a low level, but after 1937, when Iliushin's DB-3 first entered service, most resources were withdrawn from developing new heavy bombers. Instead, in October 1937 Tupolev, V. N. Petlyakov, and other designers of heavy bombers ended up in the People's Commissariat for Internal Affair's Gulag, and most proponents of strategic bombing (Lapchinsky, Khripin, and Tukhachevsky included) were arrested, executed, or "disappeared" in purges that by late 1939 would destroy some 75 percent of the senior air commanders.

As a result, Alexander Boyd concludes that the VVS "remained proportionally strong in four-engined heavy bombers by the end of the thirties, [but] the Soviet Union's strategic bomber potential had fallen drastically due to the sheer obsolescence of its machines and the correspondingly dated training of its air crews." Although a number of TB-3s saw service as bombers over Finland in 1939–1940, the majority then served as transports. By that time the DB-3 medium bomber was the workhorse of the AON, and development of the TB-7 (Pe-8) was further slowed because of engine problems and the imprisonment of its designers. Nonetheless, a second prototype passed state trials in April 1938, and in early 1939 Stalin convoked a Kremlin conference to discuss its future. Thanks to a defense by Alexander Filin, head of the VVS's Scientific Research Institute and a surviving advocate of strategic bombers, the still skeptical dictator grudgingly approved its serial production in a factory in Kazan. This began in late 1939, was halted after completion of only six aircraft, and then resumed in late 1940–early 1941. Only a handful had entered service by 22 June 1941 and, despite the emphasis placed on tactical aircraft, the plant completed another seventy-nine thereafter. Engine problems, however, plagued the TB-7/Pe-8 throughout and when production ceased in 1944, only ninety-three had been completed. Stalin's opinion of strategic bombing meanwhile had grown gloomier still and, in the wake of the Finnish War, in 1940 he again purged the VVS command and reorganized his air services. Abolishing the AON, he assigned its long-range and some medium-range bombers to the five corps and two special "independent" divisions of a new force known as the Long-Range Bomber Aviation of the High Command (DBA-GK) and gave the remaining aircraft to the tactical Frontal Aviation. After regaining its transports in May 1941, the DBA-GK had some 800 aircraft, of which 516 were the obsolescent TB-3s and only 11 were modern TB-7s (Pe-8s).

Fortunately for the DBA, its bases were in the rear of the Western Military Districts, and it suffered less than Frontal Aviation from the Luftwaffe's devastating preemptive strikes of 22 June 1941. Thanks to what is undoubtedly Stalin's greatest strategic blunder—his forward basing of his field forces, Frontal Aviation included, and his refusal to heed warnings of the coming invasion—the VVS could mount only minimal opposition to the German invaders. Consequently, over that summer the majority of DBA missions sought to slow the advancing Wehrmacht, and its losses (especially in TB-3s) mounted rapidly. By October the DBA had only 439 machines, and by 15 December a mere 182 DB-3s and 84 TB-3s. Meanwhile, on 6 July 1941 the available TB-7s were assigned to the new 412th Long-Range Bomber Regiment, which was still forming when the Luftwaffe attacked Moscow on 21 July. Determined on an immediate reprisal raid, Stalin assigned this task to fifteen naval DB-3s of the Baltic Fleet. They struck Berlin on 7 August. Although only six returned, the dictator was well satisfied with the raid's effect on Soviet morale, and he ordered a still larger attack for 11 August. On this occasion eleven TB-7s joined the DB-3s, and only five of the heavy bombers returned. Thereafter naval DB-3s briefly continued to attack targets in East Prussia and in Romania, but attacks by the DBA-GK on enemy territory ceased until it was replaced by Aviation for Distant Operations (ADD) in March 1942. Again subordinated to the high command, this new force once more sent small groups of DB-3s and TB-7s to raid Berlin, Danzig, and Konigsberg in Germany, and Romania's Ploesti oil fields, between late July and early September 1942. Thereafter it largely supported the ground forces by operational strikes behind the German front and by supplying partisans there. Finally, in December 1944 the ADD was subordinated operationally to the command of the VVS and renamed the 18th Air Army.

Having recovered from the disasters of 1941–early 1942, in part thanks to the personnel trained by *Osoaviakhim,* the Red air services gradually increased in strength and successfully fulfilled the tactical and operational roles allotted them. Many of these latter, such as the aerial blockades and frontal offensives effected from Stalingrad to Berlin, had a long-term strategic importance. But offensive strategic raids as such represented only an insignificant portion of the total missions, and usually had little value beyond propaganda. So though the ADD did employ large projectiles of up to 2,200 and 4,400 pounds (1,000 and 2,000 kilograms)—the FAB-1000 and FAB-2000—and even the 11,000-pound (5,000-kilogram) FAB-5000, its pilots usually delivered these against hardened frontal targets. Stalin and his associates meanwhile left to their allies the task of conducting strategic bombing raids on the German heartland, the value of which missions they even downplayed, and so they ended the conflict with no real strategic bombing force of their own.

Post-1945 Indian Summer

In August 1945 the American atomic strikes against Japan dramatically changed the strategic calculus. By that date bombing with conventional high-explosive and "fire" bombs had failed to achieve Douhet's promise, but the new nuclear devices seemingly did offer the silver bullet once sought from chemical weapons. The Soviet rulers, who had just emerged from a desperate struggle for survival, which left the western USSR in ruins, suddenly faced a new range of possible enemies in the form of their recent allies and a spectrum of strategic challenges unimaginable only a half decade earlier.

Stalin, however, appeared unperturbed. Dismissing the new weapon as simply another "big" bomb, he proclaimed as doctrine the thesis that victory still depended on such "permanently operating factors" as territorial area, demographic power, economic resources, and so on. Soviet military writers necessarily followed his lead and, in discussing these factors, stressed warfare's dialectical nature as demonstrated in the "strategic counteroffensive" by which Stalin, a military leader of genius, had destroyed the Nazi aggressors. Dismissing suggestions that the atomic bomb was an "absolute weapon" that allowed the United States to pressure other nations, they termed such arguments as "bourgeois" nonsense advanced by bankrupt and adventuristic Western strategists. In retrospect this response may seem eccentric, but we should note that by stonewalling suggestions of his own strategic inferiority, Stalin deprived his Western opposites of much of the political leverage they hoped to gain from their atomic weapons.

His own scientists, technicians, and weapons designers meanwhile struggled once more to catch up through a range of crash programs. These included the acquisition of massive conventional as well as nuclear bombs, the design of a strategic bomber to carry them, and the development of both cruise and ballistic missiles as alternative delivery systems. A sign of Stalin's renewed interest in strategic bombing came when, in response to the formation of the American Strategic Air Command (SAC) in 1946, he abolished the wartime ADD and transferred its bombing elements to the new, independent strategic bombing arm of Long-Range Aviation (DA). He simultaneously charged the tactical and medium bombers of the VVS's Frontal Aviation with missions "of devastating strikes in the enemy's rear," and especially with attacks on those Western air bases within range of the USSR, in an effort to destroy the enemy's "means of nuclear attack." And, finally, he reorganized the Soviet Air Defense Forces (*PVO strany*) into an integrated, nationwide system of early-warning and intercept radars, interceptors and antiaircraft guns and missiles, backed by a newly integrated nationwide system of civil defense (GO).

Western commentators once credited Soviet espionage with providing Stalin with his bomb, and German engineers and rockets with giving him jet engines and missiles. The USSR undoubtedly benefited from both, but Soviet research programs in all these fields were already well established by 1945, and they accelerated thereafter. Similarly, steps toward acquiring a new strategic bomber were already under way. Given Stalin's persistent interest in massive aircraft, it is not surprising that he envied the Americans their B-29 "Superfortresses," and he set out to obtain one for himself. His chance came in 1944 when three intact B-29s made forced landings near Vladivostok. Immediately seized by the Soviet authorities, they were flown to Moscow, where the veteran Tupolev was assigned the task of "reverse engineering." By that year's end he reported that a clone could be ready in three years. Stalin, who characteristically allowed him only two, approved the program, and in mid-1945 an order was issued for twenty preproduction models. Designated the Tu-4, this bomber made its public debut in the Aviation Day flyover in 1947, after which Western observers reported in amazement the presence of three "B-29s." The first production models entered service with DA units in 1948, and when the last Tu-4 left the line in late 1952, some one thousand had been completed. Although soon made obsolete by the American B-52 "Stratofortress," the Tu-4 enabled Soviet pilots to reach targets in the United States as well as Western Europe.

Lacking his own nuclear weapons, Stalin ordered a modernization of the VVS's conventional munitions that resulted in the M46 bomb series. Here again he revealed faith that bigger is better and, since Western bases would be "hardened," the wartime trend toward larger-caliber high-explosive weapons received free rein. Already in 1944 specifications for the Tu-4 required it be capable of delivering two high-explosive FAB-2000s or a single FAB-5000. Meanwhile, plans for the new jet bomber designated the Il-28 envisaged it carrying an FAB-3000. Finally, in lieu of an atomic device, the M46 series included the development of a truly "big" conventional bomb in the form of the massive, 19,845-pound (9,000-kilogram) FAB-9000. In the event, the successful explosion of the USSR's first atomic weapon in 1949 made this blockbuster unnecessary. Stalin also now ended talk of "devastating strikes deep in the enemy rear," for, with nuclear weapons in hand, the threat posed by his bombers suddenly acquired still greater significance for both western Europe and North America. As a result, Stalin reaped additional strategic rewards in terms of the disproportionate expenditure of resources that Western governments now devoted to air defense. Furthermore, in autumn 1950 he felt secure enough from an American strike to dispatch VVS pilots with their new MiG-15 fighters to support the Chinese air defenses in Manchuria and over North Korea. Like his earlier interventions in Spain and China, this carefully orchestrated intervention was aimed strategically at promoting Soviet foreign policy in general, at reassuring his new Red Chinese allies in particular and, in the process, at showing the Americans that the Soviets had interceptors capable of downing their strategic bombers.

Stalin, of course, was fully aware of the need to replace the Tu-4 and, in 1948, Tupolev had begun work on his twin-jet Tu-16 bomber, which appeared in 1954. Again on Stalin's direct order, Tupolev also began designing his four-engine, turboprop-powered, long-range Tu-95 in 1949, and this first flew publicly in the Aviation Day flyover of 1955. Meanwhile, the prototype of V. M. Myasishchev's four-jet M-4 strategic bomber had flown in 1954, and it soon joined Tupolev's bombers in the DA inventory. By that time the Russians had detonated their first hydrogen device, on 3 August 1953, but bombs of this type still remained too large for the available aircraft until a Tu-95 was finally modified so as to deliver a 52,900-pound (24-metric-ton) H-bomb at a test range in Novaia Zemlia in 1961. So if VVS writers later claimed that during the 1950s their bombers came "to possess an enormous striking power," the creation of a nuclear arsenal was a slow process. Thus, in 1955 the VVS reportedly had 1,276 bombers, some 400 Tu-4s and 600 Tu-16s included, targeted against western Europe, but only 324 had nuclear devices.

By the time Stalin died in March 1953 his other postwar crash programs had provided the cruise and, more important, the long-range ballistic missiles publicly heralded by the launch of *Sputnik I* in October 1957. When combined with a thermonuclear warhead, these became intercontinental offensive systems (ICBMs) that, as Douhet might have observed, could indeed get through any air defenses then imaginable. When these missiles were based on land, an enemy might hope to "preempt" them by a surprise strike. When based on the seabed as submarine-launched ballistic missiles (SLBMs), however, these became immensely more difficult if not impossible to preempt. With these new "weapons of mass destruction," the Soviet Union claimed intercontinental "strategic parity" with the United States while holding Europe hostage to its medium- or intermediate-range missile systems (MRBMs, IRBMs), as well its manned bombers.

By the late 1950s and early 1960s Soviet nuclear strategists had developed a new doctrine as well. After a thorough discussion of the advantages brought by the "scientific-technical revolution in military affairs," the missile option won political approval from the post-Stalinist "collective leadership" led by Nikita Khrushchev. Although the Tu-94 and Mya-4 bombers continued to enter service, the DA and its associated designers never recovered the elite patronage that once had spurred that arm's development. For this reason Christoph Bluth correctly concludes that "*at no time in the period under consideration did the Soviet Union deploy a substantial strategic bomber force that could play a significant role in an attack on the United States*" (emphasis in original). This has remained true since, despite the appearance of still more modern bombers (the Tu-22 and M-52) armed with cruise missiles, ballistic missiles are more than sufficient to preserve the regime of "mutually assured destruction," or MAD. Even so, bombers still provide Russia's leaders with a backup alternative to their missiles. They serve as well as a continuing support for Frontal Aviation; and, when armed with advanced conventional but strategic munitions, even this almost token strategic bomber arm retains a certain strategic value as an alternative threat vis-à-vis western Europe and China. Above all else, later Soviet and Russian statesmen probably find it diplomatically useful to retain a strategic triad (ICBMs, SLBMs, and bombers) paralleling that of the United States, if only for reasons of superpower prestige and negotiation. Yet despite their continued participation in ceremonial flyovers, once the strategic bombers lost their elite patronage under Khrushchev, this system's slide to secondary status became inevitable.

Further Reading

Strategic Bombing: If no satisfactory English-language history exists of the Russian strategic bombing arm, there are numerous studies of strategic bombing in general, as well as general histories of Russian aviation. The first group includes such works as Lee B. Kennett, *A History of Strategic Bombing* (New York, 1982); David Wragg, *The Offensive Weapon: The Strategy of Bombing* (London, 1986); and R. A. Mason, *Air Power: An Overview of Roles* (London, 1987). Otherwise, the institutional frameworks within which Russian and Soviet statesmen and strategic planners worked are conveniently outlined (with full bibliographies) in the entries under "Military Administrative and Policy-Making System," in D. R. Jones, ed., *The Military-Naval Encyclopedia of Russia and the Soviet Union,* 8 vols. (hereafter MERE) (Gulf Breeze, Fla., 1980–1998), "(Before 1917)," 2:34–169, and "(Post 1917)," 2:169–200.

A plethora of works exist on the statesmen discussed, but most biographies have little value for our purposes. On the final Romanov, the most useful are Sergei S. Oldenburg's *Last Tsar: Nicholas II, His Reign and His Russia,* 4 vols., trans. Leonid Mihalap and Patrick J. Rollins, ed. Patrick J. Rollins (Gulf Breeze, Fla., 1978), which includes "Searching for the Last Tsar" by P. J. Rollins; and Marc Ferro's *Nicholas II: The Last of the Tsars,* trans. Brian Pearce (London, 1991). This ruler's devotion to his army and sense of duty are considered in my "Nicholas II and the Supreme Command: An Investigation of Motives," *Sbornik of the Study Group on the Russian Revolution,* no. 11 (Leeds, 1985), pp. 47–83.

The classic account of the Soviet interwar period is John Erickson's *The Soviet High Command: A Military-Political History, 1918–1941* (New York, 1962), and an updated review of the Trotsky-Frunze disputes of 1923–1925 is Sally W. Stoecker's "The Historical Roots of the Current Debates on Soviet Military Doctrine," *Journal of Soviet Military Studies* 4, no. 3 (September 1990): 363–389. The military historian Dmitri Volkogonov provides an insightful portrait of the Soviet dictator in *Stalin: Triumph and Tragedy,* ed. and trans. Harold Shukman (London, 1991), and Albert Seaton presents a sometimes generous assessment of his military prowess in *Stalin as Military Commander* (New York, 1976). Memoirs of his military (airmen and a designer included) are collected in Seweryn Bialer, ed., *Stalin and His Generals* (New York, 1969), and Robert Conquest describes the purges in *The Great Terror: A Reassessment* (Oxford, 1990).

The standard histories of Russian-Soviet air forces, which often include chapters on the strategic air (and sometimes missile) branches, include Asher Lee, ed., *The Soviet Air and Rocket Forces* (London, 1959); Robert A. Kilmarx, *A History of Soviet Air Power* (London, 1962); Robin Higham and Jacob Kipp, *Soviet Aviation and Air Power: A Historical View* (Boulder, Colo., 1977); Alexander Boyd, *The Soviet Air Force since 1918* (London, 1977); Von Hardesty, *Red Phoenix: The Rise of Soviet Air Power, 1941–1945* (Washington, D.C., 1982); Paul J.

Murphy, ed., *The Soviet Air Forces* (Jefferson, N.C., 1984); and Robin Higham, John T. Greenwood, and Von Hardesty, eds., *Russian Aviation and Air Power in the Twentieth Century* (London, 1998). Also see Sergei Rudenko et al., *The Soviet Air Force in World War II: The Official History,* trans. Leland Fetzer, ed. Ray Wagner (Garden City, N.Y., 1973), and Mikhail N. Kozhevnikov, *The Command and Staff of the Soviet Army Air Force in the Great Patriotic War, 1941–1945,* trans. USAF (Washington, D.C., n.d.).

Useful studies of the actual aircraft and details of their design histories include Bill Gunston, *Aircraft of the Soviet Union* (London, 1983); Vaclav Namecek, *The History of Soviet Aircraft from 1918* (London, 1986); Lennart Andersson, *Soviet Aircraft and Aviation, 1917–1941* (London, 1994); Bill Gunston, *Tupolev Aircraft since 1922* (Annapolis, 1995); Leonid L. Kerber and Maximillian Saukke, "The Tupolev Tu-4 Story," *Bulletin of the Russian Aviation Research Group of Air Britain,* no. 113, (September 1991): 75–88, as translated by Peter Kostelnik and Maurice Wickstead from *Krylia Rodina,* no. 1 (1989); Jacques Marmain, "The Tupolev Tu-22M: A Reassessment," *Jane's Intelligence Review* 5, no. 8 (1993): 343–347; John R. Taylor, "'Blackjack' in Focus," *Jane's Soviet Intelligence Review* 1, no. 2 (1989): 54–55; Piotr Butowski, "Close-up on Tu-160 'Blackjack,'" *Jane's Intelligence Review* 4, no. 3 (1992): 119–123; Piotr Butowski and Jay Miller, *OKB MiG: A History of the Design Bureau and Its Aircraft* (Stillwater, Minn., 1991); R. A. Belyakov and Jacques Marmain, *MiG: Fifty Years of Secret Aircraft Design* (Annapolis, 1994).

A dated but still useful study of the design process is Arthur J. Alexander, *R&D in Soviet Aviation,* Rand Corporation Report R-589-PR (Santa Monica, Calif., 1970), which benefited greatly from Alexander S. Yakovlev's memoirs, *The Aim of a Lifetime: The Story of Alexander Yakovlev, Designer of the Yak Fighter Plane,* trans. Vladimir Vezey (Moscow, 1972). For the similar processes regarding aerial armaments and bombs, see the entries (with full bibliographies) in MERE: "Aerial Armament," 5:63–191, and "Aerial Bomb," 8:1–91, as well as subsequent entries on individual types of bombs. Otherwise, developments before 1917 are outlined in my "Birth of the Russian Air Weapon, 1909–1914," *Aerospace Historian* 21, no. 3 (Fall 1974): 169–181, and "The Beginnings of Russian Air Power, 1907–1922," in Higham and Kipp, *Soviet Aviation and Air Power,* pp. 15–34, as well as by Von Hardesty in "Early Flight in Russia," in Higham, Greenwood, and Hardesty, *Russian Aviation and Air Power in the Twentieth Century,* pp. 236–268. The saga of the *Il'ya Muromets* bomber is recounted in K. N. Finne, *Igor Sikorsky: The Russian Years,* trans. and adapted Von Hardesty, ed. Carl J. Bobrow and Von Hardesty (Washington, D.C., 1987).

The USSR's strategic use of geographical space and the role of transport aviation, both civil and military, are dealt with in John Ambler, Denis J. B. Shaw, and Leslie Symons, eds., *Soviet and East European Transport Problems* (London, 1985); John Stroud, *Soviet Transport Aircraft since 1945* (London, 1968); Hugh MacDonald, *Aeroflot: Soviet Air Transport since 1923* (London, 1975), and my "Rise and Fall of Aeroflot: Civil Aviation in the Soviet Union, 1920–91," in Higham, Greenwood, and Hardesty, *Russian Aviation and Air Power in the Twentieth Century,* pp. 236–268. With regard to other peripheral "strategic" issues mentioned, I deal at length with *Osoaviakhim* in my "From Disaster to Recovery: Russia's Air Forces in Two World Wars," in *Why Air Forces Fail: The Anatomy of Defeat,* ed. Robin Higham and Stephen J. Harris (Lexington, Ky., 2006), pp. 315–340. The wartime aerial blockades instituted by the VVS are detailed in MERE, vols. 6–7, and postwar strategic and diplomatic uses of aviation are reviewed in Mark A. O'Neil, "Air Combat on the Periphery: The Soviet Air Force in Action during the Cold War, 1945–1989," in Higham, Greenwood, and Hardesty, *Russian Aviation and Air Power in the Twentieth Century,* pp. 208–235. Their service over North Korea is described in detail in Yefim Gordon and Vladimir Rigmant, *MiG-15: Design, Development, and Korean War Combat History* (Osceola, Wisc., 1993), and Yuri Sutiagin and Igor Seidov, *MiG Menace over Korea: The Story of Soviet Fighter Ace Nikolai Sutiagin,* trans. and ed. Stuart Britton (Barnsley, S. Yorkshire, U.K., 2009).

Those interested in Stalin's nuclear program can begin with David Holloway, "Entering the Nuclear Arms Race: The Soviet Decision to Build the Atomic Bomb, 1939–45," *Social Studies of Science* 11, no. 2 (1981): 159–197; Andreas Heinemann-Gruder, *Die Sowjetische Atombombe* (Berlin, 1990); and David Holloway, *Stalin and the Bomb: The Soviet Union and Atomic Energy, 1939–1956* (New Haven, Conn., 1994). Additional materials on this, the Korean intervention, the Cuban Missile Crisis, and other issues appear in the *Cold War International History Project Bulletin,* published by the Woodrow Wilson Center, Washington, D.C., since 1992.

The doctrinal debates can be followed in Raymond L. Garthoff, *How Russia Makes War* (London, 1954), and his *Soviet Strategy in the Nuclear Age* (New York, 1959); William R. Kitner and Harriet Fast Scott, eds., *The Nuclear Revolution in Soviet Military Affairs* (Norman, Okla., 1968); and Vasilii D. Sokolovskii, *Soviet Military Strategy,* ed. Harriet Fast Scott, 3rd ed. (London, 1975). Their practical implications are discussed in Steven J. Zaloga's "Most Secret Weapon: The Origins of Soviet Strategic Cruise Missiles, 1945–1960," *Journal of Slavic Military Studies* 67, no. 1 (June 1993): 262–273, and his *Target America: The Soviet Union and the Strategic Arms Race, 1945–1964* (Novato, Calif., 1993). Introductions to later Soviet strategic airpower are Robert P. Berman and John C. Baker, *Soviet Strategic Forces: Requirements and Responses* (Washington, D.C., 1982); Kenneth R. Whiting, *Soviet Air Power* (Boulder, Colo., 1986); R. A. Mason and John W. Taylor, *Aircraft, Strategy and Operations of the Soviet Air Force* (London, 1986); Anthony Robinson, "The Soviet Strategic Bomber Force," *Jane's Soviet Intelligence Review* 1, no. 3 (1989): 126–127; E. S. Williams, ed., *Soviet Air Power: Prospects for the Future: Perestroika and the Soviet Air Forces* (London, 1990); Steven J. Zaloga, "Current Trends in the Soviet Strategic Bomber Force," *Jane's Soviet Intelligence Review* 2, no. 8 (1990): 338–342; and Christoph Bluth, *Soviet Strategic Arms Policy before* SALT (Cambridge, U.K., 1992); as well as the yearly assessments of the DA in D. R. Jones et al., eds., *Soviet Armed Forces Review Annual,* 14 vols. (Gulf Breeze, Fla., 1977–1999).

Suggestions for Further Research

Surprisingly little research has been devoted to the development of Russia's strategic aviation. Indeed, the only English-language study available is the U.S. Air Force's translation of Major General Boris A. Vasil'ev's slight *Dal'niaia raketonosnaia* (Moscow, 1972) as *Long-Range Missile-Equipped Machines* (Washington, D.C., n.d.), supplemented for Russian readers by Aleksei D. Tsykin's *Ot "Il'i Muromtsa" do raketonostsa. Kratkii ocherk istorii dal'nei aviatsii* (*From Il'ia Muromets to Missile-Carrier: A Brief Historical Sketch of Long-Range Aviation*) (Moscow, 1975). So though the general outlines of this arm's development are sufficiently clear, the field is wide open as the Imperial and Soviet archives allow study of the complex interplay among technical constraints, designers' inventiveness, political intrigues, and rulers' patronage.

For the Imperial period, we badly need a scholarly account of Grand Duke Alexander Mikhailovich's work as head of the Voluntary Society for Support of the Naval/Aerial Fleet, as chairman of the Imperial Aeroclub, and, finally, as wartime commander at *Stavka* of the Imperial air services—issues he virtually ignores in his own memoirs. Here his relations with Nicholas II are of particular interest, as is the wartime debate over the value of the Sikorsky bombers. For the 1920s, we need careful analysis of both archival material and contemporary published literature to reveal the extent of real interest in General Douhet's theory among Soviet airmen; biographies of A. N. Lapchinsky, V. V. Khripin, and P. I. Baranov would be particularly useful. As for the Stalin period, studies of his relationships with his designers, and especially with A. N. Tupolev, are badly needed. As his papers become more widely examined, his decisions regarding Spain and other conflicts deserve the same attention as those concerning the intervention in Korea. But if the archives for the Cold War are now less airtight than they once were regarding certain topics (such as early nuclear research and the Tu-4), it will probably be some time before the rationale and details behind decisions on today's missile-armed bomber force (DA) can be fully explicated.

5

Statesmen and Airpower in Latin America, 1945–2010

René De La Pedraja

Aviation history changed when the United States began production of the F-80 in 1945. The F-80 was the first U.S. mass-produced jet fighter and not just an experimental or pilot model. This subsonic jet fighter immediately made obsolete the world's vast fleets of propeller planes. The F-80 lifted the bar for aviation performance and forced European manufacturers to surpass or at least to match the characteristics of the F-80 in their competing aircraft. Though other countries tried to duplicate the success of the F-80, the United States itself has never ceased to design and produce newer and better jet warplanes in a seemingly endless quest for ultimate perfection in aviation.

Because the production and maintenance of fighter jets signified a quantum leap in technology, only a very small number of world powers possessed the means to manufacture these highly sophisticated machines. The United States, the Soviet Union (Russia since 1992), France, and Britain have generally been the main manufacturers, even though other countries have occasionally produced their own planes. Noteworthy in this group has been the absence of any Latin American country. Although Brazil and Argentina eventually assembled local versions of jet aircraft, the heavy reliance on foreign components, including both the crucial jet engines and the vital electronics, has rendered this seeming independence more apparent than real. For replacement parts and even for simple maintenance of fighter jets, the air forces of Latin America have remained dependent on the original manufacturers.

The appearance of the first airplanes in Latin America in the 1910s had sparked great enthusiasm for aviation in the region. Young people were fascinated with the novel airplanes, and flying clubs spontaneously appeared in many cities where persons of different social origins shared their common passion for aviation. From the very beginning of aviation history in Latin America, the number of candidates to become pilots and the number of pilots have far surpassed the available planes. Not surprisingly, the appearance of jet fighters in 1945 intensified an already great passion for flying. Blessed with an abundance of pilots, Latin America seemed poised to take maximum advantage of the jet age. Actually, the abundance was not real because the pilots spent most of their time flying obsolete airplanes. Whether because of a shortage of jet fighters or insufficient funds to operate them, the flying hours of Latin American pilots generally fell considerably below the number industrialized countries considered the norm for jet fighter planes. This limited experience forced the Argentine pilots to improvise in the Malvinas (Falklands) War of 1982, not always with positive results.

Ultimately the inability to provide proper training and preparation for pilots was symptomatic of the larger underlying problem facing the air forces of Latin America in the years of the jet warplane. During the era of the piston planes, the largest Latin American countries had been able to make modest but solid progress in establishing their first manufacturing facilities. Although some precision items had remained beyond reach, most of the technology was locally available or could be readily acquired. Most important, the costs of propeller planes were modest, and the country that did not want to produce them could acquire the planes in the world market at reasonable prices. Local shops sufficed to provide adequate maintenance and to produce spare parts. An additional attraction of the propeller planes had been their much lower price compared to that of assembling expensive navies. As a substitute for costly battleships, propeller planes seemed to offer a cheap and readily available alternative for coastal defense until 1945.

The appearance of the F-80 in 1945 immediately put jet warplanes beyond the financial reach of Latin American countries. The region simply lacked the funds to acquire these expensive weapons. The cost of keeping up with rapidly changing technology proved prohibitively expensive from the start, and only as earlier models became obsolete did the technology of jet planes filter down to local mechanics. And as the prices of new models of jet fighters climbed, the myth of replacing costly battleships with economical warplanes crumbled. Latin American countries struggled to scrape together the funds to purchase these new "battleships of the skies," whose prices often exceeded those of pre–World War II warships.

Lack of funds, a result of the general poverty in the region, remained the overriding limitation on air forces in Latin America. But because the reality of airpower could not be ignored completely, statesmen in these countries had to decide how best to provide for national defense in the age of the jet fighter. The goal of this chapter is to show how Latin American statesmen have tried to reconcile defense needs with the exorbitant costs of jet aircraft. An examination of the most important cases will show how statesmen in Latin America tried—not always successfully—to use airpower in the region. Space limitations confine the study of the role of airpower in counterinsurgencies to the section on the Cuban Revolution.[1] A roughly chronological presentation happily coincides with geography as the chapter begins initially with the Caribbean region and then shifts in the last half to South America.

Propeller Planes: Guatemala 1954

The appearance of the F-80 jet fighter in 1945 quickly destroyed any hopes of creating powerful air forces in most Latin American countries. The governments quietly resigned themselves to accepting whatever obsolete equipment the United States cared to provide. In practice this meant that propeller planes remained the only planes in most Latin American air forces until the early 1950s; in some countries this situation lasted until the 1960s and even later. Although obsolete as fighters, the propeller planes were still valuable for reconnaissance, training, and even bombing functions. Consequently, many countries eagerly received the World War II surplus planes that the U.S. government was glad to dispose of. Very revealingly, Latin America was finding its assigned place in the post-1945 world order as the final dumping ground for cast-off or secondhand equipment. The disparity in military strength between Latin America and the United States became more blatant than ever before. Until 1945 the warplanes of both regions had comprised similar types of planes, but after 1945 the jet fighters of the United States stood in sharp contrast to the propeller planes of Latin America. Not just in terms of airpower, the gap between a prosperous United States and a poor Latin America, already pronounced in many areas before 1945, became even wider and more obvious in the post–World War II period.

Of the large countries of Latin America, Mexico seemed the one best poised to attempt a successful transition to jet fighters. During the Mexican Revolution (1910–1929) airplanes had pioneered innovative combat roles.[2] In World War II Mexico had sent the 201st Fighter Squadron into combat against the Japanese, and the exploits of the Mexican airmen had earned tremendous prestige. Yet the 201st Squadron closed the heroic age of Mexican military aviation. For years after World War II, the Mexican government refused to spend any money on its deteriorating air force. Nor surprisingly, in 1951 "every aircraft of the Mexican air force [was] obsolete," and a Mexican general went so far as to describe the planes as "flying wrecks."[3]

Mexico's decision to neglect its air force had an unexpected consequence for Guatemala, its southern neighbor. This small Central American country had earlier lost considerable chunks of territory to Mexico and lived in fear of annexation by its powerful northern neighbor. The primary mission of the Guatemalan military had been to deter or defeat any invasion from Mexico. During the 1930s the expansion of Mexico's air force compelled Guatemala to acquire similar warplanes to maintain at least some semblance of air parity. But when Mexico decided not to acquire jet fighters in 1945, the pressure on Guatemala vanished. Without any Mexican danger, the government of Guatemala could rely on its traditional army and diplomacy for defense from its powerful northern neighbor. Guatemala could safely ignore the jet age in fighters. And because Mexico's propeller planes were disintegrating, Guatemala did not even feel a need to acquire surplus World War II airplanes.

The air forces of Mexico and Guatemala had sunk to abysmally low levels by 1950, and in contrast the United States had become the global superpower. This vast military imbalance constantly tempted U.S. officials to use this overwhelming force, and Guatemala gave the United States the opportunity to wield its unchecked power. In 1944 Guatemala had overthrown the dictator Jorge Ubico and entered a period of economic and political reforms. Inevitably these reforms clashed with the largest single corporation in Guatemala, the American-owned United Fruit Company. When the reformist president Jacobo Arbenz began nationalizing the banana plantations of United Fruit, the U.S. government drew on Cold War hysteria to condemn his regime falsely as "Communist." The Dwight Eisenhower administration authorized the CIA to overthrow the democratically elected regime of President Arbenz.

The nearly defunct air force of Guatemala made possible intriguing opportunities for the CIA. During the Cold War, the United States always wanted to take the high moral ground over the Soviet Union by claiming that, unlike its Communist adversary, the United States never unilaterally invaded any countries. Thus, an "open" invasion was impossible, but because the air force of Guatemala was so weak, the CIA could organize a covert operation and still deny any U.S. involvement.

Fascinating details of the CIA invasion of Guatemala continue to appear, and this chapter can only sketch that outrageous scheme. The CIA trained and equipped an invasion force of Guatemalan exiles, but its advance stalled a few kilometers after it had crossed the border from Honduras on 18 June 1954. President Arbenz, out of fear of provoking an international incident with Honduras, refused to order the Guatemalan army to crush the invaders. This blunder left the initiative to around thirty propeller planes that the CIA had provided for the invaders. After a leaflet drop over Guatemala City, the CIA planes began to strafe and bomb the capital and other towns in the country. Although the aerial bombardment was not very damaging, it spread panic throughout the civilian population and began to make the Guatemalan troops waver in their loyalty to the Arbenz regime. When the bombardment resumed the next day, Arbenz ordered his tiny, six-plane air force to fly into action, but after one of his planes was shot down, he grounded the remaining five. Although Arbenz cannot be blamed for the failure of previous governments to acquire additional planes, his decision not to use his remaining air force doomed his regime. Because antiaircraft fire had destroyed or damaged most of the CIA planes, the balance of victory was doubtful for a few days. Only when President Eisenhower approved the rush delivery of replacement airplanes did the tide finally turn. The CIA planes resumed attacks and continued to bomb the capital during subsequent days until the army withdrew its support from Arbenz, who then resigned on 27 June 1954.

Propeller planes had overthrown a government in the jet age, and this sorry spectacle reinforced the image of Latin America, and not just of Guatemala, as a region of puny and pathetic banana republics. The humiliation had been complete, and to top it off, the U.S. government was able to hide its participation for more than a decade. Local observers knew that this had been a U.S. invasion, however, and soon Latin America seethed with resentment against the United States for having bullied so shamelessly and arrogantly one of the poorest countries of the Western Hemisphere. An Argentine doctor doing humanitarian work in Guatemala vowed to do everything in his power to prevent such a blatant injustice from ever taking place again. But at that moment it was not clear how the lone Che Guevara could do anything to stop the all-powerful United States.

The Cuban Revolution and Airpower

The Cuban Insurrection

After the overthrow of Jacobo Arbenz, Che Guevara fled Guatemala and found refuge in Mexico City. There he met and struck a deep friendship with a Cuban exile named Fidel Castro. Mexico was a haven for would-be revolutionaries, and Castro had come to organize an expedition to overthrow the brutal dictator Fulgencio Batista. Che eagerly joined Castro's expedition, which was set to sail aboard the yacht *Granma* in December 1956. To avoid detection by Batista's B-26s, the *Granma* sailed considerably south of the island before reaching its destination in eastern Cuba. The yacht ran aground before reaching the coast, and disembarkation was very slow and difficult. Batista's army soon detected, attacked, and dispersed the invaders. The Batista government claimed complete victory, yet almost miraculously a group of twelve stragglers escaped to the Sierra Maestra mountain range.

Fidel Castro, his brother Raúl, and Che Guevara were among the survivors, and after receiving support from local peasants, these leaders rebuilt their strength and created a small guerrilla force. After an army campaign in early 1957 failed to find them, the military launched a larger offensive to destroy the rebels in June. For the first time the government used its B-26s to bomb suspected guerrilla positions and occasionally to drop napalm. To avoid civilian casualties, the army had evacuated all the peasant families from areas suspected of guerrilla infestation. In this free-fire zone, anything that moved was assumed to be a valid target. B-26s, ground artillery, and coastal gunboats blasted away at this zone of the Sierra Maestra just as they had earlier in the year, but the army patrols could not locate any of the guerrillas. Tired of the mounting expenses, the Batista government suspended the operation in December 1957 and proclaimed the "total extermination" of the guerrillas.[4]

Once again the victory celebrations proved premature, and the guerrillas under Castro soon regained control over the Sierra Maestra region. These rebels posed no threat to the government, and Batista could have easily ignored them and left them isolated in their mountain hideouts. Instead, Batista insisted on launching a "Final Offensive" in late May 1958 to destroy the rebels once and for all. He increased the size of the Cuban army so that he could hurl over 12,000 soldiers equipped with ample artillery and armored vehicles.

In his large attacking force, however, he neglected to increase his air force, and the trusty B-26s remained the sole aircraft supporting the ground troops. Although the B-26s dropped napalm much more abundantly than in the June 1957 offensive, the same number of bombers could not provide adequate air support for the much larger attacking force. Furthermore, the rebels had learned from the previous offensive to build bunkers as air raid shelters, and consequently none of the bombs ever caused any casualties to the guerrillas. Batista had already received his first four T-33 trainers from the United States as the initial step in the acquisition of jet fighter-bombers, but because of the arms embargo the U.S. government placed on Cuba early in 1958, the delivery of the jet fighter-bombers did not take place. Batista should have waited until he was able to obtain additional bombers or fighter-bombers from other countries. Events soon showed that sending his large army into the Sierra Maestra without adequate air cover was a big gamble.

Batista launched his Final Offensive on 24 May 1958. The little air cover the B-26s provided proved counterproductive, because the rebels used captured code books to direct the planes to bomb the army's own units. In addition, the fleeing soldiers abandoned many heavy machine guns and cannons, and the rebels turned these captured weapons against the B-26s. For the first time the bombers encountered deadly antiaircraft fire, and—not surprisingly—their pilots became wary of approaching rebel zones and instead often dropped their bombs harmlessly at sea. In less than two months, the Final Offensive had ended in complete disaster. The rebels now gained the initiative, and they proved unstoppable during the remainder of the insurrection.

As Batista's troops fled from the Sierra Maestra, the soldiers holed themselves up inside barracks and refused to face the rebels anymore. The army had lost the will to fight, and in a desperate attempt to stop the rebels, the Batista government tried to use airpower as a substitute for unreliable ground troops. As the first news of the disaster of the Final Offensive began trickling in, the Batista government feverishly scrambled to find airplanes available for immediate delivery. Fortunately for his regime, Britain was trying to dispose of the Sea Fury, perhaps the best propeller fighter-bomber ever built, and agreed in September 1958 to sell seventeen of these planes to Batista. A first lot of six arrived in early November, and the remaining eleven were being unloaded in Havana harbor on 26 November. Could these Sea Fury planes have turned the tide of battle? The rebels certainly thought so, and Castro promptly sent strongly worded protests to the British government for having sold these weapons. The insurrection announced a boycott of all British products, and because the Cubans had an intense hatred of Batista, anti-British sentiment ran high, while the United States, because of its arms embargo, also earned considerable goodwill.

The rebels did not limit themselves to protests against Britain but also sought to acquire their own air force to counter the Sea Furies. In secret negotiations with private collectors, the rebels obtained three F-51 Mustangs and illegally flew them from Florida to Cuba. The American F-51 Mustang had been the best propeller fighter of World War II, and the expected match between the American Mustang and the British Sea Fury promised to make aviation history. In reality the Sea Furies came too late to affect the outcome of the insurrection. By the time all seventeen Sea Furies were ready for action in December 1958, rebel columns were streaming westward across the island and converging on the capital, Havana. In desperation, the last die-hard defenders of the Batista regime concocted a plan for a final gamble to halt the rebels. By concentrating the Sea Furies and the B-26s for saturation bombing, the Batista high command hoped to shatter or at least delay the rebel columns long enough to restore the army's will to fight. Because cheering crowds normally greeted the rebels and welcomed them as liberators, however, any attacks had to catch the rebel columns outside the cities to minimize civilian casualties. These precautions were not enough to convince the pilots, who, sensing that the war was lost, hesitated to carry out these bombing missions. As discipline rapidly collapsed among the disintegrating Batista armed forces, nobody could be found to give the order to launch the last-ditch aerial attack on the rebels. For their part, the rebels—with immense difficulty—could make operational only two of their fighter planes, and the much-anticipated clash between the F-51 Mustang and the Sea Fury had to be postponed forever.

With the end rapidly closing in on the collapsing regime, Batista and his closest followers suddenly flew out of Cuba in the early hours of 1 January 1959. A few days later, rebel authorities had established firm control over all military installations in the island. The insurrection had triumphed and was the first popular revolt to succeed in Latin America since the start of the Mexican Revolution of 1910.

The Bay of Pigs

On the morning of 1 January 1959, as soon as news of Batista's escape flight had spread, mobs appeared in the streets to attack all symbols of the hated Batista dictatorship. A reassuring radio speech from Fidel Castro calmed the population, and gradually the crowds melted away, but not before the angry rioters had vented their fury at any British properties or companies, in particular Shell gas stations. The Cuban people did not forget that for the sake of profits Britain had supported the hated dictator, yet by an ironic twist of fate, those same Sea Fury planes in a few years saved the Cuban Revolution from a near certain demise.

In January 1959, just days after taking power, the Cuban leaders began buying weapons from the many arms merchants who had come to Havana to sell to the former dictator, Batista. Because the U.S. arms embargo remained in place, Cuba had to turn to other foreign countries and to private dealers. The revolutionary government easily placed orders for small arms, machine guns, antiaircraft weapons, and artillery pieces. Warplanes posed a bigger challenge, because arms merchants could offer for sale only propeller planes. As early as late January 1959, the revolutionary government expressed its interest in buying jet planes from Britain and in June actively sought authorization from the British government for the sale of Hunter jets.

When in May 1959 the Revolution launched its own agrarian reform and nationalized many U.S. properties (including the United Fruit Company), Cuba seemed to be following the path of the ill-fated Jacobo Arbenz in Guatemala. These Cuban actions provoked a bitter hostility from the U.S. government, and as early as the summer of 1959 the Eisenhower administration had decided to overthrow the revolutionary government and directed the CIA to prepare the requisite operation. Che Guevara had long predicted this hostile action, which the U.S. government succeeded in keeping secret from the U.S. public but not from Cuban officials. A forewarned Cuban government did everything possible to prevent a repetition of the CIA Guatemala operation in Cuba. To defend itself, Cuba intensified its search for weapons and also warplanes, but by then the United States had pressured its allies not to sell any arms to the revolutionary government.

A desperate Cuba pleaded with Britain to sell seventeen Hunter jet aircraft as replacements for the seventeen Sea Furies Batista had received in the previous November. The sale was nearly complete when at the last minute the British government caved in to U.S. pressure and canceled the sale of jets to Cuba. The U.S. government had to prevent any jet fighters from reaching the Cuban government, for otherwise the CIA's plan to overthrow the revolutionary government could not succeed. Because Cuban jet fighters could easily destroy any propeller planes the CIA purchased in the world market, the CIA could not repeat its successful 1954 Guatemalan operation in Cuba. Just as significant was the fact that any chance of deniability or secrecy had disappeared because at that time only governments could buy jet fighters, and thus the CIA could not claim that this was a privately run operation. Instead, the CIA easily purchased propeller aircraft from the lively market among museums and individual collectors that had grown up since 1945.

By January 1960 U.S. determination to overthrow the revolutionary government had forced Cuba to seek assistance from the Soviet Union as the only way to escape the fate of Jacobo Arbenz. The Soviets were more than happy to supply small arms and other land weapons, such as tanks and artillery, but the negotiations to acquire MiG jet fighters began later and took longer. Also, once the Soviet Union agreed to supply MiGs, training the Cuban pilots and ground crews with these unfamiliar aircraft required considerable time. The CIA estimated that Cuba could have MiG jets in operation as early as the summer of 1961. This date became the final deadline for the CIA to launch a Guatemalan-style operation to overthrow the Cuban revolutionary government.

An exact repetition of the Guatemala operation of 1954 in any case was not possible because Cuba posed a number of special challenges. Since Cuba was an island, any invasion required a fleet to transport equipment and troops. But merchant ships were extremely vulnerable to air attack, so any successful invasion had to destroy the revolutionary warplanes first. As a solution, the CIA acquired airplanes and prepared them to launch air strikes before the invasion force landed in Cuba. In 1959 the CIA began training Cuban exiles in a secret jungle base in Guatemala and prepared a secret staging base at Puerto Cabezas in Nicaragua. The plan called for landing 1,300 Cuban exiles on the island sometime before the MiG fighters reached Cuba in the summer of 1961.

With the election of John F. Kennedy in November 1960, the

decision to launch the CIA operation passed into the hands of the new administration. Not aware of the many close calls of the 1954 Guatemala operation and not informed of the risks of the Bay of Pigs site, such as the lack of an escape route, President Kennedy approved the operation. Early in April 1961 the invasion fleet set sail from Nicaragua, and the CIA air force in Nicaragua at Puerto Cabezas readied the first air strike. To carry out this operation and to enhance deniability, the CIA chose B-26s for the air strikes. The invasion fleet was twelve hours at sea when the B-26s struck Cuba's military air bases on 15 April 1961. Castro had long been expecting this attack, however, and, in anticipation, the Cuban air force had ringed its planes with antiaircraft batteries, built decoy planes, and dispersed the warplanes widely. Consequently, when the attack struck, the CIA's B-26s were able to inflict only slight damage.

The minor losses were still unacceptable to Fidel Castro, who was furious that his precise instructions for protecting the airplanes had not been followed exactly. He now inspected the installations himself and talked with the pilots and ground crews; he left only when he was completely convinced that every possible precaution was in place to protect the planes. The ground crews kept the fighters ready for takeoff at a moment's notice, and shifts of pilots manned the cockpits around the clock. With these and other extraordinary precautions, the returning CIA B-26s could expect to suffer crippling losses from intense antiaircraft fire and pursuing Cuban fighter planes.

But no second air strike took place. During the attack of 15 April, two B-26s were heavily damaged and could not return to their distant base at Puerto Cabezas in Nicaragua. The planes flew to nearby Key West and made an emergency landing on a civilian airstrip. Excited reporters were soon photographing the two damaged airplanes. The U.S. government put out the official cover story that the planes belonged to defectors who had tried to flee the island, but journalists recognized that the forward part of these B-26s was different from that of the B-26s Castro had inherited from Batista. A blitz of unfavorable publicity followed, and Kennedy concluded that to save the secrecy of the invasion, he had no choice but to cancel the second air strike.[5]

The CIA should have told the president that no invasion could succeed unless all the Cuban planes were destroyed, but the CIA never gave him this warning. Unaware of the extreme danger, the invasion fleet proceeded to the Bay of Pigs and began its night landing in the early hours of 17 April. The rest of the story can easily be guessed. As soon as Castro heard of the invasion, he ordered nearby troops to the landing site, and at dawn he ordered his planes to attack the invasion ships. Most of the Cuban exiles had disembarked during darkness, but almost all their supplies and ammunition remained aboard the ships. After daybreak, wave after wave of Sea Furies and B-26s bombed and strafed the ships, but the biggest shock came when jet planes appeared over the landing site. In a gross miscalculation, the CIA sloppily had forgotten to include Batista's T-33s in its estimates of the Cuban air force. The T-33, probably the most popular jet trainer in history, was in reality a version of the F-80, the first jet fighter of the U.S. Air Force. Ingenious Cuban ground crews had toiled hard to return the T-33 to its original combat role; outfitted with rockets and machine guns, the T-33 panicked the crews aboard the ships. Rockets from the T-33 hit some of the ships, but its most effective role was in shooting down the CIA's B-26s.

It was the Sea Fury, however, that delivered the most telling blows against the invasion fleet. A rocket from a Sea Fury struck one ship, which had to beach itself to prevent sinking. A rocket from another Sea Fury ignited a catastrophic explosion aboard a ship loaded with aviation fuel and bombs. The terrifying blasts demoralized the crews, who turned the remaining ships south and fled at top speed. The invasion force was left stranded, without supplies and missing most of its equipment. The battle was for all practical purposes over, but the Cuban air force still played a final indispensable role by strafing and bombing the invasion fleet whenever it attempted to return to the landing site. With no chance of receiving supplies, the invasion force gradually disintegrated and then fled into the swamps in the afternoon of 19 April. A realization of the true potential of airpower had saved the Cuban Revolution from an early destruction and prevented a repetition of the United States' easy victory over the reformer Jacobo Arbenz in Guatemala in 1954.

The failure of the Bay of Pigs did not keep the Kennedy administration from concocting an even more diabolical plan, called Operation Mongoose, to overthrow the Cuban government. Operation Mongoose was supposed to trigger an internal uprising that would serve as a pretext for a full-scale U.S. invasion of the island. Unfortunately, Operation Mongoose only triggered the chain of events that led to the Cuban Missile Crisis of 1962. The no-invasion pledge the United States gave to obtain the withdrawal of Soviet ballistic missiles from Cuba, however, did guarantee the survival of the Cuban Revolution for as long as the Soviet Union existed.

The Cuban government also insisted on having a large fleet of warplanes as an additional deterrent to any U.S. invasion. Thus, for decades the small island of Cuba possessed the most powerful air force in Latin America, and as new models of Soviet warplanes rolled off the assembly lines, Cuba regularly updated its air force. The collapse of the Soviet Union in 1991 obviously ended Soviet support and crippled the Cuban air force. Cuba's enthusiastic support for Russia in the Russia-Georgia crisis in 2008, however, has led to renewed close ties between the two countries. This new period of friendship with Russia promises to restore the Cuban air force to its previous effectiveness. Cuba knows the significance of airpower as a deterrent, and until the United States permanently abandons any hostile designs on that peaceful island, Cuba will strive to maintain one of the most powerful air forces in Latin America.

The United States and Jet Plane Rivalry in South America, 1950–1982

The lack of powerful air forces in small countries like Guatemala gave the United States the opportunity to try to overthrow their governments. In effect, all small countries remained vulnerable to U.S. covert actions, but of the large Latin American countries, only Mexico felt it did not need a jet fighter fleet to deter U.S. intervention. Instead, by 1950 the rest of the large countries and most of the middle-sized countries had come to consider an exclusive reliance on propeller planes as inadequate for their defense needs. The renewal of U.S. interventions in the Caribbean in the 1950s confirmed the worst fears about the danger from the United

States. The efforts of the U.S. government to restrict sales of jet fighters to Latin America created tremendous resentment in the region. And in a separate consideration, boundary disputes among Latin American countries sometimes sparked arms races as governments tried to match the warplane purchases of neighboring rivals.

Argentina was the Latin American country hardest hit by the shift from propeller to jet planes. Besides having one of the largest if not the largest air force in Latin America until 1945, Argentina had gone further than any other country in creating a manufacturing base to produce propeller planes. With the introduction of the F-80, the Argentine technical expertise became largely obsolete. Its airplane industry proved to be extremely resilient, however, and in one form or another has continued to produce or to assemble a variety of aircraft, but none of them has been an advanced warplane. Because of the U.S. refusal to sell jets to Argentina, its charismatic leader, Juan Perón, became the first Latin American ruler to seek an alternative supplier in Europe. He purchased nearly one hundred Gloster Meteor jet fighters from Britain in 1950. The Meteors were thus the first jet planes to enter a Latin American air force. Although they were subsonic planes, they impressed Brazil sufficiently for that nation to order the same jet fighters. For a few years aviation rivalry ensued between these two countries, but it soon fizzled. Since the mid-1950s Argentina and Brazil have maintained the closest and friendliest of relations, without even the remotest possibility existing of a war between these two countries.

Until 1979 Argentina had a territorial dispute with Chile, and because Chile has been a rival of Peru, Argentina's purchase of British jet fighters inevitably had repercussions in the Pacific Coast of South America. In the 1950s Peru was still receiving propeller planes, such as P-47 fighters and B-26s, from the United States, and not until the mid-1950s did Peru finally persuade the United States to sell it six F-86s. These jet fighters had distinguished themselves in the Korean War and normally flew at high subsonic speeds. After this initial sale, the United States reversed itself and refused to sell more of the newer F-86s to Peru, and instead sold it fourteen of the older F-80s in 1958. In response to the Peruvian purchases, Chile gradually began to acquire its own jet planes.

The purchase by Argentina of fifty A-4s from the United States in 1965 made Chile feel even more vulnerable. The A-4, a subsonic jet attack plane, has in its different models remained the veritable workhorse of the Argentine air force. In 1965 the plane seemed very menacing to Chile, whose government clamored to purchase the supersonic F-5. Large numbers of F-5s were available for sale, because the U.S. Air Force had belatedly concluded that the plane was unsuitable for combat and could provide only training functions.[6] The manufacturer was most eager to find buyers for the F-5, and soon not just Chile, but also Peru, Argentina, Brazil, and Venezuela, wanted to order large numbers of this low-priced jet fighter.

The U.S. government, however, did not want to start an arms race in South America and at least initially refused to authorize the sales. Nevertheless, Peru wanted the F-5s to offset Chilean air superiority and in desperation turned to France. In the early 1950s Britain had been the alternative supplier of jet planes to Latin America, but in the late 1960s France assumed that role. French warplanes had gained tremendous prestige when Israel used French Mirages to win a smashing victory over the Arab countries during the Six-Day War of 1967. Peru purchased 16 Mirage V fighter-bombers and announced that it possessed the best jet plane in the world. In reality it had received a stripped-down, simplified version and not the jet plane responsible for the Israeli victories. Subsequently, in 1973, Peru acquired additional Mirages to match the F-5s that Chile in the meantime had acquired from the United States.

Not just Chile, but also Venezuela and Brazil, purchased F-5s after the U.S. government lifted its restrictions on selling jet planes to Latin American countries. The United States still refused to sell to Peru, however, and turned down the final Peruvian request to acquire F-5s in 1976. By that date France was no longer the best alternative supplier of jet aircraft, and the Soviet Union had emerged as the preferred source. The Soviet Union offered not an exact substitute for the F-5 but the Sukhoi-22, a plane the Peruvians wanted for attack maneuvers at low altitude but not for challenging F-5s over Chilean airspace. The price and the financial terms were irresistible, and Peru settled for buying thirty-six of these Soviet planes. With the sale of the Sukhoi-22s, the

Soviet Union strengthened its growing commercial links with Peru but without starting an arms race in the region. Later Peru made additional arms purchases from the Soviet Union, including MiG fighters.

Threat of war hung over the region—but not between Peru and Chile. Argentina and Chile almost went to war over the Beagle Islands, but once that dispute was settled in 1979, the possibility of war between those two countries sharply declined. For Peru to win a war against Chile, an alliance with Argentina was indispensable. In a desperate gamble designed to preserve the strategic alliance with Argentina against Chile, Peru became the most enthusiastic supporter of Argentina in its brief war with Britain over the Malvinas, or Falkland Islands, in 1982. Peru went so far as to transfer several of its MiG planes to Argentina, but before these airplanes were ready to enter combat, the Argentine garrison in the Malvinas had surrendered to the British.[7] Had a less deplorable ground defense of the Malvinas gained time for the former Peruvian MiGs to enter into combat, the British attack on the islands would almost certainly have failed. Instead, the crushing defeat of Argentina left Peru alone to face any threat from Chile. The struggle for airpower in South America entered a new phase.

Rivalry of Peru with Chile and Ecuador, 1982–2010

The Malvinas war of 1982 eliminated Argentina as a competitor for regional power on the Pacific Coast of South America. That shocking defeat traumatized Argentina and marked the start of an uninterrupted decline in the country's military capacities. Peru and Chile remained the two key rivals in the struggle for air supremacy on the Pacific Coast. Without Argentina in the equation, the balance of power shifted decisively to Chile.

After 1982 Peru made little effort to improve its air force, mainly because the Peruvian army was tied down in a long and bloody struggle against the Maoist insurgency of *Sendero Luminoso,* or Shining Path. Chile correctly concluded that Peru posed no significant threat as long as the Maoist insurgency continued. But what had been a wise conclusion on Chile's part turned into recklessness on the part of Ecuador. During the 1980s Ecuador quietly began purchasing advanced weapons and in the first days of 1995 secretly made its move establishing four bases deep inside Peruvian territory. Peru had not expected any invasion in this inhospitable region, and not until February did Peruvian patrols detect the presence of Ecuadorian bases. A short and savage war under torrential rains ensued over these hellishly hot jungle outposts. Before Peru could launch a full-scale invasion of Ecuador, mediating foreign powers brokered a cease-fire.

The technological superiority of Ecuador had delayed the Peruvian recovery of those jungle outposts, and Ecuador's forces showed a surprising ability to offer real resistance. The Peruvian public, accustomed to regarding Ecuador as an unworthy opponent, was shocked by the pitiful military response of the Alberto Fujimori administration. That Chile had sold weapons to Ecuador during the 1995 war was completely predictable, but that Argentina had also sold weapons to Ecuador during the war seemed to the Peruvian public nothing less than a betrayal. Peru had supported Argentina more than any other Latin American country during the Malvinas war, and Argentina repaid the favor by selling weapons to Ecuador!

Peru now scrambled to purchase weapons, and high on the list of priorities was a new fleet of fighter-bombers. During the war with Ecuador, Peru's old Mirage planes had proven particularly vulnerable to the surface-to-air missiles (SAMs) Ecuador had acquired, and the failure to establish air control over the jungle had hindered the Peruvian counterattack enormously. Because the United States maintained its ban on the sale of advanced warplanes to Latin America, France and Russia were the only two realistic alternatives for the purchase of a new generation of warplanes. An insistent public clamored for new weapons, but unfortunately for Peru, its arms purchases were under the control of one of the most sinister persons in the history of Latin America, the Rasputin-like figure of Vladimiro Montesinos.

Sales of weapons to Latin America seem inseparable from corrupt practices, and at the very least bribes or juicy commissions characterize the shady transactions. Some of the most blatant acts of corruption took place under Montesinos, who routinely took for himself a fee of 18 percent on the value of any weapons Peru purchased. An even greater opportunity came with the purchase of fighter-bombers for Peru. Arms merchants informed Peru that Byelorussia (previously a Soviet Republic) was offering at bargain prices eighteen of the MiG-29s it had inherited from the former Soviet Union. Although the prices made the deal a giveaway, without upgrades these aging planes would soon become obsolete, and Russia, in order to push the sale of new planes from its factories, stated that it would not service these Byelorussian planes or even provide spare parts. Typically, the manufacturing country offers warranties on the planes, maintenance plans, spare parts, and the possibility of upgrades. Because the Byelorussian planes cost a small fraction of genuine Russian planes, the huge sums of money in savings went into the pockets of arms merchants and to officials in both countries. Montesinos himself received at least ten million dollars from this purchase in 1996. Because the price the Peruvian government paid was still a lot less than that of genuine Russian planes, he could still claim that he had saved Peru considerable sums of money.[8]

The newly acquired MiG-29s gave Peru complete air superiority over Ecuador and more ominously threatened Chile for the first time. Even though these planes were not the most recent version of the MiG-29s, they were still formidable weapons. The best confirmation of their great value came in 1997 when the U.S. Pentagon itself bought twenty-one MiG-29s from the former Soviet Republic of Moldavia. The Pentagon wanted to study these superb planes to extract their secrets; coincidentally, this preemptive purchase prevented other countries such as Ecuador and Iran from obtaining modern warplanes at a low price. With no other bargains on the horizon and lacking resources, Ecuador concluded that it could not win any arms race with a more powerful Peru. Without strong support from Chile and with no other allies to turn to, Ecuador had no choice but to settle the boundary dispute in the Amazon largely on Peru's terms. Actually, Peru was even more eager to dispose of this nuisance, and agreements quite favorable to Ecuador finally emerged in 1998. Ratified by both countries, this package of treaties seems to have buried the territorial dispute between both countries, and peace has prevailed, at least during the initial decades of the twenty-first century.

The rapprochement of Ecuador with Peru came too late to halt an arms race with Chile. The eighteen MiG-29s Peru had acquired in 1996 were for Chile the real legacy of Peru's war with Ecuador. Peru had never given up the hope of recovering the provinces it had lost to Chile in the peace treaty of 1883 ending the War of the Pacific, and a new dispute over maritime exclusion zones threatened to worsen an already tense situation. In a parallel development, in 1997 Argentina seemed to reenter the rivalry when it made its first major airplane acquisition in more than a decade in purchasing thirty-six A-4M fighter bombers to replace those lost during the Malvinas war. Although Chile no longer considered Argentina an enemy and had ruled out any possibility of a war with its eastern neighbor, this purchase materialized at a most inauspicious moment. The subsonic A-4Ms by themselves posed no threat to Chile, but war gaming showed that joint operations by the A-4Ms and the Peruvian MiG-29s could snatch air superiority away from Chile. Even though the possibility of a Peruvian-Argentine alliance to destroy Chile was extremely unlikely, it existed, and the temptation could prove irresistible for a bold or charismatic leader.

At this moment when Chile's armed forces were most paranoid about the country's defense, the U.S. government decided to lift the ban on selling advanced airplanes to Latin America. The Clinton administration ended this prohibition in 1997 at the request of U.S. manufacturers, who wanted to expand their sales and who were tired of leaving the market exclusively to European airplane makers. U.S. manufacturers dazzled Chilean officers at air shows with demonstrations of the feats of F-16s, and soon the Chilean military was clamoring for the purchase of those supersonic planes. To his great credit, President Eduardo Frei opposed the purchase of the F-16s and refused to start an arms race. His administration believed that war with Argentina was completely impossible and thus eliminated any chance of an Argentine alliance with Peru. Frei also believed that the existing fleet of Mirages adequately deterred Peru from wanting to start a war.

As soon as the new president, Ricardo Lagos, took office in 2000, the armed forces renewed their pressure to purchase F-16s and warships. A series of internal political events, in particular the struggle over the fate of the former dictator General Augusto Pinochet, allowed the military to bring enormous pressure on the new president, who proved less firm than his predecessor, Frei. In 2000 President Lagos stated that he would not seek any additional funds from the congress for arms purchases, but he did authorize the military to use their own earmarked funds. Chile earmarks 10 percent of the proceeds from copper, the main export of the country, to a special military fund. This arrangement is unique in Latin America and emerged out of the negotiations to dismantle the Pinochet dictatorship in 1990. This special copper fund can pay only for military expenditures, but the approval of the civilian government is required for arms purchases from abroad. Having these specially earmarked funds gives the Chilean military a tremendous advantage in seeking weapons and was the trump card that finally overcame the resistance of President Lagos.

As the generals rushed out to place orders for the first ten F-16s, only gradually did they realize that the high price of the F-16s required postponing the rest of their armament program, because the government was not providing money in addition to the copper fund. The fascination with the F-16s proved to be short-lived. In a classic example of bait and switch, the U.S. government confirmed the sale of the F-16s but announced that the plane would lack the latest weapons technology. Although many details are still secret, it was not clear whether these F-16s would have even a radar with a hundred-kilometer air range, which was already standard in the Argentine A-4Ms. Particularly troubling was the refusal of the U.S. government to hand Chile the Advanced Medium-Range Air-to-Air Missile, or AMRAAM, until another Latin American country had first acquired a similar weapon. Latin American air forces at that time had only air-to-air missiles with a maximum range of twenty kilometers, but the AMRAAM had a range of around sixty-four kilometers. The United States had been instrumental in provoking an arms race, and in a belated attempt to dampen the competition, the United States decided to withhold the delivery of the AMRAAM. Another consideration was that the U.S. Air Force was most reluctant to share its most advanced weapons technology with Chile or any other country. In reality, without the AMRAAMs the Chilean F-16s were extremely vulnerable in ranges of under twenty kilometers to the higher speed and superior maneuverability of the Peruvian MiG-29s.[9] The flaw was so obvious that the Chilean media taunted the government for having acquired "the most expensive aerobatic squadron in the world."[10] A compromise was reached that seemed to allow Chile to receive these AMRAAMs after five years, because presumably by then the U.S. Air Force would have acquired a newer and more sophisticated version of this weapon.

The good news for Chile was that Argentina openly announced that it was not concerned about the purchase of these F-16s. Instead, Peru was furious and sent many heated protests to Chile, all to no avail. Peru could not afford to buy comparable warplanes, and its military lacked any earmarked revenues such as the Chilean copper fund. In reality, the cost of the F-16s, at roughly $25 million each, was proving too much of a burden even for Chile. Sacrificing the rest of the Chilean military for the sake of ten F-16s was resulting in a very unbalanced military force. Chile still wanted advanced warships and new land weapons, because ten F-16s could provide only a very thin coverage for this very long and narrow country.

A convenient solution appeared in 2002 when the Netherlands put up for sale sixteen used F-16s slated for replacement by new planes. Chile jumped at the chance to purchase these at a bargain price, and once again Latin America returned to its traditional role as a dumping ground for secondhand or obsolescent weapons. Once Chile rediscovered this easy path to apparent military strength, there was no turning back, and in 2009 Chile purchased an additional eighteen used F-16s from the Netherlands. With a total of forty-four F-16s, Chile seemed to have the most powerful air force in South America.

The appearance may have been misleading, and not just because of the lack of the AMRAAMs indispensable for any combat with the MiG-29s. The fascination of bright, shiny weapons proved irresistible to the Chilean generals, who had starved other sectors of the military for the sake of arms purchases. Salaries remained low, and a predictable outflow of combat pilots into higher-paying jobs in the civilian sector occurred. The aviation commander claimed "to have lost an entire air force from 1980 until today."[11] The blatant attempt to pressure congress into allocating additional funds for salaries in the budget earned only scorn from a public still angry at the military's complicity with the Augusto Pinochet dictatorship. As the more experienced pilots left the air force, the combat effectiveness of the F-16s necessarily suffered.

As soon as the new planes arrived, Chile stationed all the F-16s in the north of the country, in particular in the extreme north, so that in just a few minutes these planes could be flying over Peru. Predictably, an outraged Peru sent a howl of protests after the purchase of these new planes, but the Peruvian situation had become worse than even Chile could have imagined. Although Vladimiro Montesinos was then rotting in prison, by 2008 a lack of spare parts and skilled maintenance had grounded almost all the MiG-29s he had purchased from Byelorussia. The Peruvian pilots could not meet even their minimum number of flying hours. Peru lacked the funds to buy new planes at full price, and no more discounted MiG-29s from the Soviet era were on the market. The only alternative left was to seek out Moscow to ask for forgiveness, beg for another chance, and hope for the absolution of Moscow. The twenty-first century revival of Russia as a world power made Moscow eager to find allies, friends, and customers throughout the world, and a magnanimous Moscow decided to save Peru's older MiG-29s, even though those earlier versions were no longer in production. Russian technicians went to Peru with replacement parts and an undisclosed number of upgrades for these obsolescent versions of the MiG-29. Peruvian ground crews also received training on the maintenance of these planes. If the Russians properly upgraded the planes with advanced weapons technology, the MiG-29s should once again match if not surpass the performance of Chile's F-16s. But these mere eighteen MiG-29s in the Peruvian air force served mainly as a deterrent to Chile's forty-four F-16s.

Russia hoped by its generous gesture to earn goodwill among the Peruvians, should they in the future find the funds to purchase more recent models of Russian warplanes. The imbalance in numbers of planes seems too big for Peru to let too many years pass before making a comparable purchase in response. But poverty may force Peru to resign itself to remaining largely unarmed, a policy that for wealthier Argentina has proven to be more than satisfactory.

The Rise of Venezuela

In tropical Venezuela the armed forces have always enjoyed tremendous prestige. Until 1958 the country was ruled almost continuously by *caudillos*, or army dictators, but the armed forces always managed to escape any lasting association with a fallen dictator. In a situation similar to that of General Augusto Pinochet in Chile, the military adroitly shifted blame away from itself and onto the dictator. In addition, weapons and uniforms have continued to exercise a tremendous fascination in Venezuela. Consequently, having flashy new weapons to wave at other countries was a source of pride and helped mobilize already strong feelings of nationalism among the population. And vast petroleum wealth easily financed Venezuela's purchase of expensive combat aircraft, which was rarely the case elsewhere in Latin America.

After Peru bought supersonic Mirage fighter-bombers from France in 1967, Venezuela felt the pressure to possess similar high-quality jets. Venezuela turned to France because the United States still insisted on trying to keep the most advanced jet warplanes out of Latin America. In the early 1970s Venezuela purchased sixteen Mirages, more for "keeping up with the Joneses" than for any real military reason. The Mirages should have amply satisfied the vanity needs of Venezuela, but when the first F-16s entered the U.S. Air Force in 1979, the superiority of this new plane over the older Mirages was undeniable.

Without any strategic need for the jet fighters, Venezuela should have remained content with its aging Mirages, but the glitter of the brand-new F-16s proved irresistible. As a major petroleum exporter, Venezuela had accumulated huge reserves of foreign currency during the energy crisis of 1973–1980, but in hindsight it would have made more sense to save these cash reserves for the inevitable downturn in oil prices, as happened in the 1980s. The Jimmy Carter administration had placed a ban on the sale of advanced warplanes to Latin America, and a special waiver from the U.S. Congress was necessary to carry out the sale of F-16s to Venezuela. Obviously, U.S. manufacturers were eager to place the brand-new warplane on the world markets to earn higher profits, but the question of why Venezuela needed these sophisticated weapons never received a logical and persuasive answer.

Because Venezuelan civilian rule stood in stark contrast to the military dictatorships then rampant throughout Latin America, the U.S. government could convincingly claim that selling twenty-four F-16s to Venezuela was an act in support of a democratic regime. When these planes began arriving in 1983, Venezuela made history: for the first time a Latin American country had received a brand-new advanced warplane identical to the best jets in the U.S. inventory and comparable, if not superior, to those in other air forces of the world. In an even longer historical perspective, the only other time Latin America acquired sophisticated weapons identical to those of great powers was in the pre–World War I period, when Argentina had purchased dreadnought battleships.

The arrival of F-16s was a matter of great concern to two of Venezuela's neighbors, Colombia and Guyana. Both had vigorously protested the sale of these warplanes, but to no avail. Colombia had warned about the dangers of an arms race, but very philosophically, Colombia decided to ignore those costly toys and concentrated instead on its growing guerrilla insurgency. Guyana had the most to fear, because Venezuela had on very solid grounds extended claims to nearly half the territory of Guyana, a former British colony. Because the air force of Guyana had normally consisted of only two obsolete planes, the F-16s could serve to deter Britain from coming to the rescue of its former colony in case of a Venezuelan invasion. Using force to settle territorial disputes, however, is an extremely risky action that should be taken only as a last resort and then only if the attacking country has overwhelming military superiority, as in the case of India and Goa in 1962. Venezuela, with the F-16s and its strong and mechanized army, did have the overwhelming force to recover its lost territories, yet the government never invaded Guyana.

Venezuela, with no war on the horizon and with no deterrence needed against Colombia or Guyana, found that its F-16s and its entire inventory of combat aircraft lacked a mission. The transport planes and helicopters proved invaluable in rescue operations when tropical storms ravaged Venezuela, but otherwise the air force personnel lacked a role. Without much else to do, some air force personnel and many army officers drifted into the world of politics. In the Latin American tradition, the air force became just another armed service trying to seize political power. Barracks revolts had affected Venezuela in the early 1960s and then appeared to subside, but in the late 1980s plots and conspiracies reappeared in the military bases. Two attempted coups shook Venezuela in 1992. The first, in February, was primarily an army affair and is remembered mainly because it introduced to the world Colonel Hugo Chávez Frías of the paratroopers. This coup failed because the air force conspirators had not received word on time. The second coup, in November 1992, was entirely an air force affair. Quite significantly, the coup plotters gained control of the majority of Venezuelan airplanes, but the F-16s remained loyal to the government. After inconclusive bombing of the presidential palace, the coup ended when one F-16 shot down a Brazilian-built Tucano plane and destroyed any chance of the plotters' gaining air superiority. Nobody could have guessed at the time of their purchase that the F-16s would play the key role in stopping the air force coup of November 1992.

The coup attempts were merely part of the seething discontent in Venezuela. The benefits of the petroleum wealth were flowing to the upper class and to large corporations, while the majority of the population sank into poverty. Protests became a common occurrence and indicated that Venezuela was ripe for moving in another direction. With so many internal problems facing the country, it was hard to imagine that the government could devote time to the F-16s, yet strangely enough it did. When the Clinton administration in 1997 lifted the ban on selling advanced warplanes to Latin America, Venezuela proposed buying two of the latest-model F-16s and also upgrading the original twenty-four with the most recent technology. Eventually an agreement was reached with the manufacturer to refurbish and upgrade ten of the original F-16s.

The election of the coup leader Hugo Chávez in 1998 and his assumption of office in 1999 did not signify any sharp break in policy with regard to the armed forces. Chávez inherited a substantial arsenal and a quite respectable military establishment, which at that time he considered more than adequate for Venezuela's security needs. As a paratrooper, he was well aware of airpower's potential. He duly authorized the planned refurbishing of the first ten F-16s to proceed, with the understanding that eventually the rest of the planes would receive a similar upgrade. He concentrated his energies on dealing with the economic and social problems of the country and feverishly looked for ways to bring the petroleum prosperity to the masses. As he began channeling petroleum income away from private corporations and the upper class to the rest of the population, inevitably resentment grew among the privileged groups, who began plotting with disgruntled elements in the armed forces to seek his overthrow. When a recall vote to remove Chávez from office failed, the coup plotters, helped by the United States and Spain, decided to strike. Relations between Chávez and the Clinton administration had been fine, but they turned bitterly hostile when the right-wing administration of George W. Bush came to office. When Chávez rallied world opinion against the planned U.S. invasion of Iraq, the Bush administration was furious and joined local coup plotters to try to repeat some variety of the 1954 Guatemala operation in Venezuela.

The result was the confused coup attempt of April 2002, many of whose baffling events cannot be cleared up until the United States declassifies key documents, probably not before forty years have elapsed. Chávez was arrested, removed from power, and with his family almost sent into exile. His followers spontaneously packed the streets and demanded his return to power. Junior officers refused to obey senior rebel officers, and some generals hesitated until the last moment before choosing sides. F-16 pilots loyal to Chávez were flying over the presidential palace, and the implied threat of bombing convinced the last wavering generals to proclaim their loyalty.

The coup attempt collapsed, and Chávez had survived, but he was a changed man who knew that the United States was out to destroy him, just as the United States had tried to topple Fidel Castro in Cuba for more than fifty years. From 2002 to 2009, events in Venezuela strangely paralleled those of the Cuban Revolution decades before. The armed forces of Venezuela, which had seemed sufficient to Chávez in 1999, now seemed woefully inadequate. Venezuela went on a buying spree for weapons abroad, and immediately the Bush administration did everything possible to keep Chávez from acquiring a fearsome arsenal. The United States refused to refurbish any more F-16s and halted the routine supply of spare parts. Eventually, the United States placed a formal embargo on the sale of any weapons or technology to Venezuela, but no trade embargo was possible because the United States needed Venezuela's petroleum. When Venezuela turned for airplanes to Spain, France, and Brazil, the U.S. government did everything possible to prevent the sale of any equipment with U.S. components. The Bush administration blocked even the sales of patrol aircraft and cargo planes from Spain.

During the Cuban Revolution the United States had pushed Castro toward the Soviet Union, and now in a striking parallel the United States pushed Venezuela toward Russia. Just as Nikita Khrushchev had done in 1960, in 2005 President Vladimir Putin agreed to meet Venezuela's requests for advanced weapons. Besides rifles, artillery, tanks, and helicopters, Russia sold twenty-four Sukhoi-30s, its most advanced fighter-bomber, to Venezuela. Venezuela during the Bush administration had a real reason for arming itself (as it had not when it purchased the F-16s in 1982), because Chávez feared that the United States would try to repeat in Venezuela an invasion similar to that of Iraq in 2003. Chávez needed a large military force to deter the United States from considering any invasion of Venezuela. Inadvertently, the Bush administration had given Venezuela a justification for its fleet of advanced fighter-bombers. The air force of Venezuela, just like the rest of the country's military, had a clearly defined mission of defending the country from U.S. invasion. Venezuela was not fooled into believing, as Guatemala had in 1954, that the only threat of invasion could come from a bordering country, and it concluded that the real threat came from the United States. Under the protection of his large and growing military might, Chávez has continued with his social and economic experiments to bring prosperity to a majority of the population.

Notes

1. Once published, my two-volume manuscript on the wars of Latin America, 1948–2012, will present a comprehensive overview of airpower and insurgencies. The pioneering article on this topic is James S. Corum and Wray R. Johnson, "Protracted Insurgencies: Latin American Air Forces in Counterguerrilla Operations," in *Airpower in Small Wars: Fighting Insurgents and Terrorists* (Lawrence: University Press of Kansas, 2003), pp. 325–378.

2. See René De La Pedraja, *Wars of Latin America, 1899–1941* (Jefferson, N.C.: McFarland, 2006), esp. chaps. 7 and 10.

3. "Mexico: Poor Air Force, Small and Outdated," *Aviation Week*, 26 February 1951, pp. 161–162.

4. Louis A. Pérez Jr., *Army Politics in Cuba, 1898–1958* (Pittsburgh: University of Pittsburgh Press, 1976), p. 142.

5. Critics of the Kennedy administration and of "liberals" have not ceased to portray the cancellation of the second air strike as a great betrayal and as a stab in the back that doomed the Bay of Pigs Invasion to defeat. The assumption remains that the second air strike could have turned the Bay of Pigs Invasion into a success. The condemnation of Kennedy's decision remains strong in some conservative and Republican sectors, even after evidence of Cuban preparations to neutralize and most probably destroy the planes of the second air strike has become plentiful over recent decades. Nobody has taken the time to do some simple war games to predict the range of possibilities of a second strike. To start that analysis, the text of this chapter has already shown that the Cuban air force necessarily had to escape any second CIA attack. What then remains are the four possible outcomes (1, 2, 3, and 4), which are depicted in this matrix and then discussed individually:

	Most B-26s are destroyed (most likely)	Most B-26s survive (least likely)
B-26 pilots correctly report that they were unable to destroy Cuban air force (most likely)	(1)	(3)
B-26 pilots incorrectly report that they destroyed Cuban air force (least likely)	(2)	(4)

Of course, under all four scenarios the Cuban air force necessarily escapes intact. (1) Most of the CIA's B-26s are shot down or return with major damage, and the surviving pilots report that they were unable to destroy the Cuban air force. This obvious defeat would almost certainly have led to the cancellation of the Bay of Pigs

Invasion. It was highly unlikely that the Kennedy administration would have offered replacement planes, even if they could be found in such numbers. Eisenhower had authorized sending extra planes to replace losses in the Guatemala operation of 1954, but to replace a whole fleet in 1961 was a decision of a much greater magnitude. (2) Most of the CIA's B-26s are destroyed or suffer heavy damage, but the pilots mistakenly report that they have destroyed the Cuban air force. For the purposes of determining the outcome, it does not matter why the pilots reported incorrectly, whether it was simple error or deliberate falsehood. Under this outcome the Kennedy administration would probably have leaned to cancellation. (3) The CIA's B-26s suffer few losses but report that they have been unable to destroy the Cuban air force. Proponents of the invasion could cite the survival of the B-26s as proof that the Cuban air force was overrated. The Kennedy administration most probably would have leaned toward continuing with the operation, but the invasion still had to fail because the Cuban air force easily would have sunk the invasion ships, which is what actually happened. (4) The CIA's B-26s suffer few losses but mistakenly report that they have destroyed the Cuban air force. Under this outcome the Kennedy administration would inevitably have authorized the invasion, and again the Cuban air force would have sunk the invasion ships. The most important conclusion from the matrix is that under any of the four outcomes the second air strike could not have turned the Bay of Pigs Invasion into a success. Additionally, unless the operation was canceled, the invasion would have continued on to its doomed fate.

6. The Latin American angle of this plane's history suffices to reveal major blunders in the development of the F-5. A critical scholarly analysis of the F-5 is sorely needed.

7. For a scholarly analysis of air operations in the Malvinas war, see René De La Pedraja, "The Argentine Air Force versus Britain in the Falkland Islands, 1982," in *Why Air Forces Fail: The Anatomy of Defeat,* ed. Robin Higham and Stephen J. Harris, rev. ed. (Lexington: University Press of Kentucky, 2012), pp. 227–259.

8. Vladimiro Montesinos deposited his money in accounts in a variety of countries ranging from Switzerland and Luxembourg to the United States. Although prosecutors have had difficulty reconstructing the specific steps, the general outline of the corrupt deal is very clear. As an indication of the magnitude of the deposits, Switzerland in 2002 returned to the Peruvian government nearly $50 million from illegal accounts of Montesinos.

9. This inferiority of the F-16 at short ranges has been at the root of the insistent demand of the U.S. Air Force for new generations of supersonic jet fighters. Constant upgrades in avionics have preserved the superiority of the F-16 at long ranges, but superiority may be lost at any moment to countries such as Russia and China, which have tremendous and growing computer capabilities.

10. *La nación* (Buenos Aires), 6 January 2001.

11. *La nación* (Buenos Aires), 23 March 2008.

Further Reading

Only a handful of useful titles exist in English, and the number of publications in Spanish is very limited. The Spanish publications always refer to just one country. Although some of the publications in Spanish claim to be official histories, they generally are a combination of yearbooks and photo albums. Real official histories that are comparable to those in the United States, Canada, and western Europe do not exist. For the few countries that have them, however, the Spanish publications provide a starting point and contain useful information, if usually in the form of raw data.

English

Dienst, John, and Dan Hagedorn. *North American F-51 Mustangs in Latin American Air Force Service.* Arlington, Tex.: Aerofax, 1985.
Corum, James S., and Wray R. Johnson. "Protracted Insurgencies: Latin American Air Forces in Counterguerrilla Operations." In their *Airpower in Small Wars: Fighting Insurgents and Terrorists.* Lawrence: University Press of Kansas, 2003, pp. 325–378.
Ethell, Jeffrey, and Alfred Price, *Air War South Atlantic.* New York: Macmillan, 1983.

Spanish

Ayala Paredes, César M. *Panorámica ensayo: La Fuerza Aérea Ecuatoriana, 50 años en la vida nacional.* Quito: Editorial Don Bosco, 1971.
Echavarría Barrientos, Raúl. *Fuerza Aérea Colombiana, su epopeya y grandeza 1919–1974.* Bogotá: Fondo Rotatorio de la Fuerza Aérea Colombiana, 1974.
Fernández Prada, E. Alberto. *La aviación en el Peru.* 2 vols. Lima: CIMP, 1966–1975.
Quellet, Ricardo Luis. *Historia de la Fuerza Aérea Argentina.* 8 vols. to date. Buenos Aires: Fuerza Aérea Argentina, 1997–2008.

Suggestions for Further Research

Almost the entire field of Latin American military aviation remains open for research and study. The little scholarly work done has taken place as part of general military histories, such as my *Wars of Latin America, 1899–1941* or in reference to a specific war. The absence of scholarly studies applies to the entire history of aviation in Latin America since its inception in the 1910s, but it is even more acute for the period after 1945. Additionally, a critical scholarly analysis of the F-5 plane would be most welcome.

The need for further research is obvious, but the extreme scarcity of sources, both published and archival, has crippled research efforts. This chapter is a reduced version of a longer text I hope to expand into a book if time and other commitments make this possible.

6

Presidential Statesmen and U.S. Airpower

Personalities and Perceptions

Jeffery S. Underwood

The first duty the Constitution requires of a president is to swear an oath to "preserve, protect and defend the Constitution of the United States." Next it names the president as the "Commander in Chief" of U.S. military and naval forces, but the thirty-four words in Article II, Section 2, granting that power provide no guidance on how to use those forces. Before the Spanish-American War, American presidents had to concern themselves only with land and naval warfare largely restricted to the North American continent or the Western Hemisphere. Throughout the twentieth century, however, presidents increasingly ventured into the third dimension of warfare: airpower. How each president employed airpower often depended more on his personality or perceptions about what airpower could achieve than on a deeply considered assessment of how airpower could achieve national goals.

The first president to use airpower was Abraham Lincoln when he appointed Thaddeus Lowe as the chief aeronaut of the Army of the Potomac to conduct aerial balloon reconnaissance of Confederate troops. There was precedent for using balloons. The French army had used them in the 1790s, and the Austrians had unsuccessfully used balloons to bomb Venice in 1849. Nevertheless, Lincoln's support of Lowe's balloon corps probably indicates his willingness to employ any means to preserve the republic more than any presidential conceptualization of airpower. Under President William McKinley in 1898, brief observation support was provided to American troops in Cuba during the Spanish-American War. In both cases, this limited use of balloons was more a footnote than a presidential use of airpower.

In actuality, President Woodrow Wilson became the first American president to employ military aerial forces, initially with the flimsy, underpowered aircraft the U.S. Army sent to Mexico in support of the 1916 Punitive Expedition. With American entry into World War I, the Wilson administration planned to use the nation's industrial might to create a massive aerial armada of American-built airplanes that would darken the skies over Europe. In the first great lesson about the difficulty of quickly building an air force, American industry failed to meet the expected production, which forced American military and naval aviators to rely mainly on European-built aircraft. Significant numbers of American-built warplanes began arriving in the war zone just before the Armistice, and had the war continued into 1919, the dream of American military aviation might have been fulfilled.

The Armistice spared the Wilson administration from addressing the question of how American bombers would be used: tactically against military targets near the front lines or strategically against enemy industry, the latter accompanied by its inherent threat to civilians. The decision had already been made, however. Austro-Hungarian fliers had bombed Italian cities with little effect, but the Italians responded, guided by the advocate of strategic bombing, Giulio Douhet. Americans serving with the Italians, including the U.S. congressman and future mayor of New York City, Fiorello LaGuardia, had flown Italian Caproni bombers on strategic bombing attacks against the Austrians. German air raids on London with zeppelins and Gotha bombers and the creation of the Inter-Allied Independent Air Force commanded by the Royal Air Force's Major General Hugh Trenchard indicated the direction that aerial warfare had taken. In a total war, civilian industry and populations had become targets.

In France, Brigadier General William "Billy" Mitchell, who commanded the U.S. Army Air Service for the First Army Group in that country, had been influenced by Trenchard's ideas on the offensive use of airpower. He and other American military commanders supported the strategic bombardment effort. Just as it had refused to condone unrestricted submarine warfare, however, the Wilson administration would not approve the aerial bombardment of civilian populations. On 8 November 1918 Secretary of War Newton D. Baker told American military commanders that the United States would not take part in any plans for the "promiscuous bombing upon industry, commerce, or population, in enemy countries disassociated from obvious military needs to be served by such action."[1] The Armistice ended the Independent Air Force and prevented an open breach between the American military leaders in France and the political leaders at home over the conduct of the war.

As it had after every previous war, the United States demobilized following the Armistice, and remaining true to the republic's longstanding disdain for standing armies, Congress reduced the army and navy into little more than constabulary forces. Military and naval aviation, which had had little visible effect on the war's outcome, received proportionate reductions. Rejecting the collective security offered by the League of Nations in favor of an isolationist foreign policy, the Republican-dominated Congress and White House of the 1920s and early 1930s relied on the Atlantic and Pacific oceans to protect America from foreign threats. This dependence on natural barriers perfectly matched the Harding, Coolidge, and Hoover administrations' emphasis on economy, small government, small military establishments, and naval disarmament. Thus, the international naval disarmament treaties adopted in the 1920s supported Republican policies in two ways. First, smaller foreign navies made the oceans more effective as defensive barriers. Second, a smaller U.S. Navy required fewer tax dollars.

Billy Mitchell and other airpower advocates returned from the Great War convinced by Trenchard and Douhet that strategic bombardment provided the best way to prevent another bloody war of attrition. By destroying an enemy's industrial capacity to produce weapons, even at the cost of civilian lives and property, strategic bombing would shorten any future war and save countless lives. American voters, however, chose a government that adopted a defensive military policy based on isolationism and oceanic barriers for defense. As Americans became disillusioned about the war and suspicions grew that "merchants of death" had maneuvered the nation into Europe's war to sell more weapons, the idea of developing offensive weapons like strategic bombers was viewed unfavorably in America. Furthermore, the small budgets given to the army and navy provided little funding for weapons development and procurement, which forced military aviators to find a legitimate mission or incur further reductions. Unable to build a strategic air arm, they settled on coastal defense as the mission to which military aviation was best suited, but this strategy did not match defense policies adopted by the Republican administrations in the 1920s.

Convinced that the Atlantic and Pacific provided adequate defense, the Republican administrations discounted the claims of Mitchell and other airpower advocates that oceanic barriers would soon crumble to technology. For Mitchell and his supporters, offensive airpower offered the best and least expensive way to defend the country. Mitchell's successful sinking of the German battleship *Ostfriesland* in 1921 tests showed that airplanes could sink battleships, and many more record-setting flights by the U.S. Army Air Service demonstrated the growing capabilities of airpower. The flight to Alaska in 1920 and the first non-stop transcontinental flight in 1923 gave the first inklings that things had changed. Then the Army Air Service's first flight around the world in 1924, followed by Lindbergh's solo crossing of the Atlantic and the first flight from California to Hawaii, both in 1927, showed that the oceans were shrinking in the face of aeronautical advances.

The Republican presidents clearly recognized the rapidly growing capacities of military aircraft, but they also understood the reality of the world situation. President Calvin Coolidge had greeted the 1924 round-the-world fliers when they landed in Washington, D.C., but he correctly perceived that the United States had no serious foreign threats at that time. Once asked to explain his unwillingness to spend tax money on the military, Coolidge succinctly answered: "Who's gonna fight us?"[2] Within just a few years, the world situation changed dramatically, but Coolidge's assessment was understandable for the time. Rebuffed by the presidents, Congress, and the War Department, Mitchell and other airpower advocates became convinced that the only way airpower could achieve its fullest potential was through the creation of a separate air force. Their public campaign for independence brought them into direct conflict with the commander in chief.

Sinking the *Ostfriesland* gave Mitchell powerful evidence in support of airpower, but his unrelenting drive for a separate air force created a fresh rift between the military aviators and the politicians. His increasing advocacy for using strategic bombing of civilian as well as military targets to prevent any future war or to end one quickly ran directly counter to American foreign and diplomatic policy. For the Republican presidents, and Calvin Coolidge in particular, Mitchell's campaigning presented a direct challenge to their constitutional authority. Mitchell finally pushed too far after the crash of the airship USS *Shenandoah* in 1925, when he essentially accused his superiors of treason. The Coolidge administration and the War Department reacted swiftly by court-martialing Mitchell and "exiling" his supporter Henry H. "Hap" Arnold, who later commanded the U.S. Army Air Forces in World War II, to Kansas. In his memoirs Arnold admitted that the War Department did not profit from the Mitchell period. Members of the War Department, he wrote, "seemed to set their mouths tighter, draw more into their shell, and if anything, take even a narrower point of view of aviation as an offensive power in warfare."[3]

A decade of international disarmament efforts culminated at the 1932 League of Nations' Conference for the Reduction and Limitation of Armaments, better known as the Geneva Disarmament Conference. Although not a member of the League, the United States sent observers to the conference, where the limitation of air forces became a major topic of negotiation. President Herbert Hoover proposed the total elimination of all military aircraft, except scouting planes for naval vessels, but international efforts to limit or eliminate air forces collapsed. No nation really wanted to give up its air force. In spite of his laissez-faire policies, Hoover's willingness to regulate commercial aviation and to do away completely with America's military aviation in 1932 clearly showed his perception of airpower as something that could be regulated like commercial aviation.[4]

The election of Franklin D. Roosevelt in 1932 fundamentally altered the way that American presidents perceive and use airpower. Often dismissed by contemporaries and historians as "pro-navy," Roosevelt perceived that airpower could be used to shape military and foreign policy. In the months before the United States entered World War II, Roosevelt's perceptions and experiences shaped his responses toward aggression in Europe and Asia. His personality inclined him toward accepting technological solutions to problems—whether it be using hand controls to drive a car after polio left his legs paralyzed, the radio to reach Americans quickly with "fireside chats," or American airpower to overcome two decades of military unpreparedness.

Early in his political career, Assistant Secretary of the Navy Roosevelt recognized that aviation could bring significant changes in national defense policy. In 1917 he witnessed firsthand the potential use of aviation in naval operations when he flew in a U.S. Navy airship. Then in 1919, two years before the sinking of the *Ostfriesland*, FDR testified before Congress that "in the future, aviation might make surface ships practically impossible to be used as an Arm."[5] By 1932 he clearly perceived that aviation had forever altered the United States, which was demonstrated when he became the first American presidential candidate to fly to a nominating convention. To his contemporaries, that flight from Albany to Chicago to accept the Democratic Party nomination demonstrated Roosevelt to be "air-minded." Unaware that polio had rendered air travel difficult for FDR, the army, navy, and Commerce Department tussled to become the sole agency to provide airlift for the new president. The aircraft of the 1930s lacked accommodations for persons with disabilities, however, and Roosevelt pragmatically traveled within the United States on trains, automobiles, and boats. During World War II necessity dictated that he take a flying boat to the Casablanca Conference to avoid the threat of German submarines, and FDR took the first aircraft built specifically for the president, the Douglas VC-54C, nicknamed the *Sacred Cow*, to the Yalta Conference in 1945.

More important than inaugurating the first presidential airlift was FDR's redirection of American military, naval, and foreign policy toward an increased reliance on airpower. Initially, President Roosevelt had been unwilling to expand either army or navy aviation, but the need for strong air forces became apparent because of rising German, Japanese, and Italian militarism. In 1932 Stanley Baldwin had warned the British Parliament that bombers would always get through air defenses, and the British began an expansion of the Royal Air Force in 1934. The United States took notice of the rising threats. Three new aircraft carriers, which had not been prohibited in the naval disarmament treaties of the 1920s, were commissioned during the Roosevelt administration: the USS *Ranger,* the U.S. Navy's first ship specifically built as an aircraft carrier (1934); the USS *Yorktown* (1937); and the USS *Enterprise* (1938). To provide an adequate supply of navy and marine corps pilots, Roosevelt approved the Aviation Cadet Act in 1935. The Munich Crisis of 1938 provided the catalyst, but aerial achievements by the army air corps laid the foundation for FDR's shift in defense policy. In 1937 the highly publicized interception of the Italian ocean liner *Rex* by three of the army's new Boeing B-17 "Flying Fortress" bombers, and the secret interception of the USS *Utah* by army air corps bombers during war games conducted off the California coast, demonstrated to the president that the air corps could find an attacking enemy fleet long before it could reach America's coastlines.

Just as important was Roosevelt's approval of the use of Flying Fortresses to counter the German and Italian propaganda threatening democracy in Latin America. The U.S. government had already supported the expansion of the Pan American Airways' civilian routes into Colombia to prevent the German-owned Colombian airline SCADTA (*Sociedad Colombo-Alemana de Transportes Aereos,* or Colombian-German Air Transport Society) from creating a monopoly on aerial routes between Latin America and the United States. The Roosevelt administration used military airpower in a peaceful way, however, to support its foreign and defense policies in the region. In January 1938 Bruno Mussolini, the dictator's son, led a flight of three Italian bombers from Rome to Rio de Janeiro across Africa and the Atlantic, and at the request of the State Department, the air corps dispatched six B-17s to Buenos Aires, Argentina, to attend the inauguration of President Roberto M. Ortiz, who had been democratically elected, the following month. Turned into a goodwill tour of South America, this highly publicized trip included a nonstop flight of 2,695 miles from Miami, Florida, to Lima, Peru. This goodwill flight not only supported the FDR administration's efforts to foster democracy—and aircraft sales—in South America, but also proved that the air corps could quickly reach any place in the Western Hemisphere. The Buenos Aries flight and follow-up B-17 flights to other South American nations helped cement the air corps's role in the hemispheric defense adopted by the United States as the rest of the world tumbled toward another world war.

In 1935 Adolf Hitler touted the rebirth of Germany's air force, which had been banned by the Treaty of Versailles. The Luftwaffe was not as powerful as the Nazis proclaimed, but their propaganda efforts had convinced Europe that German airpower was a dangerous threat. Fear of deadly air attacks on their cities had shaped the Western democracies' response to Hitler's demands during the Munich Crisis. In part, the British and French unwillingness to fight over Czechoslovakia in 1938 had been molded by the threat of German bombers. Belatedly realizing how ill prepared their air forces had become, both nations embarked on large-scale aerial rearmament projects. America became a source for airplanes, and Roosevelt actively supported the sale of military aircraft to the Allies. Knowing that the Neutrality Law of 1937 would have compelled him to stop the flow of American aircraft to France and Great Britain if war broke out, FDR supported repeal of the law. Furthermore, he personally supported French efforts to purchase American combat planes. After hearing Hitler's Nuremberg speech on 12 September 1938, Roosevelt concluded that war would inevitably come, and he sent Harry Hopkins to the West Coast to survey the American aircraft industry with a view toward expanding the production of military aircraft.

At the height of the Munich Crisis, FDR's concept of airpower had crystallized. In a private conversation with Harold Ickes, Roosevelt stated that, if he were leading the Western democracies, he would fight a defensive war. First, he would inform the German people that there were no designs on German territory, to calm their fears and undermine their morale. Second, he would blockade Germany. Third, Roosevelt would make it principally an air war. With Great Britain, France, and Russia pounding Germany from the air, Germany would be unable to defend itself. Anticipating that the German air force would attack, Roosevelt believed that the German civilians would crack before the French and British. Roosevelt said that an air war would cost less, have comparatively fewer casualties, and be more likely to succeed than a traditional land and sea war.[6] Clearly, the president had listened to the supporters of strategic bombardment like Billy Mitchell—who had campaigned for him during the 1932 presidential election.

Cognizant of the important role airpower would play in the war he anticipated, Roosevelt instituted a program to expand American aircraft production. At a secret meeting with his top military, naval, and governmental officials on 14 November 1938, the president stated that the United States needed an air force large enough to protect the Western Hemisphere. Warning that America must not repeat its 1918 failure to provide airplanes, he directed that production for the army air corps aircraft be expanded to 10,000 per year, a huge increase after the previous twenty years, during which few aircraft were produced. Hap Arnold, commander of the army air corps, later recalled that he left the White House feeling that the army air corps had finally "achieved its 'Magna Carta.'" Within a few months, however, Roosevelt, who had promised to keep American boys out of foreign wars, began shifting the new aircraft toward the British and French. He placed much of the cost for expanding the capacity of America's aircraft industry on the British and French, who, with FDR's support, began purchasing hundreds of millions of dollars' worth of American military aircraft. Providing the Western democracies with these weapons might prevent the need to send American boys overseas. Thus avoiding America's aircraft production failures of the First World War, Roosevelt had already put into motion before war erupted in Europe the expansion plan that would eventually provide the tens of thousands of combat aircraft the United States needed to win World War II.

The successful application of airpower by Germany in the war in Europe, in particular against British naval forces off Norway in 1940 and Crete in 1941, persuaded Roosevelt and his administration to alter war plans that had been in place since the end of World War I. The fundamental strategy in War Plan Orange, which prepared for a war between the United States and Japan, called for American and Philippine forces to hold Corregidor until the U.S. Navy could destroy the Japanese fleet and return to Manila Bay. The success of the German Luftwaffe in driving the Royal Navy from the waters off Norway and the key role British airplanes played in hunting down the German battleship *Bismarck,* however, convinced the War Department and the Roosevelt administration that airpower could defend the Philippines from a Japanese invasion fleet and could prevent Japanese naval forces from reaching the oil fields in the Dutch East Indies. This change from War Plan Orange allowed the U.S. Navy to move warships from the Pacific to the Atlantic to protect the sea-lanes to Great Britain. Furthermore, new long-range army air corps bombers like the B-17 and the new B-24 could reach the southernmost part of Japan from the Philippines, and American foreign policy shifted to incorporate the new capability. In November 1941 the army's Chief of Staff General George C. Marshall privately briefed members of the American press that the United States was prepared to use the threat of airpower to deter the Japanese from further aggression. If they did not comply, Marshall explained, the American bombers would attack Japan and set their wooden cities on fire. The United States was already rushing its new, long-range bombers to the Philippines in preparation for giving the Japanese an ultimatum by April 1942. Unfortunately for the American planners, the Japanese struck first at Pearl Harbor and in the Philippines in early December 1941. Nevertheless, Roosevelt became the first American president to employ the threat of airpower as a deterrent. For him, airpower had become another tool for achieving national goals.

Once America had entered World War II, Roosevelt left the conduct of the war to his military and naval commanders, and he focused on grand-strategic and diplomatic matters. Therefore, unlike their counterparts in World War I, American military aviators were left largely free to conduct the strategic bombing campaigns they wanted. By the time FDR died in April 1945, three years of war had reshaped the American perception of how to use airpower. Concern over bombing civilians to achieve military objectives, which the U.S. government had rejected in

General Dwight Eisenhower (*left*) meeting with U.S. Army Air Forces Commander Henry H. "Hap" Arnold in Sicily after the Casablanca Conference, 1943. (National Museum of the USAF)

the First World War, no longer constrained Roosevelt's successor, Harry S. Truman, or most American politicians. It had become a fact during the increasingly bloody Second World War, even if bombing civilians was not openly described in such a manner. Enough euphemisms were available, such as "precision bombing," used to describe one-thousand-plane bombing raids, and "de-housing," for attacks on civilian housing.

Personal experiences during service in France in World War I had shaped Truman's perception of how to employ airpower. Having seen firsthand the horrors of modern warfare, he considered airpower to be a means for saving American lives and ending the war as quickly as possible, thereby saving other lives, as had been argued by Mitchell, Douhet, and Trenchard. The merging of the two most technologically advanced weapons the United States developed during the war, the atomic bomb and the Boeing B-29 bomber to deliver it, made it possible for Truman

President Harry S. Truman (*left*) and General Dwight Eisenhower at the Congressional Air Demonstration held at Andrews Air Force Base, Maryland, in February 1949. This occasion showed the president and members of Congress the frontline aircraft of the U.S. Air Force. (National Museum of the USAF)

to do both. After deciding to use the atomic bomb on Japan, he never second-guessed that decision. It saved American lives, brought the war to a rapid conclusion, and thereby also saved countless Japanese lives that would have been lost in an invasion.

By 1945 the prophecies of Mitchell and the other airpower advocates of the 1920s and 1930s had come true. An air force could win a war before surface forces could ever come into contact. In part, this realization sustained the effort to create a separate U.S. Air Force in September 1947, which Truman supported.

As relations with the Soviet Union deteriorated, the Truman administration rejected the isolationist policies of the interwar years in favor of collective security offered through international cooperation in the United Nations and military alliances such as the North Atlantic Treaty Organization (NATO) in 1949. Furthermore, his strategy of using American military, economic, and diplomatic power to contain the spread of Communism was matched by the Truman Doctrine's pledge to support "free peoples who are resisting attempted subjugation by armed minorities or by outside pressures." The Republican victory in the 1946 Congressional mid-term elections, however, limited what Truman could do. Budget-minded, the Republicans rebuffed his efforts to institute a universal draft to man an army large enough to contain the spread of Communism, and budgetary constraints forced a bitter budget fight between the navy and the air force. Denied a large standing army and unable to fund both the air force's B-36 Peacemaker strategic bombers and the navy's super aircraft carriers, the Truman administration favored the B-36 and canceled the super carriers. Missiles with intercontinental range, developed from captured German V-2s, were not viable at that time. Also, the establishment of an effective continental air defense system took a lower priority because the Distant Early Warning (DEW) Radar Line across the Northern Hemisphere needed years of additional development. Central to the defense system, the DEW Line would have required years of costly development at the expense of other weapon systems. Containment backed by a nuclear deterrent rather than a large standing army became U.S. policy, and the Strategic Air Command's (SAC) nuclear-armed strategic bombers became the chief instrument of deterrence under the Truman administration.

To be successful, containment had to avoid a third world war, and airpower allowed Truman to do so in two ways. First, in what became the initiation of the new U.S. Air Force, airpower in the form of airlift thwarted the Soviet blockade of Berlin. The Berlin Airlift sustained the city and peacefully forced the Soviets to back down, but this employment of airpower on an extended, routine basis required stubbornness, a trait often attributed to Truman. Second, during the Korean War Truman obstinately resisted calls to use nuclear weapons on the Communists. Such a move would have expanded the conflict beyond the Korean peninsula and probably started another world war, an unthinkable option once the Soviets acquired the atomic bomb in 1949. Furthermore, it would have depleted SAC's still limited number of nuclear weapons, which were seen as necessary to deter the spread of Communism into western Europe. Either way, resorting to nuclear warfare would have been a failure of his containment policy.

When he took the oath of office in 1953, President Dwight Eisenhower entered office with probably more knowledge about military affairs, including the capabilities and limitations of airpower, than any other president of the United States. He had campaigned, however, on the promise of economy in government and a balanced federal budget. Accordingly, Eisenhower reduced the Truman administration's planned expansion of the air force to only 143 wings. The armistice ending the fighting in Korea promised further savings, but the Soviet detonation of a hydrogen bomb that year reshaped the balance of power between the two superpowers. It seemed that the Soviets had achieved nuclear parity with the United States, and the arms race intensified. Trying to maintain budget reductions while responding to the new Soviet threat, the Eisenhower administration adopted its "New Look" defense policy of deemphasizing conventional forces and emphasizing nuclear weapons carried by SAC bombers. As a result, army budgets declined, navy budgets remained relatively constant, but air force budgets grew. The navy managed to keep its current level of aircraft carriers and fund a third USS *Forrestal*–class carrier and a third atomic-powered submarine by reducing its auxiliary and amphibious warfare vessels. The New Look, as enunciated by Secretary of State John Foster Dulles, promised "instant, massive retaliation" against Soviet cities in response to an attack on the United States. It also brought the assertion by Secretary of Defense Charles Wilson that this policy would bring a "bigger bang for the buck" into the defense budget.

Ironically, the New Look's focus on massive retaliation through airpower to keep the federal budget under control mirrored Billy Mitchell's argument decades earlier that airpower could defend the nation much more cheaply than traditional land or sea forces. What had changed, however, was that airpower could deliver on its promise. Nobody doubted that SAC bomber crews could reach and destroy their targets with nuclear weapons.

It seems odd that Eisenhower, a five-star general in the U.S. Army, would willingly divert funding from the army to the air force. His perception of military power, however, had been broadened by his commanding the 1944 Allied invasion of France, leading his victorious forces into Germany, and afterward being the first supreme commander of NATO. These positions gave him a rare overview of military power, one perhaps found only in nineteenth-century military commanders such as Napoleon Bonaparte, who had mastered the employment of all combatant arms—infantry, cavalry, and artillery—to meet battlefield situations. Trained as a ground force commander, Eisenhower displayed an understanding of airpower's role in modern warfare, which was demonstrated by his support for the creation of an independent U.S. Air Force. Eisenhower perhaps surpassed even Napoleon, who had difficulty grasping the importance of sea power in maintaining his Continental empire. Yet President Eisenhower's drive for economy nearly negated his great command skill and frequently reduced him to reacting to Communist moves.

As a commander of land, sea, and air forces in Europe, Eisenhower knew too well the horrors that modern warfare had unleashed, but he perceived the threat of massive retaliation by American airpower as the guardian of peace. The adage that the best defense is a strong offense clearly applies to Eisenhower's New Look, but his military experience showed him that bombers alone would not deter a determined Soviet attack. Quick retaliatory strikes deep into the Soviet Union by intercontinental ballistic missiles (ICBMs) would have enhanced the New Look threat of "instant, massive retaliation," but since ICBMs had limited accuracy and could deliver only small payloads, funding these weapons remained a lower priority. The rapid development of light-weight, high-yield thermonuclear weapons compensated for the missiles' inaccuracy, and Eisenhower made the ICBM program a top priority, especially after intelligence sources suggested in 1955 that the Soviets had a jumped far ahead in ICBM development. The air force's ICBM program took a major step forward in 1954 when General Bernard A. Schriever became the chief architect of the air force's early ballistic missile and space programs. In the coming years, he oversaw the development of the Thor, Atlas, Titan, and Minuteman missile systems, which became key elements of deterrence. Because these operational ICBMs would not be available for a number of years, the administration pressed for the development of transitional, air-breathing, unpiloted missiles such as the SM-62 Snark, intermediate-range ballistic missiles (IRBMs), and the Mach-3 XB-70 Valkyrie manned bomber. The cost to develop each of these systems concurrently, not to mention the defensive systems to counter a Soviet attack, became enormous.

Air defense of North America made headway under Eisenhower with the building of the DEW Line, the construction of the semiautomatic ground environment (SAGE) system to handle interceptors, and the formation of the U.S.–Canadian North American Aerospace Defense Command (NORAD). The air force's Air Defense Command (ADC), like the Tactical Air Command, however, still received less funding than SAC. When the air force had to decide whether to fund the Mach-3 XB-70 bomber or the Mach-3 XF-108 interceptor, it chose the nuclear bomber. Besides, as is usually the case, the defensive systems always seemed to be chasing the offensive systems. When it appeared that the air system could handle the propeller-driven Tu-95, the Soviets introduced jet bombers. When the SAGE system emerged to handle the jets, the Soviets turned increasingly toward ICBMs. General Curtis LeMay, the SAC commander and later chief of staff of the air force, believed the best thing ADC could do was give his bombers as much warning of a Soviet attack as possible.

Responding to the perceived threat of Soviet ICBMs, Eisenhower turned to the oldest element of airpower, aerial reconnaissance, to provide reliable information on Soviet capabilities and targets, without which no retaliatory plan could succeed. A private pilot before World War II and the first American president to fly in a helicopter, Eisenhower had an appreciation of aviation that none of his presidential predecessors had had. Furthermore, he indicated his appreciation for aerial reconnaissance with his unauthorized flight in the backseat of a modified P-51 Mustang behind German lines in France after D-Day.

Desperate for reliable information about the Soviet missiles, in 1954 Eisenhower approved the development of the Lockheed U-2 to conduct strategic reconnaissance flights over the Soviet Union. The first U-2 overflight occurred in 1956, but the shooting down of Gary Powers's U-2 in 1960 ended that source of intelligence information. After the Soviet refusal to allow "open sky" overflights, Eisenhower extended airpower into space with the development of "spy" satellites, but he remained concerned about the legality of sending satellites over Soviet territory. This problem disappeared when the Soviets launched *Sputnik* on October 4, 1957, as part of the International Geophysical Year. With *Sputnik*'s flight over American territory, the Soviets established the right for satellites to pass over other nations.

Serious questions arose owing to the New Look's reliance on deterrence through the threat of massive nuclear retaliation at the expense of conventional forces. How would the United States respond in a crisis created by a Communist move into a small country? Would a small country be worth a full-scale nuclear war? For many observers and most critics of the New Look policy, those questions were answered by the Eisenhower administration's very restrained response to Soviet forces crushing the uprisings in Hungary and the alignment of Fidel Castro's Cuba with the Soviet Union. By the end of Eisenhower's presidency, many analysts had concluded that the New Look had left the Free World susceptible to a "domino effect" of Communist revolutions and invasions. They argued that the United States could avoid the escalation of a local, Communist-inspired war into a nuclear world war only by using conventional air and ground forces. Termed "Flexible Response," this strategy became a political issue during the 1960 presidential election.

Upon taking office, President John F. Kennedy adopted Flexible Response as the nation's defensive policy and prepared to meet any Communist aggression with an appropriate level of military force. Flexible Response required the United States to maintain its strategic nuclear deterrence, reinvigorate its conventional forces, and develop the capability to conduct counterinsurgency operations. Into this policy Kennedy mixed his idealistic goal of improving the world, for example by creating

President John F. Kennedy (*center*) at Homestead Air Force Base, Florida, after the Cuban Missile Crisis. In the background are U.S. Air Force RF-101 reconnaissance aircraft. (National Museum of the USAF)

the Peace Corps, and his desire to end oppression, which led the United States along the road to Vietnam.

Kennedy did not remain in office long enough to have much influence on American airpower, but his and President Lyndon B. Johnson's secretary of defense, Robert S. McNamara, shaped its direction for decades to follow. A statistical analyst with the U.S. Army Air Forces in World War II and an efficiency expert in the corporate world, McNamara sought to limit expenditures through consolidating programs and offices and instituting budget planning within the Department of Defense. In addition to canceling expensive, ineffective, and outdated systems (the Snark and XB-70 under development in the previous administration), McNamara forced the air force and navy to accept a common aircraft, the F-111. The savings were applied to other systems, such as the Minuteman missile. Eventually, McNamara increased the ICBM force to more than what the Eisenhower administration had wanted for the New Look, but he also reduced the number of strategic bombers requested by the air force.

The Limited Test Ban Treaty of 1963 took the first step toward putting the nuclear genie back into its bottle. With a resolution of the nuclear arms race seemingly on track, funds became available for McNamara to begin the buildup of conventional forces necessary for Flexible Response. Also, the Kennedy administration steered the military toward an unprecedented level of mobility. The army received its own "air force" with the decision to give it control of almost all helicopters, both attack and transport. In return, the air force took control of most fixed-wing cargo aircraft. The creation of army air assault divisions capable of moving infantry troops quickly into battle while "air cavalry" units attacked the enemy became a cornerstone of army doctrine throughout the rest of the twentieth century. Concurrently, the air force maintained its close air support mission and developed a true strategic airlift capability with its jet transport aircraft, the C-141 Starlifter and C-5 Galaxy. The navy's nuclear-powered submarines and aircraft carriers rounded out this revolution in military, naval, and airpower of the United States.

This revolution gave the Kennedy and Johnson administrations the ability to put Flexible Response into action in Southeast Asia. The escalation of America's military involvement in Vietnam before the Tonkin Gulf Incident is well known. First, military advisers were sent to train the Army of the Republic of Vietnam; then, air force instructors and aircraft were delivered to the South Vietnamese air force; and finally, Americans became involved in combat with Communist forces. The Flexible Response policy, however much it reflected his desire to end Communist oppression throughout the world, also provided Kennedy with the ability to exercise restraint, as he did during the Bay of Pigs Invasion of 1961, the Berlin Crisis of 1961, and the Cuban Missile Crisis of 1962. He decided that supporting the Cuban exiles with American airpower was not in America's best interests, and once the Communists blocked East Berlin and constructed the Berlin Wall, Kennedy chose not to risk a general war. When the Soviets attempted to place nuclear-armed missiles in Cuba, Kennedy acted forcefully by instituting a quarantine of Cuba and putting SAC forces on highest alert. He refused, however, to launch the preemptive air attack advocated by many of his military and political advisers. He also chose not to retaliate when Soviet SA-2 surface-to-air missiles shot down an Air Force U-2 over Cuba and killed the pilot, Major Rudolf Anderson Jr. The diplomatic settlement of the Cuban Missile Crisis demonstrated that nuclear deterrence worked. The threat of using American strategic bomber and missile forces against the Soviet Union and tactical airpower against Cuba deterred the Soviets from escalating the crisis. Deterrence was a dual-edged sword because the Soviet nuclear threat tempered American responses. Neither super-power wanted a thermonuclear conflagration, and the threat of airpower forced both parties to agree on that common ground as a starting point for negotiations.

As President Johnson decided on his course of action in Vietnam, the memory of thousands of Chinese soldiers attacking across the Yalu River in the Korean War was still fresh in the minds of most American politicians. As a result, he attempted to lessen the risk of escalating a regional war into a general thermonuclear war. Using limited, retalia-tory air strikes against North Vietnamese naval bases in response to the 1964 Tonkin Gulf Incident displayed much about Johnson's personality.

As a U.S. congressman from Texas during World War II, Johnson became a reserve naval officer for a brief period after Pearl Harbor until President Roosevelt ordered all members of Congress back to Washington in July 1942. During his short naval career, Johnson toured the combat zone in the Southwest Pacific, and he saw firsthand the importance of airpower in the Pacific. As a U.S. senator, he learned how to marshal support for legislation through the gradual application of increasing pressure until an opponent acquiesced. The Operation Rolling Thun-der aerial campaign vividly demonstrated how Johnson's personal and political experiences shaped his perceptions of airpower. He would ap-ply gradual pressure with increasingly severe air strikes until it became unbearable for the North Vietnamese, and they would be forced to stop supporting the Communist insurgency in South Vietnam. The North Vietnamese, meanwhile, chose to accept whatever pain the Americans inflicted to reach their goal of a unified Vietnam. In the Cuban Missile

Crisis the two sides had had common ground on which to negotiate; this decisive element was lacking in Vietnam, and so the war continued.

President Richard Nixon's political style, like LBJ's, carried over into his perception of how best to use American airpower in Vietnam. Always willing to strike his political opponents hard and mercilessly until they surrendered to his will, Nixon applied that approach to the air war in Southeast Asia. He responded to the North Vietnamese's Easter Offensive in 1972 with an immediate and crushing aerial assault limited only by his desire to avoid Chinese military intervention, to keep alive his efforts at détente and strategic arms limitation (SALT Treaty) with the Soviet Union, and to extricate the United States from the Southeast Asia War. His "Vietnamization" plan to withdraw American forces and give more responsibility to the South Vietnamese for their own defense proceeded unchecked. For Operations Linebacker and Linebacker II, Nixon allowed air force and navy aircraft to attack targets previously off-limits. Military targets in Hanoi and other cities were struck by as many B-52s as possible, North Vietnamese harbors were mined, and the North Vietnamese were forced to the peace table. The Paris Peace Accords ended American military involvement in Vietnam, but it did not end the North Vietnamese desire to unify Vietnam. They accomplished that goal within a few years, but the American approach toward the use of airpower seemed to have forever changed. Thereafter, applying the so-called lesson of Vietnam, American airpower would be used with overwhelming force to reach national goals quickly, but it was suitable only in situations where national goals involved another government. With the spread of terrorist organizations across international boundaries at the end of the twentieth century, the lesson became difficult to apply.

Less well remembered than either Operation Rolling Thunder or Operation Linebacker II, Operation Nickel Grass, the airlifting of military matériel to Israel during the 1973 Yom Kippur War, elevated American airlift capability into an intercontinental form of diplomatic airpower that only the United States had the facility to sustain. Nixon's order to the air force to use "everything that can fly" to airlift critical weapons and supplies to Israel, which were also needed by the South Vietnamese, demonstrated his single-minded willingness to use every resource available to achieve his political and foreign policy goals. The lack of usable overseas bases for staging areas unmasked a weakness in American airlift capability, and this deficiency was remedied by improving the aerial refueling abilities of the C-141, C-5, and eventually C-17 airlifters. The capacity to move men and supplies, for military or humanitarian purposes, by air on a transcontinental scale gave American presidents another powerful arrow in the quiver of airpower.

The final quarter of the twentieth century presented challenges to American presidents that seemed similar to those of the post–World War I decades. As before, the American people had grown weary of war and military expenditures. Unelected to the office, President Gerald Ford had to deal with a Congress unwilling to provide additional military support for South Vietnam. In addition, he had to spend most of his political effort at ending the nation's long nightmare of Watergate. Nevertheless, as president, Ford had to deal with an unexpected crisis when Cambodian Khmer Rouge forces seized the American container ship SS *Mayaguez* in international waters in May 1975. The United States had no formal diplomatic connections with the Khmer Rouge, and President Ford believed that the collapse of South Vietnam just weeks earlier had left him no option. Forgoing diplomacy, Ford responded with military force to retake the ship and its crew. A former navy officer who had served in combat on an aircraft carrier in the Pacific, he employed one of the most visible demonstrations of American airpower and ordered the aircraft carrier USS *Coral Sea* to the area, but air force aircraft provided most of the air support. In the ensuing joint rescue operation, which included the insertion of U.S. Marines by air force special operations helicopters, the *Mayaguez* and its crew were rescued. This action was seen as a demonstration of American resolve after the Communist victories in Cambodia and South Vietnam, but the cost was high: American casualties totaled forty-one killed, including twenty-three in a noncombat-related helicopter crash, and forty-nine wounded.

American public opinion, more noninterventionist after the Southeast Asia War than isolationist (as it had been in the 1920s), expected the European nations to assume a more active role in their own defense, and this atmosphere carried over to the administration of President James

A NATO F-4 Phantom II shadows a Soviet Tu-95 "Bear" reconnaissance aircraft over the North Sea in 1973. (USN 1153213 photo by Robert G. Edmonson)

"Jimmy" Carter. Oil embargos, stagflation, unemployment, the national debt, and a host of other issues took center stage.

Carter attempted to use moral suasion in foreign policy and to reduce military expenditures, especially for nuclear weapons. By this time both the East and the West had carried their production of nuclear weapons to the point of absurdity, technically referred to as mutually assured destruction (MAD), and military strategists could envision only the building of more weapons. Furthermore, the precision attained by ICBMs, enhanced by the development of multiple independently targetable reentry vehicle (MIRV) warheads, made it conceivable that either side could destroy the other's ICBM in a surprise first strike, a threat that had driven the development of SAC and the American nuclear triad of manned bombers, missile launching submarines, and ICBMs.

A former engineer and nuclear submarine commander, Carter turned an engineer's eye toward weapons development and procurement. Despite achieving only limited success in nuclear arms reduction, he succeeded in reducing military budgets while incurring only a slight decline in real expenditures proposed by the Ford administration. In actuality, the air force's budget topped $30 billion for the first time under President Carter, and it exceeded $40 billion by the time he left office. Unfortunately, the wild inflation of the 1970s deeply eroded the real purchasing power of the air force's budgets.[7]

President Carter achieved his goal of fiscal responsibility while increasing the military budget amid monetary inflation by canceling expensive programs such as the B-1, reducing the navy's shipbuilding plans, slowing the rate of other programs, and holding down the growth of military pay. In the process, Carter gained an undeserved reputation for having gutted the military. The controversial decision to end the B-1 program was offset by his decision to acquire nuclear-armed, air-launched cruise missiles (ALCM), to be launched from existing and proven B-52s and the B-2 stealth bomber. The nonnuclear version, the conventional air-launched cruise missile (CALCM), gained great fame during Operation Desert Storm in Iraq and became the presidential weapon of choice for precision strikes during the 1990s. The Northrop B-2 proved highly adaptable and became a key weapon for delivering precision-guided weapons in Serbia, Afghanistan, and Iraq.

The Soviet development of SS-20 missiles, armed with MIRV warheads for tactical use in Europe, and aggression in Afghanistan forced Carter to move away from his strategic arms limitation efforts. The so-called SALT II treaty was never ratified, and Carter approved the development of American weapons to match the Soviet SS-20s, the intermediate-range Pershing II and the BGM-108 Gryphon ground-launched cruise missile (GLCM). Deployed under the next administration, these two systems played a significant part in reaching arms reduction agreements with the Soviet Union in the 1980s. The failed attempt to rescue American hostages in Iran with helicopters, however, had much greater influence on how people remember Carter's administration.

President Ronald Reagan came into office in 1981 promising increased military expenditures for all the services, and during the first three years of his administration American airpower received large funding increases. The air force's appropriations alone rose to $65 billion by fiscal year 1982. His administration continued the long-standing policy of containing and deterring the Soviet Union, but it took a more aggressive direction. American military power would be projected overseas to a much greater extent around the world, from the Middle East to Latin America. Furthermore, his administration wholeheartedly supported the development of an antiballistic missile defense system to negate the Soviets' ICBM threat. For all his rhetoric and hard-line stance about confronting Communism and the Soviet Union, however, Reagan never took overt military action against the Soviets. Rather, his administration provided economic and military support to the governments of El Salvador, Guatemala, and Honduras, and to the anti-Sandinistas in Nicaragua.

How Reagan actually employed American military power suggests a growing reliance on airpower. The deployment of peacekeeping forces to Lebanon in 1982 ended disastrously the following year with the bombing of the Marine barracks in Beirut, but the air force's ability to airlift American ground forces to Grenada in 1983 contributed tremendously to the success of Operation Urgent Fury. The Reagan administration's best-remembered use of force occurred after a series of Libyan military and terrorist attacks against Americans. Operation Eldorado Canyon employed navy and air force aircraft to strike targets in Libya in 1985. The president specified the targets, terrorist facilities and Libyan air defenses, and the U.S. European Command planned and executed the operation. Deciding that inserting special forces would take too long and that Tomahawk cruise missiles were too valuable to be used on these targets, the European Command settled on a mixed-strike package of navy carrier aircraft and air force F-111Fs armed with laser-guided bombs from RAF Lakenheath in Great Britain. The refusal of European nations to allow overflights of their territory and the capability to conduct aerial refueling were additional factors. This action demonstrated America's resolution to respond to terrorist attacks and its ability to use military force effectively around the globe. American aerial refueling capability made this long-range operation possible. Precision-guided munitions (PGMs), first used effectively at the end of the Southeast Asia War, had become reliable and dangerous weapons. Moreover, PGMs "limited" the damage to nearby civilians and property, which also reduced the threat of public backlashes to video of dead and wounded civilians on television. These technological improvements provided increased range and greater accuracy, but they also increased the likelihood of a president's choosing a military response over other economic or diplomatic options in a crisis.

Toward the end of Reagan's first term, deficit spending had increased the national debt sharply, and the American people and Congress concluded that too many tax dollars were being spent on the military. The Soviet-built shoulder-launched SA-7 Grail surface-to-air missiles used with great effect against American aircraft by the North Vietnamese at the end of the war meant that simply refurbishing older aircraft was not a feasible option. Compounding the problem was the escalating cost of developing and procuring weapons systems. Increasing complexity lengthened the time needed to research, design, and test weapons and was accompanied by a corresponding rise in funding needs. By way of comparison, the air force acquired 2,041 Boeing B-47 Stratojet bombers between 1947 and 1956 at a cost of about $2 million each, but only 100 Rockwell B-1B Lancer bombers from 1985 to 1988 at $200 million each. Inflation accounted for much of the increasing costs, and the B-1B offered greater flexibility and longevity in service. Also, the improved accuracy of precision-guided weapons meant that fewer aircraft and crews would be necessary to perform the same mission. One aircraft could now do the same job that would have required a thousand B-17 and B-24 bombers in World War II. Nevertheless, the rising cost of weapons research and development cut deeply into the number of weapons procured over time, and the Reagan administration's Strategic Defense Initiative (SDI), commonly referred to as "Star Wars," exemplified that dilemma. Mostly theoretical, the SDI program promised expensive development costs before a workable system could be fielded—at the same time the administration's other weapon systems were being funded through deficit spending and cuts in social programs. Fiscal realities eventually led to the adoption of a less ambitious missile defense program, but future administrations would be forced to choose between buying new weapons for field units or putting those dollars toward research and development.

President George H. W. Bush took office with a slipping economy and a Congress motivated to rein in deficit spending. A reduction in military spending became inevitable, especially after the Communist regimes began to disintegrate in Europe. The withdrawal of Soviet forces, best illustrated in Germany when the people tore down the Berlin Wall, signaled the end of the Cold War. After forty years, the American military and diplomatic policy of containment and deterrence prevailed. The United States had been embroiled in two wars of containment, the Korean War and the Southeast Asia War, and many other military actions, but the overall policy had succeeded. Contained and prevented from expanding, Communism collapsed from within. Moreover, the Western democracies won without suffering the cataclysmic nuclear holocaust feared by so many for so long.

The end of the Cold War left the United States as the world's only superpower and provided the Bush administration with an opportunity to reassess military policy. It also freed that government to seek a "peace dividend" through reduced military expenditures and a gradual drawdown of forces. Starting in 1991, the Base Realignment and Closure (BRAC) process reduced the Department of Defense's operation and maintenance expenditures by closing excess bases and consolidating assets onto fewer bases.

Not too surprisingly, the importance of airpower to American presidents continued to grow in the post–Cold War years. President Bush used airpower to subdue Manuel Noriega's forces in Panama, and the United States unveiled the radical new technology of "stealth" to the world with the operational debut of the F-117 stealth fighter. Airpower became an even more important factor when Iraqi forces challenged the United Nations and the United States by invading Kuwait in 1990. When Saddam Hussein refused the UN demand to withdraw, the U.S.–led coalition forces drove the Iraqis out in a hundred-hour land assault. This phenomenal military success was made possible by the air campaign launched against Saddam's forces, which made one of the world's largest and best-equipped military forces virtually irrelevant. It began by disrupting Iraq's command and control system, starting with CALCMs launched from B-52s flying nonstop from Barksdale Air Force Base, Louisiana, to the Middle East. Then the Iraqi air force and air defenses were destroyed, which gave the coalition air forces virtual air superiority. These coalition air forces, led by U.S. Air Force, Navy, and Marine aircraft using "smart bombs" to great advantage, destroyed the Iraqi army in place, cut its supply lines, and decimated any forces that tried to escape. The air war devastated the Iraqi military before the ground forces came into combat and validated the argument for airpower expounded by Billy Mitchell seventy years earlier. Operation Desert Storm demonstrated to all that conventional airpower, correctly applied, could do to land or sea forces what the atomic bomb could do to a city: bring total destruction. For the public and politicians, however, who saw mainly the "video game" images of PGMs making direct strikes on specific targets while inflicting almost no collateral damage, airpower regained a reputation for cleanliness that it had not enjoyed since the World War II–era myth that the Norden bombsight could drop a bomb into a pickle barrel.

The Bush administration's drawdown of forces continued under President William "Bill" Clinton, but Clinton continued to use America's aerial might for diplomatic purposes. In addition to continuing the no-fly zones over northern and southern Iraq to enforce the UN resolutions, Clinton also used airpower to counter Saddam Hussein's military adventurism, Operation Desert Fox in December 1998 being one example. Again, cruise missiles and PGMs remained the weapons of choice. These weapons proved highly accurate and effective, put fewer aircrews at risk of being shot down and captured, and cost much less than conventional land and sea forces. In the Balkans airpower kept American ground forces largely out of the fighting, first by the humanitarian airlift to Sarajevo and later in the skies over Serbia. The most spectacular loss came when the Serbs shot down an F-117 stealth fighter, but the Serbs lost a major propaganda coup when they failed to capture the pilot.

For President George W. Bush, the role of airpower in American military actions had become firmly entrenched. The American response to the terrorist attacks of 11 September 2001, Operation Enduring Freedom took combat forces to Afghanistan, but instead of large numbers of ground troops, the Bush administration chose to use special forces and airpower to support the Northern Alliance's assault on Al Qaeda and the Taliban. In Operation Iraqi Freedom, airpower again provided the pivotal edge after the administration chose to send fewer troops on the drive to Baghdad and to airdrop combat-ready paratroopers into Kurdish northern Iraq. The clarity of airpower's domination in traditional clashes of surface forces disappeared once the insurgency began. Just as they had in Southeast Asia, where American soldiers and marines had to put "boots on the ground" to defeat the insurgents, who looked the same as the general populace, aerial forces became an important and often crucial element in support of ground forces.

A notable anniversary occurred in September 2009. It marked the one hundredth anniversary of the purchase of the world's first military airplane by the U.S. Army Signal Corps. In just a century, military aviation had grown from a single, rudimentary flying machine built by the Wright brothers in Dayton, Ohio, with a top speed of about forty miles per hour to complex aerial fleets capable of destroying cities with a single bomb, shooting down enemy aircraft so far away that the pilots cannot see them without radar, or quickly transporting soldiers and supplies anywhere in the world on short notice. Other innovations have affected warfare, but very few of these weapons created such a major change in such a short time. American presidents have constantly adjusted to technological advancement, some more quickly than others. Those who adapted their policies to take the fullest advantage of airpower's potential, whether combat effectiveness or the potential threat, generally have had the greatest diplomatic and military success.

Just as it seems that American presidents have learned the secrets of blending airpower into their statecraft, the playing field has again shifted under the dynamic power of advancing technology. When Harry Truman decided to use atomic weapons, he changed the battlefield forever, and his decision remains controversial. The increasing reliance on unmanned aerial vehicles (UAVs) will bring new challenges. Will it become too easy for a remote pilot, half a world away with insufficient information, to strike a target? Will some future president face the same problem as Woodrow Wilson when the Germans employed unrestricted submarine warfare? Legal, moral, and public opinions had not caught up to the new technology, and Wilson had to worry about the actions not of the German government but of some submarine captain who had the power to take America into the Great War. Smart weapons offer the tantalizing prospect of destroying a single target, living or inanimate, with no civilian casualties, which could be displayed on television for propaganda purposes, as the North Vietnamese did during Operation Linebacker II and the Serbians did when faulty intelligence led to bombing the Chinese embassy with Global Positioning System–guided PGMs. Future presidents will have to make difficult decisions about the use of these weapons. As is true of any decision, a president's personality will always influence his or her choices, and that fact will never change. How presidents perceive the implications of employing airpower can and will be altered by events, the recommendations of military and political advisers, political calculations, and public opinion. They will have to choose between being politicians seeking short-term gains or being statesmen or stateswomen looking at the long view of their oath to defend and protect the Constitution and thereby the republic. Only a populace well educated in the history and roles of airpower can force the latter.

Notes

1. Alfred F. Hurley, *Billy Mitchell: Crusader for Air Power* (New York: Franklin Watts, 1964), p. 37.

2. Wesley Frank Craven and James Lea Cate, eds., *The Army Air Force in World War II*, 6 vols. (Chicago: University of Chicago Press, 1948–1955), 2:28–29; Edwin H. Rutkowsky, *The Politics of Military Aviation Procurement, 1926–1934: A Study in the Political Assertion of Consensual Values* (Columbus: Ohio State University Press, 1966), pp. 20, 59–61.

3. Henry H. Arnold, *Global Mission* (New York: Harper and Brothers, 1949), p. 122.

4. David Lee, "Herbert Hoover and Commercial Aviation Policy, 1921–1933," in *Reconsidering a Century of Flight*, ed. Roger D. Launius and Janet R. Daly Bednarek (Chapel Hill: University of North Carolina Press, 2003), pp. 89–117.

5. Benjamin D. Foulois with C. V. Glines, *From the Wright Brothers to the Astronauts: The Memoirs of Major General Benjamin D. Foulois* (New York: McGraw-Hill, 1968), pp. 185–186; Arnold, *Global Mission,* p. 97.

6. Harold L. Ickes, *The Secret Diary of Harold L. Ickes,* vol. 2, *The Inside Struggle, 1936–1939* (New York: Simon and Schuster, 1954) pp. 467–469.

7. Bernard C. Nalty, ed., *Winged Shield, Winged Sword: A History of the United States Air Force, 1907–1997,* 2 vols. (Washington, D.C.: Air Force History and Museums Program, 1997), 2:348–349.

Research Reading

By the end of the twentieth century aviation had become a ubiquitous element of American life. No longer would people travel for miles to marvel at a flying machine; they could simply look overhead. Outside a classroom or a military or naval base, a person would be hard pressed to hear a conversation about the future of aviation or the proper application of airpower. Moreover, airpower has been generally subsumed into the overarching label of "military power." This change has been for the better because it illustrates how completely airpower has become equal in every sense to ground and sea power. Therefore, airpower in itself is no longer a political issue or a topic about which presidents may expect to field questions from the press. As a result, researchers will face much more difficulty in determining what is more important in a president's decisions: personality or perceptions. Nevertheless, the pursuit of that answer should continue to interest historians, and a few suggestions for further reading follow: David Lee, "Herbert Hoover and Commercial Aviation Policy, 1921–1933," in *Reconsidering a Century of Flight,* ed. Roger D. Launius and Janet R. Daly Bednarek (Chapel Hill: University of North Carolina Press, 2003), pp. 89–117; Jeffery S. Underwood, *Wings of Democracy: The Influence of Air Power on the Roosevelt Administration, 1933–1941* (College Station: Texas A&M University Press, 1991); Mark Clodfelter, *The Limits of Air Power: The American Bombing of North Vietnam* (New York: Free Press, 1989); Stephen P. Randolph, *Powerful and Brutal Weapons: Nixon, Kissinger, and the Easter Offensive* (Cambridge: Harvard University Press, 2007); John Darrell Sherwood, *Nixon's Trident: Naval Power in Southeast Asia, 1968–1972* (Washington, D.C.: Naval History & Heritage Command, Dept. of the Navy, 2009); Robert F. Futrell, *Ideas, Concepts, Doctrine: Basic Thinking in the United States Air Force,* 2 vols. (Maxwell Air Force Base, Ala.: Air University Press, 1989); Michael M. Boll, *National Security Planning: Roosevelt through Reagan* (Lexington: University Press of Kentucky, 1988); Nicholas Laham, *The American Bombing of Libya: A Study of the Force of Miscalculation in Reagan Foreign Policy* (Jefferson, N.C.: McFarland, 2008); Jeffrey Record, *Making War, Thinking History: Munich, Vietnam, and Presidential Uses of Force from Korea to Kosovo* (Annapolis: Naval Institute Press, 2002); Joseph G. Dawson III, ed., *Com-*

manders in Chief: Presidential Leadership in Modern Wars (Lawrence: University Press of Kansas, 1993); Richard P. Hallion, *Storm over Iraq: Air Power and the Gulf War* (Washington D.C.: Smithsonian Institution Press, 1992); and P. W. Singer, *Wired for War: The Robotics Revolution and Conflict in the 21st Century* (New York: Penguin, 2009).

7

Gunboat Diplomacy

Presidential Use of Aircraft Carriers and Their Embarked Air Wings

Douglas V. Smith and Kent S. Coleman

I believe that America's birthrights of freedom and liberty have been in large part secured through air power. One of the first questions I always asked as Commander-in-Chief when American interests were threatened around the globe was "*Where are our aircraft carriers?*" The ability to project power from the sea—free from the restrictions of international political maneuvering—has repeatedly played a key part in crisis management and in securing vital U.S. interests.

> —President George Herbert Walker Bush,
> Lieutenant, U.S. Navy Reserve

So starts the majority of articles on U.S. carrier airpower since World War II. Yet others would disagree, citing the huge cost of the carrier, cruisers, destroyers, and submarines to screen and protect it; the men and women who crew these ships; and the expensive infrastructure and logistical apparatus necessary to support, sustain, and provide petroleum for a Carrier Strike Group at sea. The naysayers claim that sending a Carrier Strike Group in a crisis situation is usually done by a weak president wanting to demonstrate his resolve to the American people

210 Douglas V. Smith and Kent S. Coleman

but without any intention of actually engaging the enemy in combat. Moreover, they would say that there is no way at all to establish that a Carrier Strike Group actually achieved the desired political outcome even if that outcome is favorable, and that other forms of military power could often have secured America's interests at a much lesser cost. The only way to examine these two contending viewpoints is to look at some of the crisis situations that have faced America since World War II to see how presidents approached them and to evaluate how crucial to a positive diplomatic outcome aircraft carriers and their air wings actually were.

Whenever a crisis arises for an American president, many questions have to be answered quickly. First and foremost among these is whether the crisis requires force for resolution or for enabling other diplomatic options through threat of its use. If the answer to this is yes, then a whole series of questions follows. What is the geographical location of the crisis, and what forces does the United States have nearby to respond? How capable is the opposition military, and what types and quality of forces does it comprise? How can the required forces be logistically sustained while waiting to be employed, which may be for an extended period, and how will they be sustained once engaged with the enemy? What kind of lift will be needed to deploy and sustain American forces? Does the United States have one or more allies in the vicinity of the crisis likely to support an American decision to use force? What specific diplomatic measures will the United States need to take for force emplacement and sustenance during hostilities? Can America station the forces in proximity to the enemy without alerting the adversary of intended strategies or letting it know the size of the force and the specific units that will constitute it?

In this age of rapid movement of all types of military and paramilitary forces and equipment, the vast majority of crisis situations will require the use of airpower. The question then becomes what type of airpower, that is, what air capabilities are needed? These "net assessment" questions necessarily presage employment of gunboat diplomacy—the use or threatened use of force—to secure American interests in a specific crisis.

Carrier aviation became available as a diplomatic tool after World War II had demonstrated its tremendous military clout and after the technology had matured (mirror landings, angled decks, steam catapults, increasing range), and following the postwar determination of the U.S. Navy to fight for the nuclear delivery mission. Add to this the onset of the Cold War just as the decline of the British Empire and other great powers were thrusting the United States into the role of leadership of the Free World.

Just four months after America's entry into the Second World War, on 18 April 1942 sixteen B-25B "Mitchell" medium-range bombers lifted off from the carrier *Hornet,* bound for Tokyo and Nagoya. Though the damage they inflicted was minimal, this minor raid gave a tremendous boost to American public morale and shattered the Japanese people's impression of the invulnerability of their emperor. When asked by reporters where the attack had originated, Roosevelt responded, "They came from our secret base at Shangri-La." Faced with a mythical air base within range of Tokyo, the Japanese had to return fighter squadrons to defend the emperor and military targets in the vicinity of his palace. While not creating it, the Doolittle Raid certainly hardened the Imperial Japanese Navy's resolve to embrace Admiral Isoroku Yamamoto's plan to move east and take Midway, which resulted in a critical reduction of their *kido butai,* the carrier mobile striking force. Thus, at a critical juncture in World War II, the utility of the aircraft carrier, albeit with army air corps planes, was clearly demonstrated. More to the point, the incident demonstrated the strategic effect of carrier forces.

Not always involving carriers or aircraft, gunboat diplomacy can have great efficacy in peacetime as well. On 5 April 1946 the battleship USS *Missouri* returned the body of the deceased Turkish ambassador to the United States, Mehmet Münir Ertegün, to Istanbul. The diplomatic significance of the move was not lost on Joseph Stalin and his Politburo as they were then pressuring Turkey into conceding two provinces in the Dardanelles region. The *Missouri*'s arrival in Istanbul gave the Soviet leadership pause to rethink its strategy. Was this bold move a signal that Soviet pressure on its neighbors might cause President Truman to reconsider his stated intention of removing U.S. troops from Europe within two years of the war's end—a necessary precursor to Soviet political domination of Eastern Europe? For this and perhaps other reasons, Stalin refrained from military actions against Turkey.[1]

While cause and effect in these two crisis situations are impossible to establish unequivocally, the pattern that emerges is clear: highly visible and rapid positioning of one or more powerful navy combatant vessels precedes resolution of a crisis on terms favorable to the United States. These were not isolated instances. Between January 1946, when a coup in Haiti resulted in considerable civil strife, and May 1975, when the merchant ship *Mayaguez* and its crew were taken hostage by Cambodian gunboats (labeled "pirates" by President Gerald Ford) near Koh Tang Island, outside Cambodian waters, American presidents have faced 215 documented crisis situations.[2] Of these 215, naval forces were involved in 177, or slightly over 82 percent, and aircraft carriers took part in 106, or slightly fewer than half of all crises.[3] From January 1976 to July 1985, another 51 situations required responses by American presidents. Carrier Strike Groups took part in 35 of them.[4] Thus, from January 1946 to July 1985, a period of just under forty years, American Carrier Strike Groups responded to 141 of 266 national crises, an impressive 53 percent of all such situations.

In the post–World War II era there have been twelve American presidents. Ten of these had served in the military: six in the navy, three in the army or army air corps, and one in the Air National Guard. The president's background colored his proclivity for resorting to gunboat diplomacy in time of crisis.

President Harry S. Truman served in the Army National Guard from 1905 to 1911, and in World War I from 1917 to 1919, during which he saw action. He remained in the Army Reserves from 1919 to 1953, rising to the rank of colonel. During Truman's presidency there were thirty-five crisis situations. Of these the most critical to American security were the 1946–1949 civil war in China, the Berlin Airlift in 1948–1949, and the North Korean invasion of South Korea initiated on 25 June 1950.

When the Chinese civil war between the Communists and Nationalists resumed after Japan's defeat in World War II, President Truman's advisers contemplated the use of American troops to preserve U.S. interests in China. The sheer vastness of China and its huge distance from American shores quickly led to the discarding of this option.

The Berlin crisis of 1948–1949 was a different story, however. At the end of World War II, the United States, Great Britain, and France found themselves staring at the troops of their former ally, the Soviet Union, over makeshift borders in Germany and elsewhere. The incumbent Truman administration had been unable to prevent Joseph Stalin's Soviet state from occupying Poland, Czechoslovakia, Hungary, Romania, and Bulgaria, and cooperation on stabilizing the defeated German state was stymied by Stalin's political objective of keeping Germany weak by sustaining its postwar recession. Disagreements over German currency reform led to increased tensions by 1948. In mid-June the Soviet Union began requiring that all convoys destined for Berlin be searched, and rail and autobahn traffic to the western sectors of Berlin were cut completely on 27 June. The response was immediate. An airlift was mounted to the two grass airstrips in the western sectors of Berlin—Tempelhof, with one runway in the U.S. sector, and Gatow, with one runway in the British sector. Often landing at three-minute intervals, the airlift provided nearly eight thousand tons of food and supplies daily. More than 277,000 flights to Berlin provided over two million tons of sustenance. The Soviets finally lifted the blockade on 12 May 1949. Though no carrier or naval involvement had been used, airpower ended the Berlin crisis on a positive note for America and its occupation partners.

Certainly American military power, including aircraft carriers, was critical to supporting President Syngman Rhee and his South Korean nation when Kim Il-sung invaded from the north with seven divisions on 25 June 1950. Carriers would be key to the U.S. response. At the end of World War II the navy had possessed over a hundred aircraft carriers. Postwar force draw-downs had reduced to five the number of fleet carriers capable of operating the new jet fighters.[5] The first major U.S. event of the shooting war was an attack on the North Korean capital city of Pyongyang by aircraft from the *Valley Forge,* which destroyed much of the North Korean air force.[6] Carrier strikes were critical to enabling General Walton Walker, commander of the U.S. Eighth Army, to stabilize a perimeter around Pusan after having been repeatedly driven back by the North Koreans. Having three aircraft carriers on station by the end of September 1950 to provide air support and attack the North Korean supply routes was essential to maintaining the Pusan perimeter.[7]

During the Korean conflict, nineteen *Essex*-class carriers were taken out of mothballs, and in all twenty-one carriers of all types served.[8] This made it possible to have four carriers on station in the waters off the Korean peninsula and two additional carriers in the Mediterranean Sea. Major General Field Harris, USMC, commanding general of all marine aviation in Korea, credited close carrier air support from Task Group 96.8 escort carriers with enabling the marines of the 1st Marine Division to withdraw from the Chosin Reservoir, testimony to the utility of carrier aircraft during this critical period.

President Dwight D. Eisenhower graduated from the United States Military Academy at West Point and rose to the rank of general of the army after serving as Supreme Allied Commander during World War II. There were sixty crisis situations during his two terms as president. A host of complex problems confronted the Eisenhower administrations, but terminating the conflict in Korea, the China-Taiwan confrontation over the islands of Quemoy and Matsu, and Fidel Castro's installation of a Communist government in Cuba, just ninety miles off the coast of Florida, in January 1959 may well have been the most serious.

During Eisenhower's first term in office the Korean conflict was successfully concluded. More than 30 percent of all combat sorties during the Korean conflict were performed by carrier aircraft.[9]

An armistice in the Korean conflict was signed on 27 July 1953. On 11 August 1954 a potentially much more serious crisis arose when the People's Republic of China (PRC) employed force to try to regain the islands of Quemoy and Matsu near mainland China. While in office President Truman had resisted calls by congressional hard-liners to unleash Chiang Kai-shek against the PRC, but shortly after his inauguration, on 2 February 1953, President Eisenhower lifted the U.S. Navy blockade of Taiwan, which had prevented Chiang's force from attacking mainland China. Chiang moved 58,000 troops to Quemoy and 15,000 to Matsu in August 1954. China's Zhou Enlai responded by declaring that Taiwan had to be liberated from Chiang's Nationalists. The United States warned the PRC against military action, but on 3 September the Communists began an artillery bombardment of Quemoy, and in November People's Liberation Army planes bombed the Tachen Islands. The U.S. Joint Chiefs of Staff (JCS) recommended using nuclear weapons against the PRC, but President Eisenhower refused to bomb mainland China or use American troops to resolve the crisis. The United States ultimately signed the Mutual Defense Treaty with the Nationalist government on Taiwan on 2 December 1954. U.S. support for Nationalist Taiwan against a PRC attempt to repatriate the disputed islands and a mutual U.S.-Taiwanese amphibious exercise staged at the time combined to put Communist China in an untenable situation. Thus the Quemoy-Matsu crisis was ultimately resolved when the Chinese leadership, fearing war with the United States, backed down.

Critical to resolution of this crisis was the massing of naval power in what Vice Admiral Wallace Beakley, commander of the Seventh Fleet, called "the largest integrated naval force ever assembled in peacetime history."[10]

Within a day of the renewal of the bombardments [of Quemoy and Matsu], steps were undertaken in the Taiwan area to reaffirm U.S. defense commitments and supplement existing forces so as to suggest an extension of such obligations. On August 24 the Seventh Fleet was alerted in what were described as "normal precautionary defense measures." In addition, the American aircraft carrier *Essex* and four destroyers from the Sixth [Mediterranean] Fleet were ordered to augment vessels from the Seventh Fleet already in the Taiwan area. Two additional aircraft carrier groups were added to the Taiwan Strait patrol. A U.S. air defense exercise was also held over Taiwan.[11]

By 29 August 1954, with the reassignment of the aircraft carrier *Midway* and the heavy cruiser *Los Angeles,* the total number of American ships in the Taiwan Strait area surpassed fifty. This armada included six aircraft carriers with five hundred fighter and bomber aircraft.[12] This is an instance that, with the potential for nuclear war, was solved almost exclusively by aircraft carriers of the U.S. Seventh Fleet.

Fidel Alejandra Castro Ruz was the illegitimate but privileged son of a Spanish immigrant to Cuba. A University of Havana graduate with a law degree, he became involved with violent and radical political groups. On 26 July 1953 Castro, pursuing a political agenda of his own, attacked Moncada Barracks, President Fulgencio Batista's military stronghold, with a hundred followers. The ill-advised attack resulted in around eighty of the attackers dead and Fidel himself captured. Though sentenced to prison for fifteen years for staging this coup, he was pardoned by President Batista after just two years. He then went to Mexico to regroup and restrategize.

Castro returned from Mexico as leader of a group of about a hundred revolutionary exiles. They gradually wore down Batista's forces in a guerrilla war. On 1 January 1959 President Batista fled Cuba to the Dominican Republic. Castro arrived in Havana a week later and assumed first the position of commander in chief of Cuba's armed forces and shortly thereafter that of prime minister. Fidel Castro had stated in his victory speech, "This new revolution will not be like 1898, when the North Americans came and made themselves masters of our country."[13] Eschewing an earlier promise to hold democratic elections, Castro embraced Communism and began expropriating land, including that owned by American citizens. This prompted President Eisenhower to greatly reduce Cuban exports to the United States, of which sugar was the most important to the Cuban economy.

Though President Eisenhower resented all that Castro stood for, and particularly his overtures to Soviet Premier Nikita Khrushchev, he refrained from using American military power to remove him. The United States retained its naval base at Guantánamo Bay, but airpower was not employed against Castro except for reconnaissance during the coup against President Batista.

John F. Kennedy had risen to the rank of lieutenant while serving in the navy in World War II. He was awarded the Purple Heart and Navy and Marine Corps Medal for heroic action in the PT-109 incident. During Kennedy's short time as president, there were thirty-eight crises. While his administration was absorbed with the political and military situation in Vietnam, perhaps the most important issues with which it had to deal were a series of crises surrounding Cuba, especially the 1961 Bay of Pigs incident and 1962 Cuban Missile Crisis.

Though many of President Kennedy's top advisers weighed in against a military move to topple the Castro regime in Cuba, Kennedy ultimately approved the Central Intelligence Agency's (CIA) operation, an insertion of Cuban exiles as a catalyst for an expected uprising by disenfranchised Cuban nationals. On 30 March 1961 Senator J. William Fulbright, chairman of the Senate Foreign Relations Committee, handed President Kennedy a 3,766-word memorandum on the planned invasion. In it he outlined many things that could go wrong. Foremost among these was that it would be impossible to conceal U.S. involvement in the invasion. He also warned of "the prospect . . . that an invasion of Cuba by exiles would encounter formidable resistance which the exiles, by themselves, might not be able to overcome. The question would then arise of whether the United States would be willing to let the enterprise fail . . . or . . . would respond with progressive assistance as necessary to insure success."[14]

U.S. Navy forces provided naval support for the CIA's operation. One destroyer was needed to escort the Cuban Expeditionary Force (CEF) ships to the three-mile limit of Cuban territorial waters. A landing ship dock (LSD) then delivered landing craft to the area of the operation. The navy was also expected to supply air cover for the CEF ships until completion of the landings, which were planned for 10 April 1961.[15]

Reconnaissance flights indicating that the Cubans had thirty-six combat aircraft to contest the CEF landings prompted an increase of American air support from six to eight aircraft.[16] The flights of CEF aircraft that followed claimed to have eliminated 75–80 percent of these on the ground in preparation for the landings, but later photo intelligence revealed that these pilot estimates were significantly exaggerated.

After the landings, as the situation soured for the CEF, Admiral Arleigh Burke asked President Kennedy to "let me take two jets and shoot down the enemy aircraft."[17] President Kennedy said that he would not commit U.S. forces to combat. Kennedy did, however, authorize six unmarked jets from USS *Essex* to provide air cover for the invading CEF at 0630–0730 on the morning of the invasion, with the provision that they neither engage in air combat nor attack ground targets. These limitations resulted in the loss of nine of the sixteen CEF B-26 bombers.[18]

The Bay of Pigs operation failed disastrously. In three days of fighting, 89 men of the invading CEF were killed and 1,197 taken prisoner. Castro lost 157 killed.[19] In this crisis so close to American shores, only one hour of navy carrier aircraft "surveillance" took place because of Kennedy's imposed constraints. Yet navy ship power was more than sufficient to keep Castro from contemplating a move to oust Americans from Guantánamo Bay, and one cannot help feeling that U.S. troop intervention, without question supported by U.S. carrier aircraft, would have brought an end to Fidel Castro's Communist regime in Cuba.

Sunday afternoon, 21 October 1962, brought another crisis with Cuba. President John F. Kennedy received definitive intelligence that medium-range ballistic missiles (MRBMs), intermediate-range ballistic missiles (IRBMs), and Il-28 bombers with a thousand-mile range were arriving on the island. Kennedy and his advisers decided to implement a quarantine of Cuba. To conduct the quarantine, Vice Admiral Alfred G. Ward commanded Task Force 136, comprising the cruiser *Canberra,* the support carrier *Essex,* several squadrons of destroyers, and supporting vessels.[20] In addition, Rear Admiral John T. Hayward led Task Force 135, with one hundred navy and marine F8U, F4E, A4D, A3J, and AD-6 aircraft aboard the *Enterprise.*[21] The USS *Independence,* with one hundred aircraft, including F8Us, F3Hs, and WF2s, was available for additional support.

Navy and marine pilots flew six million miles during the crisis, and each of the carriers steamed more than ten thousand miles; but U.S. Air Force aircraft flew about 80 percent of all the American hours.[22] Yet by the time President Kennedy announced to the American public on 20 November that a nuclear exchange had been averted and the Soviet Union had agreed to remove their threatening forces from Cuba, navy carriers and their air groups had clearly played a dominant role in de-escalating the crisis. The proximity of these units to Cuba and the ability of naval units to fire shots across the bows of Soviet merchant ships were what made the quarantine a success.

Lyndon Baines Johnson, successor to the presidency upon Kennedy's assassination in November 1963, had served in the navy in World War II and had been awarded the Army Silver Star by General Douglas MacArthur for his actions on a B-26 bomber mission. Johnson had entered the navy while a member of Congress in June 1940. After two years he was transferred to the Navy Reserve, where he remained until his resignation upon becoming president.

As president, Johnson faced forty-eight crisis situations. He was consumed with the continuing situation in Vietnam and particularly with the Gulf of Tonkin incident in August 1964. The evolving trouble among Cyprus, Greece, and Turkey and the seizure of the USS *Pueblo* by North Korea in January 1968 were other noted crises his administration faced.

On 2 August 1964 three North Vietnamese P-4 torpedo boats allegedly attacked the American destroyer *Maddox* in the Gulf of Tonkin, well outside Vietnamese waters. A purported second attack two days later is roundly held to be a misrepresentation of events. During the first assault, four navy F-8 Crusader jets from the USS *Ticonderoga* attacked the retiring North Vietnamese torpedo boats, claiming one sunk and one heavily damaged. There was no visual indication of a P-4 having been sunk or damaged during inspection of the area the following day, however, and even the captain of the *Maddox* questioned the claim of the second attack. This did not stop President Johnson from announcing that these two "attacks" were being retaliated for by Operation Pierce Arrow, part of which was an attack on North Vietnamese torpedo boat bases and fuel facilities by U.S. carrier aircraft. These events in turn led to a widening of the conflict and ultimately to deployment of ground troops by the United States, followed by air campaigns such as Flaming Dart (7–11 February 1965), Rolling Thunder (2 March 1965–31 October 1968), Linebacker I (9 May–22 October 1972), and Linebacker II (18–29 December 1972).

In the afternoon of 22 January 1968, two Democratic People's Republic of Korea (DPRK) Lenta-class fishing trawlers passed within close proximity of the USS *Pueblo* (AGER-2), which was on an intelligence mission. That same day a North Korean unit had made an assassination attempt on the South Korean president, Park Chung-Hee, but the crew of the *Pueblo* was not informed of the attempt.

On 23 January 1968, according to the American account, the USS *Pueblo* was engaged in intelligence activities well outside the internationally respected twelve-mile limit of North Korean waters but probably within the fifty-mile limit claimed by the DPRK. When a sub chaser approached the *Pueblo* and challenged its nationality, the *Pueblo* responded by raising the U.S. flag. The DPRK vessel then ordered it to stand down, but the *Pueblo* attempted to maneuver away. The *Pueblo*, however, was considerably slower than the sub chaser, which was soon joined by a second sub chaser, four torpedo boats, and two MiG-21 fighters. Commander Lloyd M. Bucher of the *Pueblo* was forced to heave to and follow the DPRK vessels into a North Korean port.

The *Pueblo* was in radio contact with the U.S. Naval Security Group in Kamiseya, Japan, during the entire incident, so the Seventh Fleet was fully aware of the *Pueblo*'s evolving situation. Bucher was promised air support, but it never arrived. The USS *Enterprise* was over five hundred miles south of the *Pueblo,* and its aircraft munitions were not configured for surface targets, so help could not be sent for hours. The Fifth Air Force was in a similar situation, having no aircraft on strip alert. By the time President Johnson was awakened, the *Pueblo* had been captured. With the *Pueblo* well inside DPRK waters, a rescue attempt would have been futile.

President Richard M. Nixon, like his predecessor in office, had served in the Pacific during World War II, where he became a lieutenant commander in the Navy Reserve. He was mainly on the islands of the South Pacific, where he was a combat Air Transport Command officer. Nixon was promoted to commander before his resignation from the reserves in 1953. Records show Lieutenant Commander Richard Nixon took a course in international law at the Naval War College while he was vice president.

President Nixon had to handle twenty-nine crisis situations. Key among them were the India-Pakistan (Bangladesh) War of December 1971, a major North Vietnamese offensive in South Vietnam (Easter Offensive) in the spring of 1972 that led to a breakdown of the peace talks with North Vietnam, and the Arab-Israeli War of October 1973.

India and Pakistan had been adversaries since they had become independent nations following World War II. In 1947 and again in 1965 they had fought over control of Kashmir, which lies between northwest India and what was then West Pakistan. The East Pakistani delegation to the national assembly elected in 1970 consisted of nearly all Hindu Bengali nationalists, an unlikely development, as the majorities in both East and West Pakistan were Muslim. This in turn greatly fueled the long-standing separatist movement for an autonomous East Pakistan.

West Pakistan responded in March 1971 by sending 80,000 troops to East Pakistan to put down the separatist Bengali movement. The brutality they showed toward the Bengali minority caused mass population migrations to India, which by early December totaled an estimated 9.5 million. This put considerable stress on the Indian economy and held the prospect of becoming a permanent problem. Exiled Bengali freedom fighters launched attacks on the West Pakistani troops in East Pakistan, and there were bombardments, tank engagements, and aerial dogfights along the East Pakistan border.[23]

In this convoluted political environment, India signed the twenty-year Treaty of Peace, Friendship, and Cooperation with the Soviet Union on 9 August, prompting the West Pakistanis to enlist Chinese support. Though Pakistan was a Southeast Asia Treaty Organization (SEATO) ally, the U.S. Congress banned offensive arms transfers to West Pakistan.[24] The crisis deepened that autumn, and West Pakistan on 3 December launched a major offensive, which went badly from the first.[25] India formally recognized the independent state of Bangladesh only three days into the war, and Pakistan terminated diplomatic relations with India.[26]

The Soviet Union sent a small task force into the Indian Ocean, and the rapidity with which the Soviets' client India achieved military advantage was worrisome. President Nixon had the Department of Defense expand the Seventh Fleet area of operations into the Indian Ocean and dispatched a Carrier Strike Group around the USS *Enterprise* from Vietnamese waters to the Bay of Bengal to deter Indian territorial expansion at the expense of Pakistan, the American ally. "The effects of this U.S. military action were to prompt precautionary military countermeasures by India, intensify Indian animosity toward the United States, increase

Indian-Russian diplomatic and military cooperation, and encourage Pakistani leaders to delay the transfer of power in the East to Bengali nationalists."[27] The *Enterprise* strike group left Vietnamese waters on 10 December and arrived in the Bay of Bengal on 15 December. The next day West Pakistani forces in East Pakistan surrendered after only thirteen days of fighting. Fortunately, Prime Minister Gandhi refrained from annexing any West Pakistani territory, so the *Enterprise* force may have conveyed a positive political signal. Yet the blow to U.S. relations with India and the increased Soviet influence might have been less severe if carrier power had not been used.

As the India-Pakistan conflict was reaching its resolution, North Vietnamese leaders greeted 1972 with hopes for victory at last in their long war. They considered the Army of the Republic of Vietnam (ARVN) to be overstretched and ready to be broken, and they believed that a significant victory could influence the 1972 U.S. presidential election as well as improve the North's bargaining position at the Paris Peace Talks. On Good Friday, 30 March 1972, the 324B North Vietnamese Army (NVA) Division, reinforced by two hundred tanks and two additional infantry regiments, engaged the 1st ARVN Division, widely considered to be the ARVN's best, in what has come to be known as the Easter Offensive. The North Vietnamese units made rapid advances but were stopped and driven back, owing primarily to the massive employment of American airpower. Most important was the constant pounding of the NVA by air force B-52 aircraft in Operation Linebacker, the first comprehensive bombing of North Vietnam's transportation, storage, and air defense systems. Besides tactical missions, B-52s flew 2,724 sorties.

At the height of the offensive three U.S. cruisers and thirty-eight destroyers were providing naval gunfire support. As the weather cleared, the number of aircraft employed soared. Between April and June, U.S. and Allied aircraft flew 18,000 combat sorties in support of ARVN defenders, 45 percent by the U.S. Air Force, 30 percent by the navy and marine corps, and 25 percent by the South Vietnamese air force.

Task Force 77, cruising at "Yankee Station," had four carriers assigned, but only two, *Coral Sea* and *Hancock,* were on station when the NVA offensive started. Their air wings totaled 140 strike aircraft.

The Seventh Fleet was quickly augmented with the four Carrier Strike Groups, including the USS *Saratoga, Kitty Hawk, Constellation,* and *Midway.* Four of the six carriers were available at any one time for strike operations. During the Vietnam conflict, Task Force 77 conducted carrier strike operations from the Gulf of Tonkin and South China Sea for nine years (1964–1973). Twenty-one of the navy's twenty-three operational carriers made at least one cruise with Task Force 77 and served over 9,100 days on the battle line.

The 1973 Arab-Israeli War was fought from 6 to 26 October between Israel and a coalition of Arab states led by Egypt and Syria. The conflict created a severe international crisis that almost escalated into a confrontation between the two nuclear superpowers. Both launched massive resupply efforts to support their respective allies during the conflict. The war began with a massive and successful Egyptian attack across the heavily fortified Suez Canal on Yom Kippur, Judaism's holiest day, which happened to coincide with the Muslim holy month of Ramadan. Egypt swept into the Israeli-held Sinai Peninsula, which had been captured in the 1967 Six-Day War and occupied ever since.

The attackers advanced for three days and then dug in, creating a stalemate along Israel's southern front. In the north the Syrians attacked the critical Golan Heights, another area seized by the Israelis six years earlier, and initially achieved significant gains, but soon their momentum waned. Within a week Israel blunted the Syrian attack and launched a four-day counteroffensive, driving deep into Syria. The Egyptians renewed their offensive to relieve the Israeli pressure on Syria but were checked by an Israeli counterattack that split the seam between the two Egyptian armies. Advancing southward and eastward, the Israelis encircled elements of Egypt's Third Army. But both sides agreed to abide by a United Nations ceasefire resolution imposed on 25 October, thus ending the war. When the fighting stopped, Israeli forces were only twenty-five miles from Damascus and sixty-three miles from Cairo.

Early on 9 October President Nixon ordered the commencement of an American airlift to replace all of Israel's matériel losses. By the time the resupply operation ended, the United States had shipped 22,400 tons of matériel to Israel, but only 8,750 tons had arrived during the war. American C-141 Starlifter and C-5 Galaxy aircraft flew 567 missions during the airlift, and the Israeli national airline, El Al, flew 170 flights in its own airlift, delivering 5,500 additional tons of matériel. The United States also mounted a seaborne supply operation delivering 33,210 tons of matériel to Israel during the war and 90,000 tons overall by early December. By then Israel had received a hundred aircraft and helicopters, 450 combat vehicles, and numerous other weapons, including some missile systems that had only recently entered service, and advanced electronic jamming equipment, but much of it arrived after the fighting had stopped. Almost all the combat airplanes arrived during the war, and many were taken directly from U.S. Air Force units. Throughout this crisis the only aircraft carrier involved was on normal patrol in the eastern Mediterranean.

Another of President Nixon's world crises was the 1974 Greek situation, shortly before his resignation. The Turks had seized Cyprus in the sixteenth century, but Britain assumed administrative control in 1878 to prevent Ottoman holdings from falling into Russian hands following the Congress of Berlin. Subsequently, the Greek Cypriot majority on the island, about two-thirds of the population, pressed increasingly for "enosis," or political union with Greece. This movement boiled over in July 1974, when the military junta in Athens, citing Cyprus's President Makarios's alleged pro-Communist leanings and perceived abandonment of enosis, sponsored a coup by extremist Greek Cypriots to effect the union of Cyprus with mainland Greece. In response, Turkey intervened militarily to protect Turkish Cypriots, noting that the 1960 Treaty of Guarantee, signed by Great Britain, Greece, Turkey, Greek Cypriots, and the Turkish Cypriots, ensured "the recognition and maintenance of the independence, territorial integrity, and security of Cyprus by preventing direct or indirect partition or annexation of it by any guarantor state." Hoping to avoid a reason for an increase of NATO's power in the region, the Soviet Union refrained from interfering. Thus, the U.S. military response was limited to naval forces evacuating American civilians from the island during the crisis.

Vice President Gerald R. Ford Jr. became president upon the resignation of Richard Nixon, and he was sworn in on 9 August 1974. He had served in the navy in World War II and had seen extensive action as a junior officer aboard the light carrier *Monterey*. Ford left active service as a lieutenant commander in early 1946 but remained in the Navy Reserve until June 1963.

Of the crises while Ford was president, most significant were the collapse of the regime in South Vietnam in March 1975 and the resultant requirement for evacuation of American personnel, the implosion of the regime in Cambodia in April 1975, and the seizure of the U.S. merchant ship *Mayaguez* the following month.

Airpower had played a prominent role in the U.S. military's involvement in Vietnam. Throughout the entire nine years of operations, navy aircraft flew more than half of the combat sorties into North Vietnam.[28] This was because most strikes against North Vietnam were undertaken by a few aircraft at a time, a pattern well suited to carrier operations. In addition, carriers could operate up to a few dozen miles from the Vietnamese coast, whereas U.S. Air Force aircraft were based in Thailand and thus required in-flight refueling to attack targets in North Vietnam.[29]

As Americans were getting out of Vietnam in the spring of 1975, all remaining U.S. personnel hurriedly departed Phnom Penh on 17 April, just ahead of the advancing Cambodian revolutionaries. This was followed rapidly on 12 May 1975—only twelve days after the last American had been evacuated from Saigon—by the Cambodian seizure of the American merchant ship *Mayaguez* in a heavily traveled shipping lane in what President Gerald Ford labeled an "act of piracy."[30] Thirty-nine crewmen of the *Mayaguez* were taken prisoner.

With this crisis coming so close to two major reverses in Vietnam and Cambodia, President Ford was compelled to take firm and rapid measures to bolster perceptions of U.S. continued commitment to its allies. He was also forced to consider the possibility that the hostages might be taken to the Cambodian mainland, precipitating a repeat of the lengthy *Pueblo* incident. He quickly ordered the USS *Coral Sea* strike group and 1,100 marines from Okinawa into the area. Air surveillance of the *Mayaguez*'s movements had already been ordered.[31] Subsequently, the carrier *Midway* was ordered into the vicinity for additional support of the recovery operations.[32]

Unknown to President Ford or his advisers was an emerging pattern of seizing commercial ships by Cambodian gunboats. Thai, Panamanian, and Swedish commercial vessels had been fired on or briefly detained in the period between 2 and 13 May.[33] Thus, there should have been every expectation that the *Mayaguez* and its crew would be released unharmed in short order. Nevertheless, President Ford launched an attack on Koh Tang Island, off the Cambodian coast, on the second day after the *Mayaguez* was seized. Around two hundred marines landed by helicopter and attacked the island in the late evening. Two helicopters were shot down, and a third was lost near shore when the pilot swamped it while trying to offload marines.[34] The approximately 150 Cambodian defenders of the island were heavily armed, which resulted in the loss of forty-one Americans' lives.[35] By 0920 the next morning the marines had departed Koh Tang Island and were safe on the *Coral Sea*.[36]

Within an hour of the marines' taking ground on Koh Tang Island, other marines boarded the *Mayaguez* and found it empty. The sad part of the story is that Phnom Penh had announced, by radio broadcast, that the *Mayaguez* crewmen would be released. They were actually released about 2000 on 14 May, just before the marines hit Koh Tang Island. Thus, the military response to this crisis could have been avoided with better intelligence or a less rapid response. During the critical seventy-eight hours, American forces flew 479 helicopter and fixed-wing sorties, of which 300 were of a tactical nature. This included strikes at Ream airbase, where seventeen Cambodian aircraft were destroyed and facilities damaged, and at Sihanoukville.[37]

Some criticized the president for failure to consult Congress, but that body roundly applauded the decisive use of force. Similarly, this operation bolstered Americans' confidence after the severe reverses in Vietnam and Cambodia of the same month. Though intended to reassure allies internationally and Southeast Asia regional partners in particular of U.S. resolve, the *Mayaguez* recovery action—seen by many nations as a spasmodic reaction borne of failure—probably had the opposite result. Certainly this decisive action by President Ford lessened the possibility of being repeatedly tested by weak adversaries, though forty-one American deaths was a high price to pay.

President James Earl "Jimmy" Carter remains the only president who is a graduate of the United States Naval Academy, 59th in a class of 820 in 1946. Carter served first on battleships and later in submarines. In 1953 he was selected for the nascent nuclear power program by Admiral Hyman Rickover, but soon thereafter he retired from the service to run the family farm after the death of his father. Interestingly, Carter was the fifth consecutive American president who had served in the navy.

The one noted crisis during the Carter administration was the Iranian hostage rescue attempt on 24 April 1980, Operation Eagle Claw. On 11 February 1979 a popular revolution had swept the shah of Iran, a close American ally, out of power. A national referendum was held on 1 April 1979, resulting in Iran's becoming an Islamic republic with a new theocratic constitution under which the Ayatollah Khomeini became supreme leader of the country. On 4 November 1979 Iranian students backing the new revolutionary Islamic government stormed the U.S. embassy in Teheran and took hostage the fifty-two members of the staff and U.S. Marine Corps security contingent. Poor intelligence left it unclear whether the hostages were being tortured or readied for execution. After five months of failed negotiations, the United States broke diplomatic relations with Iran in early April 1980, and the U.S. Army Special Forces Operational Detachment-Delta (Airborne) prepared for a helicopter-assisted rescue attempt; the JCS gave the go-ahead on 16 April 1980. All four U.S. military services were involved in the rescue attempt, including the aircraft carriers USS *Nimitz* (CVN-68) and USS *Coral Sea* (CV-43).

The plan was to infiltrate operators into Iran the night before the assault and get them to Teheran, and to bring the hostages home after the assault. Unfortunately, a sandstorm caused a helicopter-aircraft collision, which killed eight, and as other helicopters were inoperative for various reasons, the mission was scrubbed. Instead, on 20 January 1981, on their 444th day of captivity and the day of Reagan's inauguration, the hostages were finally ransomed and sent home.

President Ronald W. Reagan had served in the army air corps during World War II, rising to the rank of captain in the Army Reserve. Barred from combat because of poor eyesight, he narrated training and recruitment films with the Army Air Forces Motion Picture Unit.

The first employment of carriers in combat during President Reagan's tenure occurred in what is known as the First Gulf of Sidra Incident. In 1981, to counter excessive Libyan claims in the Gulf of Sidra, President Reagan ordered the *Forrestal* and *Nimitz* carrier groups to conduct missile exercises in what the United States considered international waters. Libyan fighter and attack aircraft repeatedly approached the area during U.S. forces' operations. Many were intercepted and escorted away by U.S. carrier aircraft, and two Libyan planes were shot down when they fired on the American interceptors.[38]

Later in Reagan's first term, the *Independence* carrier group supported Operation Urgent Fury, the U.S. invasion of the Caribbean island of Grenada, in October 1983.[39] Then, in December, strike aircraft from the USS *John F. Kennedy*, patrolling the Mediterranean in response to the bombing of the Marine barracks in Beirut, attacked Syrian antiaircraft positions in Lebanon that had fired on U.S. patrol aircraft.[40] In October 1985 F-14s from USS *Saratoga* intercepted an Egyptian airliner carrying the terrorists who had seized the Italian cruise ship *Achille Lauro* and murdered a U.S. citizen; the F-14s forced the airliner to land in Sicily, where the terrorists were arrested.[41]

The year 1986 was one of major confrontation between Libya and the United States; carriers were on the front line. In March a task force comprising the *Coral Sea, America,* and *Saratoga* carrier groups again challenged Libyan claims to international waters in the Gulf of Sidra by crossing the so-called line of death in Operation Prairie Fire. In a two-day series of engagements, Libyan missile patrol boats fired on American aircraft, and U.S. planes sank some of the patrol boats and attacked numerous shore-based surface-to-air missile sites.[42] There followed Operation Eldorado Canyon, in which air force and navy aircraft struck terrorist and military targets in Libya in retaliation for terrorist attacks against Americans in Berlin.[43]

When war between Iran and Iraq threatened the flow of oil through the Strait of Hormuz, carrier-led American naval forces arrived to protect Kuwaiti tankers. After months of tanker passage through Hormuz without incident, friction with the Iranians mounted in April 1988. The sides traded minings and attacks on offshore oil platforms until the

Iranian navy sortied in force. The USS *Enterprise* aircraft sank a gunboat and a frigate and heavily damaged another frigate.[44]

President Reagan's administration ended with an incident similar to the one at the beginning. F-14s of the *John F. Kennedy* carrier group shot down two Libyan planes threatening the U.S. task force in waters north of the Libyan coast.[45] Although President Reagan was a former army air corps officer, his administrations, more than any other president's since World War II, relied on carrier airpower in crisis situations.

George Herbert Walker Bush was a decorated U.S. Navy aviator. The youngest man ever to receive his navy wings, he served aboard the USS *San Jacinto* during the War in the Pacific. He flew fifty-eight combat missions, for which he received the Distinguished Flying Cross, three Air Medals, and the Presidential Unit Citation awarded to the *San Jacinto*. He was honorably discharged in September 1945, but he continued in active service with the Navy Reserve until 1955, attaining the rank of lieutenant commander.

Prominent among the crises faced by President George H. W. Bush were actions to oust the dictator Manuel Noriega of Panama and Operations Desert Shield and Desert Storm, launched in response to the invasion of Kuwait by Saddam Hussein of Iraq. Early in George H. W. Bush's tenure, carriers were considered for, but ultimately not included in, Operation Just Cause, the U.S. invasion of Panama to topple Manuel Noriega.[46] Carriers were, however, heavily involved in Operations Desert Shield and Desert Storm. Within five days of the August 1990 Iraqi invasion of Kuwait, the *Independence* and *Dwight D. Eisenhower* carrier groups were within range to confront Iraqi forces had they continued their advance into Saudi Arabia.[47] On 2 October the USS *Independence* entered the Persian Gulf, the first carrier to do so since 1976. The risks of operations in the constricted waters of the gulf and multicarrier operations have been taken in the gulf on many occasions since. When coalition forces launched the campaign to liberate Kuwait in January 1991, aircraft from the carriers *John F. Kennedy, Saratoga, America, Ranger, Midway,* and *Theodore Roosevelt,*[48] all on station in the Red Sea and Persian Gulf, executed sea control, counterair, and strike missions in Kuwait and Iraq. Although command and control and other joint doctrinal issues affected the ability to employ carrier aircraft, they were a significant portion of the air campaign against Iraq.

President William Jefferson "Bill" Clinton saw no military service, having received a draft deferment during the Vietnam conflict. Carriers were regularly employed during the Clinton administrations, and carrier aircraft contributed to Operation Southern Watch patrols in support of United Nations sanctions against Iraq over the no-fly zone in the southern part of the country. Carriers conducted further operations against Iraq in response to separate Iraqi actions in 1996 and 1998.[49] Carrier aircraft were also employed when the USS *Abraham Lincoln* supported American operations in Somalia in October 1993.[50] In the Balkans carrier aircraft helped enforce no-fly zones over Bosnia in 1993–1995. The USS *Theodore Roosevelt* and *America* aircraft struck Bosnian Serb military targets in a 1995 NATO operation designed to persuade Serbian and Bosnian Serb leaders to engage in peace negotiations.[51] The following year saw two carrier groups deployed in the vicinity of Taiwan in response to provocative missile tests by China in a show of force during a tense period leading up to Taiwan's presidential elections.[52]

At the end of Clinton's presidency, focus shifted back to the Balkans and the dispute over control of the Serbian province of Kosovo. Aircraft from the USS *Theodore Roosevelt* hit targets in Kosovo and Serbia proper as part of a NATO air campaign crafted to dissuade Serbia's President Slobodan Milošević from continuing ethnic cleansing in the province.[53]

President George W. Bush, son of President George H. W. Bush, performed limited duty in the Texas Air National Guard as an F-102 pilot during the Vietnam conflict but saw no action. As part of the response to the terrorist attacks of 11 September 2001, the United States under President Bush's watch actively assisted the rebellion to topple the terrorist-supportive Taliban regime in Afghanistan. The United States had very limited access to air bases within tactical range of Afghanistan, so aircraft carriers were vital to the campaign. By March 2002 six different carriers had been employed in operations in the northern Arabian Sea; the USS *Kitty Hawk* served as a forward operating base for U.S. Special Forces. The flexibility of carriers was shown once again during Operation Iraqi Freedom, which began 20 March 2003. The USS *Abraham Lincoln,*

Constellation, and *Kitty Hawk*, stationed in the Persian Gulf, and the *Theodore Roosevelt* and *Harry S. Truman*, in the eastern Mediterranean Sea, provided a large component of the airpower employed against Saddam Hussein's forces during the successful operation.[54]

Another example of the flexibility of aircraft carriers was the humanitarian relief operations on the Indonesian island of Sumatra. A devastating tsunami struck the eastern Indian Ocean on 26 December 2004. In response, the *Abraham Lincoln* carrier group soon arrived and provided vital organizational, logistical, and medical support to time-critical relief operations, heavily utilizing its air wing's two helicopter squadrons.[55]

President Barack Obama has seen no military service. In his short time as president, however, he has used aircraft carriers to support the crises he inherited in Iraq and Afghanistan. Carrier-based aerial forces were also central to two of the more celebrated foreign affairs events of his administration: the assassination of Osama bin Laden and the toppling of the Muammar Gaddafi regime in Libya.

It is interesting that no clear patterns of presidential use of aircraft carriers since the Second World War have emerged. One would expect that presidents would feel most comfortable with and draw most heavily on forces from their own branch of military service in crisis situations, and so the six of the twelve presidents since World War II who served in the navy would be presupposed to rely most heavily on the use of carriers. Yet the evidence does not support that thesis. Then what conclusions can be drawn concerning presidential use of carriers in crises?

There appear to be three dominant determinants of presidential use of carriers. First, carriers appear to be used most frequently when they can arrive at the scene of a crisis earlier than other forms of military power. This is particularly true when crises such as the USS *Pueblo* and *Mayaguez* incidents offer only a finite amount of time in which to respond. Second, carriers seem to be used more frequently when there are no assurances of proximate allies supporting American military operations staged from their soil. Third, carriers are more likely to be employed when sustainable air operations are required. Carriers afford the advantage of deploying a sizable number of aircraft without necessitating and waiting for a logistics train or negotiating land-basing rights with third parties to commence operations. When combinations of these determinates exist, American presidents appear to be predisposed to the use of carriers and their embarked air wings in times of crisis.

Admiral Alfred Thayer Mahan was among the first to recognize that a very large proportion of the population of planet Earth lives close to the sea. It is estimated today that approximately 80 percent of the earth's population lives within two hundred miles of a major body of water, and it is a fact that no point of land on Earth is more than 1,700 miles from an ocean. That, in part, accounts for use of naval forces in crisis situations. So, too, does geography play an important part in presidential selection of an appropriate military component to respond to a given crisis situation.

One other consideration regarding presidential use of aircraft carriers in crises is doctrine. Operating from higher altitudes with weapons technologically configured for the purpose, air force squadrons at the outset of a confrontation are well suited and doctrinally focused to be able to hit and destroy strategic targets far inland. Navy and marine corps air assets are doctrinally disposed, on the other hand, to "roll up" the opposition from the shore before transitioning to a strategic role. This requires elimination of enemy radar and aircraft vectoring sites and suppression of missile sites and major gun emplacements, considerations that would inhibit a subsequent amphibious landing. Thus, depending on how a crisis is unfolding, the air force may be the service of choice if high stakes demand immediate strategic targeting, whereas the navy–marine corps team might be the choice for an unfolding scenario where a footprint on land may ultimately be required.

From the scenarios considered above, it appears that carriers, or at least naval forces, have been used when crises arise at sea, or on or around islands and near-shore locations. Surely the USS *Mayaguez*, Quemoy-Matsu, Cuba, Cyprus, and Gulf of Sidra operations bear out this pattern, as do the handling of the *Achille Lauro* recovery operations and the Egypt Air airliner interception operations. Each revealed a situation quickly accessible in the maritime regional domain. Moreover, each of these situations necessitated employment of a force that could apply airpower consistently over an extended period. Geography, initial proximity of force, sustainability in theater, and the diplomatic option quickly to remove the force all factored into the presidential decisions concerned.

On the other hand, air force air assets are normally employed by presidents when immediate strategic targeting is necessary, or when strategic and operational air lift is needed, particularly over an extended period, such as is currently the case in Iraq. Certainly the Cuban Missile Crisis bears out the former, and the Berlin Airlift the latter.

Oddly, proximity to target has also played an important part when presidents and their top advisers are tailoring a force package in a crisis. For instance, since air force bases were so far away from many targets in Vietnam, single or multiple refuelings of a strike package were required to reach their targets. Aircraft carriers, owing to their mobility, could be positioned much closer to remote targets and were therefore the force of choice when distances and fuel consumption were major considerations. Similarly, in Afghanistan initial unavailability of land bases made aircraft carriers the only viable source of requisite airpower. There geography and sustainability of persistent firepower combined to form a pattern of presidential preference.

In all this it appears that presidents and their principal advisers select force packages in large part on the basis of expert advice they are given by the service chiefs and their top staff members. Airpower options are tailored to necessity, and the unique abilities of all the services are considered and combined to optimize combat power and availability in response to the unfolding military and diplomatic considerations. As noted, American aircraft carriers have been called on by presidents in roughly half of all crises since World War II. The ability they have given to manage crisis situations without placing a firmer and more provocative "trip wire" on contested soil was particularly useful to U.S. presidents and their top advisers during the Cold War, when concerns about Soviet crisis escalation were paramount.

Virtually all the individual crises discussed above serve to validate the utility of airpower delivered from aircraft carriers when the situation warrants it. The combination of factors that make carrier airpower attractive to American presidents and their advisers is considerable, but it certainly validates the flexibility of employment that is often required when American interests are at risk around the globe.

Notes

The epigraph is from George H. W. Bush's foreword to Douglas V. Smith, ed., *One Hundred Years of U.S. Navy Air Power* (Annapolis: Naval Institute Press, 2010), p. 1.

1. Barry M. Blechman and Stephen S. Kaplan, *The Use of the Armed Forces as a Political Instrument* (Washington, D.C.: Brookings Institution, 1976), pp. 1–2.

2. Ibid., pp. A-2–A-10.

3. Ibid., p. IV-4.

4. Scott C. Truver, "Where Are the Carriers?" *U.S. Naval Institute Proceedings* 112 (October 1986): 63.

5. James L. Holloway III, *Aircraft Carriers at War: A Personal Retrospective of Korea, Vietnam, and the Soviet Confrontation* (Annapolis: Naval Institute Press, 2007), pp. 44–45.

6. Ibid., p. 46. It should be noted that by this time each aircraft carrier of two squadrons had jet fighter aircraft—the new Grumman F9F-2 Panthers and McDonnell F2H-2 Banshee—assigned on board.

7. Ibid., pp. 47–48.

8. Ibid., p. xii.

9. Ibid.

10. Jonathan T. Howe, *Multicrises: Sea Power and Global Politics in the Missile Age* (Cambridge: MIT Press, 1971), p. 247.

11. Jonathan D. Pollack, *Perception and Action in Chinese Foreign Policy: The Quemoy Decision,* 2 vols. (Ann Arbor: UMI Dissertation Services, 1976), 1:163.

12. Ibid., p. 168.

13. National Security Archive, "Bay of Pigs 40 Years After—Chronology," www.gwu.edu/~nsarchiv/bayofpigs/chron.html.

14. Fulbright Memorandum, Cuba Policy, 29 March 1961, National Security Archive.

15. U.S. Navy Memorandum for the Record, 4 April 1961, Rules of Engagement Operation Bumpy Road, pp. 1–4, National Security Archive.

16. National Security Archive, "Bay of Pigs 40 Years After."

17. Ibid.

18. Ibid.

19. Ibid.

20. Department of Defense, news release, 29 November 1962, Department of Defense, Office of Public Affairs, no. 1942–72, Oxford 53201, 53176, pp. 4, 5.

21. Ibid.

22. Ibid., p.10.

23. Blechman and Kaplan, *The Use of the Armed Forces as a Political Instrument*, pp. IX-30, 32, and 41.

24. Ibid., p. IX-41.

25. Ibid., p. IX-32.

26. Ibid.

27. Ibid., p. XI-33.

28. Holloway, *Aircraft Carriers at War*, p. 246.

29. Ibid., pp. 246–247.

30. Blechman and Kaplan, *The Use of the Armed Forces as a Political Instrument*, p. XIV-25.

31. I was mission commander of the second P-3 aircraft on top of the USS *Mayaguez* and arrived on station just as the ship was approaching its anchorage about a mile off Koh Tang Island. When VP-4 crew 5 relieved the VP-17 aircraft that was first on station, we were asked to use our aviation sextant to determine the area of damage caused by a twenty-millimeter round taken through the tail. Unfortunately, relative aircraft speeds made this impossible. Upon landing, VP-17 determined their aircraft had taken a single round through the center of the tail section in a nonvital spot that was three inches in diameter.

32. Blechman and Kaplan, *The Use of the Armed Forces as a Political Instrument*, p. XIV-27.

33. Ibid., p. XIV-30.

34. See note 32. This material comes from the official debrief of the action around Koh Tang Island to members of VP-4 participating in the *Mayaguez* recovery.

35. Blechman and Kaplan, *The Use of the Armed Forces as a Political Instrument*, p. XIV-28.

36. Ibid.

37. Ibid.

38. Edward J. Marolda, "Cold War to Violent Peace: 1945–1991," in *The Navy*, ed. W. J. Holland Jr. (Washington, D.C.: Naval Historical Foundation, 2000), pp. 184–186.

39. Ibid., p. 187.

40. Ibid., p. 186.

41. Ibid., p. 188.

42. Ibid.

43. Ibid., pp. 188–189.

44. Craig L. Symonds, *Decision at Sea: Five Naval Battles That Shaped American History* (New York: Oxford University Press, 2005), part 5.

45. John F. Morton, "The U.S. Navy in Review," *U.S. Naval Institute Proceedings* 116, no. 5 (May 1990): 174.

46. Malcolm McConnell, *Just Cause: The Real Story of America's High-Tech Invasion of Panama* (New York: St. Martin's Press, 1991), p. 54.

47. Marvin Pokrant, *Desert Shield at Sea: What the Navy Really Did* (Westport, Conn.: Greenwood Press, 1999), pp. 3–4.

48. Ibid., p. 3.

49. Robert J. Schneller Jr., *Anchor of Resolve: A History of U.S. Naval Forces Central Command/Fifth Fleet* (Washington, D.C.: Naval Historical Center, 2007), pp. 60–62.

50. Walter S. Poole, *The Effort to Save Somalia: August 1992–March 1994* (Washington, D.C.: Joint History Office, 2005), p. 59.

51. Robert C. Owen, *Deliberate Force: A Case Study in Effective Air Campaigning* (Maxwell Air Force Base, Ala.: Air University Press, 2000), p. 202.

52. Suisheng Zhao, *Across the Taiwan Strait: Mainland China, Taiwan, and the 1995–1996 Crisis* (New York: Routledge, 1999), p. 1.

53. A. L. Stigler, "The Kosovo Conflict," in *Naval Coalition Warfare: From the Napoleonic War to Operation Iraqi Freedom,* ed. Bruce A. Elleman and S. C. M. Paine (New York: Routledge, 2008), pp. 184–185.

54. Benjamin S. Lambeth, *American Carrier Air Power: At the Dawn of a New Century* (Santa Monica, Calif.: Rand, 2005), pp. x–xii.

55. Bruce A. Elleman, *Waves of Hope: The U.S. Navy's Response to the Tsunami in Northern Indonesia* (Newport, R.I.: Naval War College Press, 2007), p. 10.

Suggestions for Further Research

There is almost nothing written on presidential use of aircraft carriers in crises, and most of what does exist is in unpublished manuscripts. This chapter has used literally all that could be found, and the notes indicate the sources. On the other hand, there is a great deal of material on individual crises in which aircraft carriers were used. One could spend days compiling source material just on the crises included in this chapter.

Of particular value would be studies of presidential decisions concerning the employment of carrier-based airpower on the basis of the individual presidents' military experiences and political party affiliations. Another topic meriting more thorough investigation is the recent trend to employ land-based airpower (now with greater ranges because of in-flight refueling and greater accuracy because of "smart" technology) for missions for which carrier-based airpower had been traditionally better suited.

Topics that require further investigation include the average number of hours taken to put a carrier on a crisis station, the logistics of carrier groups, analysis of carrier commanders' decision making, and congressional concerns and actions.

8

Chinese Statesmen and the Use of Airpower

Andrew S. Erickson

The development of airpower and its influence on history has been primarily a Western narrative, with American, European, and even Russian centers. Aside from Japan's operationally brilliant but strategically unsustainable military employment in the Pacific War, no Asian power has been a significant airpower beyond its immediate region.[1] China, though it has regained much of its pre-nineteenth-century economic significance and plays an increasingly important geopolitical role, still has not fully proven itself in the realm of airpower.[2] That may finally be changing, and if so, the ramifications could be considerable.

Today Beijing's military air components are finally on the verge of giving the country's leaders something they have dreamed of since before the 1949 founding of the People's Republic of China: a reliable instrument of national power. Though civil and military aviation have long been a tool of national consolidation and development, and the latter has played a vital if limited role in many of China's twentieth-century military campaigns, both started from virtually nothing, and the journey upward has been arduous indeed. From the Chinese Communist Party (CCP)'s failure to reunify Taiwan to its awkward reliance on Soviet aid during the Korean War to its truncated invasion of Vietnam, airpower can be said to have been at least as much a limiting factor as an enabler. Yet China's leaders used it as best they could, as part of a larger pattern of foreign policy in which they played a weak but strengthening hand with notable skill to consolidate China's autonomy and advance its strategic interests. In its six decades of existence, the People's Liberation Army Air Force (PLAAF) claims to have shot down 1,474 aircraft and damaged 2,344, for a total of 3,818.[3] Airpower has thus been at the heart of modern Chinese statecraft, and for that reason alone its evolution and use merits careful examination.

Founded during the Nanchang Uprising on 1 August 1927, the Red Army gradually incorporated subordinate units throughout the Long March of 1934–1935, the War of Resistance against Japan in 1937–1945, and the War of Liberation in 1945–1949, until the PRC's establishment on 1 October 1949. The term *People's Liberation Army* was used to describe individual units as early as 1945, but only the Central Military Commission (CMC) order on 1 November 1948 made the term PLA broadly applicable to CCP armed forces.

Founded on 11 November 1949, the PLAAF began operations with captured Nationalist and Japanese aircraft. Like the PLA Navy (PLAN, which had been established on 23 April 1949), its early leaders had only ground experience; this persisted until the mid-1980s, since which time all commanders have been former pilots. The PLAAF, PLAN, and Second Artillery—established in 1966 and responsible for most ballistic missiles—were subordinated to the ground forces through the end of the Cold War. A survey of PLA uses of force during the latter half of the twentieth century reveals primarily ground force actions on China's land borders with some degree of air "support" (albeit never close air support near ground troops), as well as several efforts to assert sovereignty over disputed islands (although China's air forces did not generally fly over water until the late 1990s). PLAAF wartime operations have followed a general pattern in which a sudden political decision forces rapid preparation and deployment of underprepared PLAAF forces, facilitated by political work, and guided by nuanced rules of engagement established by the PLA's highest decision-making body, the CMC. Using Chinese territory as a sanctuary, the PLAAF deploys hundreds of aircraft to a border zone. Conflict operations are then used both to achieve military objectives and to train pilots and support personnel.[4]

Under Soviet guidance, the PLA established the Naval Aviation Force in 1951. Apparently subordinated to the PLAAF initially, it subsequently was divided into three fleet air divisions. In 1950 a naval air academy was established in Qingdao to provide fifteen months of primarily technical instruction. By January 1953 PLA Naval Aviation had established a fighter and a light bomber division. Its 80 aircraft were Tu-2 bombers, MiG-15 fighters, and Il-28 bombers. By 1958 the force had grown to a shore-based 470 aircraft charged with coastal air defense. The separate PLA Air Defense Force was merged into the PLAAF in 1957.

It is surface-to-air missiles (SAMs) and antiaircraft artillery (AAA), not aircraft, that have provided primary air defense. The PLAAF has long employed both; Naval Aviation relies primarily on AAA and has largely phased out its SAMs. The extent to which PLAAF and Naval Aviation aircraft are capable of flying in airspace covered by the various services' SAMs remains unclear.

Paramount leaders have always had disproportionate influence on the PLA because it is a party army. Mao Zedong (1893–1976) is the most prominent example of the interrelation between PRC political and military leadership. He led the CCP to victory in the anti-Japanese and civil wars and was China's principal leader from 1949 to 1976. During that time he commanded the PLA as head of the CMC and served as China's foremost military strategist. In developing PLA tactics, Mao drew on both traditions of peasant insurgency and guerrilla warfare experience, which he privileged under the aegis of "People's War" at the expense of technological emphasis. In doing so, he limited possibilities for Chinese airpower development even as he presided over its one significant use in conflict, in Korea. However they decide to manage affairs of state in the future, Mao's successors will finally have significant aviation assets at their disposal.

Doctrine and Trends

Nations develop airpower in different ways, but they are guided by broadly overlapping doctrine. The U.S. Air Force (USAF) basic doctrine document cites General H. H. "Hap" Arnold's definition: "Air power is not made up of airplanes alone. Air power is a composite of airplanes, air crews, maintenance crews, air bases, air supply, and sufficient replacements in both planes and crews to maintain a constant fighting strength, regardless of what losses may be inflicted by the enemy. In addition to that, we must have the backing of a large aircraft industry in the United States to provide all kinds of equipment, and a large training establishment that can furnish the personnel when called upon."[5]

The closest Chinese equivalent of *airpower* is *kōngzhōng lìliàng*.[6] This term is a foreign derivative, however, and the more commonly used Chinese term is *zhìkōngquán*, or "command of the air."[7] Like the USAF concept of "air dominance," this is defined as control over air operations "over [at least] a critical or limited area for [at least] a short period of time."[8] The scope of this definition has expanded as increasingly well-armed Chinese aircraft are able to go farther, fly higher, and stay up longer, all while under better protection. The organizational components of Chinese airpower include the PLAAF, Naval Aviation, Army Aviation, and, in some respects, the Second Artillery. This chapter focuses only on the first two.

The USAF also frequently cites General Arnold's observation that "offense is the essence of air power."[9] As modern airpower is defined by offensive (or what the United States euphemistically terms "defensive and offensive counterair operations"), it is only logical that the PLAAF has gradually begun its shift from purely defensive operations to simultaneous offensive and defensive operations. Likewise, Naval Aviation's "doctrine" fits into the PLAN's overall doctrine of "near seas active defense." This doctrine does not mention offensive capabilities, but successful aircraft carrier group development would give China that capability.

In the summer of 2004 the CMC authorized the PLAAF, for the first time in its history, to have its own service-specific aerospace strategy known as "integrated air and space operations, simultaneous offensive and defensive operations." China's 2004 Defense White Paper was the first to mention "conducting both offensive and defensive operations," which was actually formulated around 1987 under PLAAF Commander General Wang Hai (1985–1992). Although it was not mentioned in the 2006 paper, it was included in the 2008 and 2010 papers. The

2008 report was the first to put it in a strategic context as "the strategic requirements of conducting both offensive and defensive operations." This appears to have come out at about the same time PLAAF strategists began writing increasingly about becoming a "strategic air force."

Yet although there was considerable press coverage and speculation surrounding PLAAF Commander General Xu Qiliang's (2007–) mention of space during the PLAAF's sixtieth anniversary in November 2009, none of China's white papers has mentioned "integrated air and space" in the PLAAF section or any other section. Other services and organizations, including the General Armaments Department and the Second Artillery, are competing for control of China's emerging space capabilities, while the PLAN may have a much greater role in air capabilities as Chinese deck aviation progresses. Since even Chinese leaders probably do not know yet how these factors will ultimately play out, it is useful to review how their predecessors have attempted to develop and employ airpower, and the interests and challenges that have shaped their actions.

Background

Long a dream of Chinese statesmen, Chinese airpower emerged from virtually nothing and experienced many false starts. Sun Zhongshan (Sun Yat-sen, 1866–1925), the founder of modern China, promoted airpower as a key to liberating and modernizing his nation. In 1917 his Guangzhou Revolutionary Government established an aviation bureau, flying squadron, and aviation school. A Western arms embargo stunted Sun's efforts, however.

Subsequently, the Guomindang (GMD, or Nationalists; also known as the Kuomintang, or KMT) obtained aircraft and instructors from Moscow. Jiang Jieshi (Chiang Kai-shek, 1887–1975), who would emerge as the leader of the GMD and later of the Republic of China on Taiwan, used Russian-supplied aircraft in his Northern Expedition to recapture China from local warlords, albeit with limited effect. Nevertheless, Jiang accorded priority to development of an air force, first to reunify China and later as the only hope of rapidly raising military capabilities against the Japanese. His efforts were facilitated by the lifting of the Western-imposed arms embargo in 1929; the introduction of U.S. and Italian military aircraft and professionals followed in 1932. In a substantial achievement for the time, seven hundred pilots and six hundred aircraft were assembled, only to be destroyed in substantial part shortly after Japan invaded China on 7 July 1937.

Soviet assistance arrived by late 1937, and U.S. assistance by 1942, giving the Nationalists more than one thousand aircraft by 1945. These proved to be of little use in the subsequent civil war with the CCP. By 1937 three hundred aircraft had been lost to CCP destruction and poor maintenance; the remainder were used primarily for resupply, not to attack CCP forces directly. By the time the CCP seized complete control of mainland China and Mao Zedong established the People's Republic on 1 October 1949, most GMD aircraft and pilots had been sent to Taiwan; the CCP assumed use of their abandoned facilities.

Like its GMD rival, the CCP traces its aviation experience to a Russian-established aviation school. In 1925–1926, eighteen cadets (nine GMD, nine CCP) were sent to the USSR for advanced flight training. Two CCP cadets, Chang Qiankun and Wang Bi, would play a foundational role in PLAAF development. After the 1927 GMD-CCP split, two CCP groups of nineteen each enrolled in Soviet air force schools for further training; this was the cradle of early PLAAF leadership. A guerrilla army, the PLA captured its first GMD aircraft in February 1930. In 1937 the CCP cooperated with a local warlord to receive Soviet aircraft. The resulting Xinjiang Aviation Unit was cut off from Soviet supplies in 1941–1942 and disbanded in 1942, however. The following year Mao authorized special negotiations with the GMD for the freedom of the unit's personnel, who were then granted three months' special living conditions during which to recover. In 1941, with Mao's guarded approval, the CMC established an aviation engineering school; it was suspended in 1943. In May 1944, at the CCP headquarters of Yan'an, the CMC founded an aviation section. Wang and Chang became its director and deputy director, respectively.

On 28 August 1945, on the way to American-sponsored negotiation efforts with the GMD, Mao made his first plane flight. Even before this, he was a supporter of aviation development. Like Sun Zhongshan and Jiang Jieshi, he saw an air force as vital to national unity, economic development, and defense. But, perhaps in part because he had witnessed his predecessors' failures, Mao was also cautious and pragmatic. He realized that China's backwardness and resource constraints would limit the speed with which it could progress in this area, and he believed that a "People's War" approach, which emphasized human capital and ideology over technology, was the only choice for China.

Nevertheless, after Japan's surrender left the GMD as the CCP's primary threat, the CMC established an airfield at Yan'an and sent staff to Manchuria to gather Japanese equipment and begin flight training. These efforts were aided further when fifty-four GMD air force pilots defected, bringing twenty planes with them. On 1 March 1946 the Northeast Aviation School was established in Tonghua, Jilin Province. It drew on forty Japanese aircraft, captured Japanese pilots and ground crews, Nationalist defectors, and some 660 Chinese personnel. On 17 March 1949 the CMC upgraded its aviation section to an Aviation Bureau; Chang served as the director and Wang the political commissar. The bureau assumed control of GMD personnel, equipment, and facilities; on 4 May it established the CCP's first combat squadron.

With its control over mainland China imminent, the CCP made a concerted effort to acquire Soviet aid. In July 1949, at Mao's direction, Vice Chairman of the Central People's Government Liu Shaoqi traveled to Moscow to request fighters, bombers, help in training pilots and mechanics, and Soviet air force officers to assist. Stalin approved, thereby initiating a decade of Soviet aid that would afford China the foundations of an air force and an aviation industry, but would be fraught with tension and limited in critical ways. Finally, on 11 November 1949, the CMC formally disestablished the Aviation Bureau and established the PLAAF, with army unit commanders Liu Yalou (1949–1965) and Xiao Hua (1949–1950) as its first commander and political commissar, respectively; Chang and Wang became their deputies. Liu was subsequently accorded the rank of general; the PLA had no ranks at that time, instated them during 1955–1965, and reinstated them in 1988. He had Soviet training, was politically correct, and enjoyed good connections with Mao.

The Mao Era

In its initial decades, the Red Army (PLA) had considerable leadership continuity, as commanders of the campaigns from the 1930s to the 1950s largely rose through the ranks together in the same military regions and forged a variety of reciprocal bonds. Schooled on the battleground of the People's War, these first-generation commanders had very little naval or air experience. They also played a major role in affairs of state: Mao and Deng Xiaoping became national leaders, Zhou Enlai became premier, and Chen Yi became foreign minister.

Three other PLA leaders merit special mention. Zhu De (1886–1976), one of the few early PLA leaders to receive a professional military education, arguably founded the Red Army, commanded the Eighth Route Army, and later became PLA commander in chief. Peng Dehuai (1901–1974) commanded the Chinese People's Volunteers (CPV) in Korea in 1951. In 1954 he returned from Korea and was appointed minister of national defense and National Defense Council vice chairman. Having criticized Mao's disastrous policies at the 1959 Lushan Conference, Peng was purged and further repressed during the Cultural Revolution. Lin Biao (1907–1971) was educated at the Whampoa Academy and served the CCP in a variety of early military commands. Lin was named vice premier and National Defense Council vice chairman in 1954. As minister of national defense (1959–1971), Lin rose to great power and was designated Mao's successor. He died in September 1971 when his aircraft crashed under mysterious circumstances in Mongolia, after he allegedly plotted a coup against Mao. This incident would marginalize the PLAAF as a politically unreliable organization until after Mao's death, in 1976, and even the rehabilitation of his successor Deng Xiaoping (1904–1997) in 1978.[10]

Leadership and political reliability have long been important limiting factors for China's air forces. Emphasis on political reliability is evidenced by the fact that the PLAAF had no confirmed pilot commanders until Wang Hai in 1985, though some sources suggest that Ma Ning (1973–1977) was also a pilot. PLAAF Commander Wu Faxian's (1965–1971; 1915–2004) involvement with Defense Minister Lin

Biao harmed his force's development severely. In May 1965 Wu Faxian (PLAAF political commissar 1957–1965) was appointed PLAAF commander and was concurrently assigned as a deputy chief of the General Staff and a deputy director of the CMC's General Office. While so empowered, he became a member of Defense Minister Lin Biao's clique. Upon Lin's demise, Wu Faxian was arrested immediately. He was tried ten years later and sentenced to seventeen years in prison.[11] The PLAAF was not assigned a new commander until eighteen months after Wu's arrest, when Ma Ning was appointed in May 1973.[12]

Establishment of a Military Aviation Industry

China emerged from the Anti-Japanese War and the civil war as it had entered them: impoverished, largely uneducated, and virtually unindustrialized. Limited resource-extraction and processing facilities had been established in coastal areas by foreign enterprises and in scattered interior locations by warlords. Overall, however, China's unevenly located resources were underexploited and disconnected for want of infrastructure. Lacking even relevant raw materials and trained pilots, the People's Republic had to create an aviation industry from virtually nothing.

These deficiencies necessitated significant Soviet guidance and assistance, which were secured by the February 1950 Treaty of Friendship, Alliance, and Mutual Assistance. The CCP launched its first Five Year Plan for industrial and agricultural development and production in 1949. In 1951 Premier Zhou Enlai called for licensed production of Soviet fighters and trainers by 1954–1956. That same year Minister of Heavy Industry He Changgong led a delegation to Moscow to seek technology transfer. In 1952 Li Fuchun and Marshal Nie Rongzhen (1899–1996) led a study of how to develop the industry. On 8 January 1953 Zhou convened a meeting concerning the defense industrial aspects of China's first Five Year Plan.

Limited funds were allocated to establish an aviation industry with a relatively comprehensive, if rudimentary, infrastructure. By soliciting extensive Soviet aid and focusing on development of heavy industrial plants and equipment, China doubled industrial capacity within five years. Nie Rongzhen was the first major PLA technocrat, heading the National Defense Industry Office and its successor, the National Defense Science and Technology Commission, in the 1950s and 1960s.

This early progress (albeit from a very low baseline) would be squandered by counterproductive Maoist policies. Mao's Great Leap Forward (1958–1960)—which sought to render China self-sufficient through labor-intensive light industrialization, agricultural collectivization, and military production—wasted limited resources and undermined economic development. Mao repressed Peng Dehuai and others who opposed these policies, which included devoting significant PLA focus to agricultural production. Soviet advisers were expelled in 1960 following deterioration of the bilateral relationship. Soviet withdrawal interrupted transfer of aviation expertise and imposed an ethos of self-reliance on China's aviation industry; but independent, inefficient factories failed to meet the PLAAF's needs.

Subsequent preparation for "early war, big war, and all-out nuclear war" caused Mao to order roughly half of military production dispersed among a "Third Line" network in China's vast interior. This process, which occupied much of the 1960s and 1970s, may have consumed as much as half of defense expenditures, unquestionably dispersed scarce human and material resources inefficiently, and further overextended China's limited transportation infrastructure. The Cultural Revolution (1966–1976) threw all but the highest-priority weapons program into disarray, dividing bureaus into rival factions and even threatening rail links critical to the development of advanced weapons systems. Though Zhou Enlai's intervention protected missile development, and even that of satellites to some extent, aircraft development suffered greatly.

The military importance of aircraft was recognized, but limited resources were squandered by Marshal Lin Biao's unrealistic production targets for the industry and subsequent implication in the alleged "571" coup attempt in 1971. Lin's doctrine of imminent war during the Cultural Revolution was particularly damaging to the PLAAF, which suffered from low training and high accident rates of aircraft that were poorly constructed and maintained and supplied with insufficient fuel and spare parts. In 1969, for instance, the PLAAF shuttered twelve of its twenty-nine schools. In 1970 pilots averaged 30–40 flight hours annually, far below the 123 hours mandated by regulations. The aircraft industry's organization, and the quality of its products, remained poor.

The Korean War, 1950–1953

The Korean War, known in China as the War to Resist U.S. Aggression and Aid Korea, is the only war that the PLAAF has ever fought in its six-decade history. It thus merits special examination. The motives of Mao and Stalin, and what they knew of Kim Il-sung's invasion plans, remain debated by scholars. What is agreed is that Mao attempted to caution the United States that its forces should not enter North Korea, Washington dismissed these warnings, and the CPV crossed the Yalu in late October 1950, later to be supported indirectly by Soviet pilots, as well as the PLAAF.

PLAAF participation in Korea may be divided into three eras. First, from late October 1950 to July 1951 the PLAAF developed its capabilities rapidly in preparation for conflict. Second, from September 1951 to May 1952 the PLAAF and Soviet forces provided air defense in parallel. This limited role resulted from political restrictions that confined the Soviets to providing rear air defense, the MiG-15's short range, and lack of working airfields in North Korea. Third, from July 1952 to the 27 June 1953 armistice, the PLAAF engaged in more independent air operations.[13]

Whereas American and Soviet forces were self-limited by political concerns, the PLAAF was limited primarily by inability and inexperience. It had only begun large-scale development the previous year, with crash programs to establish aviation schools and select young, politically reliable cadets; and even that had initially been focused on Mao's planned invasion of Taiwan. Airfields inherited from the GMD were generally in poor condition; upgrades were prioritized carefully. Drawing on captured supplies, the PLAAF developed support, maintenance, and logistics units.

PLAAF Commander Liu Yalou and his staff emphasized fighters over bombers; their goals were attaining air superiority over the GMD, supporting an amphibious assault on Taiwan, and defending a reunified China's airspace (including that over water). Now, in the new Korean context, PLA leaders suddenly found their ground forces vulnerable to air attack, but they lacked airpower experience and concepts. The Korean War provided strong impetus to develop the PLAAF rapidly, but its leaders failed to understand the tremendous challenges involved. At the same time, Soviet influence and PLA perceptions led to the PLAAF's being envisioned as a tactical support unit for the ground forces; other roles were unexplored.

As they weighed whether to intervene in the Korean War in October 1950, Chinese leaders were particularly concerned about the lack of air support available to them. Here Stalin's desire to divert America and its allies with an Asian conflict without directly involving the USSR and facing retaliation provided critical but limited support; this was to become a double-edged sword that would ultimately help catalyze the 1960 Sino-Soviet split. To secure nine Chinese divisions on the Sino-Korean border, Stalin had offered air support, in the form of a 124-plane MiG division. Russian pilots would train their Chinese counterparts, then transfer the aircraft to them after two to three months. As early as 21 July 1950 a Soviet air unit arrived in northeast China; this played a critical role in convincing Chinese troops not to fear a U.S. air attack. Mao used Soviet loans and citizens' contributions to purchase Soviet aircraft—a total of 2,470—after China entered the Korean War in October 1950.

Though China's leadership agreed that PLAAF development was important and was generally unified in policy approaches, some predictable differences did emerge along bureaucratic lines. As part of a larger pattern throughout the war, CPV Commander Peng Dehuai, faced with uncertainty regarding ground–air force coordination and Soviet assistance, requested maximum air support for the ground forces under his command, repeatedly pressed Mao for additional resources, and even threatened to resign on one occasion. Zhou Enlai and Liu Yalou, by contrast, did not want to risk the nascent PLAAF that they were working so hard to build. Mao, responsible for overall national decision making and acutely aware of China's limited international leverage and domestic resources, communicated with Stalin, dispatched Zhou Enlai to seek Soviet aid, and adjusted strategy and policy as necessary. Like Stalin, he faced his own escalation concerns. Mao requested Soviet air support to safeguard rear supply lines, not to support ground operations. Though the latter might have been impossible to achieve in any case, Mao might have further restrained himself in this area because he feared Soviet-American confrontation. Believing that airpower did not negate his doctrine of People's War, Mao used airpower as a defensive deterrent and sought to avoid conflict with the United States. He kept his strategic focus almost exclusively on his ground forces, even though doing so imposed heavy costs and limited his ability to achieve his wartime goals.[14]

Air defense (as provided by antiaircraft artillery, not by aircraft, as was the case in the Soviet Air Defense Forces, or APVO) was a fundamental concern for the CCP, which did not initially control the airspace over China's coastal cities. On 6 February 1950 Nationalist aircraft bombed Shanghai, killing 1,400 and threatening CCP governance. Following strong Chinese requests, later that month Moscow provided advanced MiG-15s for air defense of Shanghai. But Stalin declined to support Mao's plans for a Taiwan campaign and prohibited the MiG-15s from flying beyond China's coastline. In September 1950 the PLA Air Defense Headquarters was established to defend major cities.

Differences between Stalin's and Mao's strategic objectives emerged almost immediately; repeated diplomatic negotiations could not fully resolve them. In what Mao must have considered a geopolitical bait and switch to bring China into the war, Stalin declined to deliver the air support that China expected, providing instead training and air defense. Soviet pilots were initially prohibited from flying beyond the Yalu River; Stalin wanted to avoid fighting the Americans, and he pushed the Chinese to do so instead. Even as Soviet air operations extended over the Yalu, they provided little air support for CPV ground troops. Caution was taken to an impractical degree: Soviet planes carried North Korean insignia; pilots wore Chinese uniforms, were supposed to speak Chinese in radio communications, and were instructed to identify themselves as "Eurasian Chinese of Soviet extraction" if captured.[15]

Nevertheless, Soviet assistance was massive and provided tangible benefits almost immediately. Beginning on 1 November 1950, UN air superiority was challenged by Russian-piloted MiG-15s. By mid-November Moscow had sent six MiG-9 fighter divisions, two MiG-15 divisions, eleven antiaircraft and artillery regiments, and several searchlight and radar battalions to China. Within a month, these were joined by one La-9 division, one Il-10 division, and one Tu-2 bomber division to bolster air defense. Chinese air and ground crews were provided with training. Following debate, and with these new assets in hand, Mao approved Peng's request for air support of ground forces on 4 December 1950.[16]

In early 1951, using most of its staff officers, the PLAAF formed the CPV Air Force Headquarters. The CPV joint command Air Force Headquarters was officially formed on 25 April, and China attempted to place air divisions under its authority, but in practice operations with Soviet and North Korean air forces were not formally coordinated. Citing political reasons, Soviet pilots refused to join. The small number of North Korean pilots played a minimal role in the war, as Kim Il-sung husbanded his nation's few remaining aircraft after his air force was decimated in early Allied raids.

Before China officially entered the air war, starting on 28 December 1950, small PLAAF units tried to gain combat experience under the cover of Soviet planes but met with limited success. The first PLAAF combat with American planes occurred on 12 September 1951. That these efforts occurred at all was testimony to Beijing's tenacity; the asymmetry its air force faced was staggering. The PLAAF had fewer than one-fifth of the USAF's aircraft; its pilots had one-tenth the flying hours and no air combat experience whatsoever. Problems with Soviet advisers, rapid training, and limited flight hours produced a high PLAAF accident rate. Critically limiting the PLAAF's range, as Mao himself recognized, was the lack of usable airfields in North Korea, and the lack of reliable air cover to repair them. Thanks to UN bombing operations, in which airfields under construction were bombed no fewer than 119 times, this would remain a limiting factor throughout the war. As a result, the PLAAF was confined to Chinese airfields, making the MiG-15's hundred-mile range a determining factor. This forced the CMC to change the PLAAF's mission from supporting ground forces directly through a progression of repaired airfields in North Korea to "maintaining air superiority in northwestern Korea, providing point protection of key transportation lines and military and industrial targets, and providing indirect support for the ground forces."[17]

Almost immediately Mao attempted to use airpower to further his political objectives. As an armistice seemed increasingly possible in late 1951 and early 1952, he ordered the PLAAF to obtain more combat experience. On 1 November 1951 the PLAAF deployed Tu-2 bombers against South Korean radar and radio monitoring sites at Taehwa-do to aid negotiations at Panmunjom. The mission failed disastrously when mistiming facilitated a devastating Allied air attack; the PLAAF never again used bombers in daylight raids.

Despite this setback, PLAAF efforts finally began to pay off in a series of modest but politically significant victories. On 10 February 1952 Zhang Jihui was credited with shooting down a top U.S. ace, Major George Davis; several similar kills followed. As is true of many such events in the Korean War, confirming evidence remains unclear; regardless, such achievements represented a major propaganda coup at the time. This was part of a larger pattern in which the PLAAF was treated as a symbolic bellwether and indication of CCP competence: "If the Communists could make airplanes work, they could make anything work."[18]

In another sign of the connection between airpower and statecraft, China's leadership imposed strict rules of engagement, including a prohibition on striking below the 38th parallel. This restriction of operations to a "MiG Alley" over North Korea spared Chinese airfields and aircraft from retaliatory strikes and made virtue of the reality that, with no unbombed North Korean airfields to utilize, PLAAF aircraft lacked the range to return unrefueled from striking South Korea. Beijing likewise restricted air operations in response to enemy restraint. In February 1952, for example, Zhou Enlai called off an attack on Kimpo Airfield, located in a safe haven south of the 38th parallel, after Washington restricted bombing north of the Yalu. The following year Beijing resisted North Korean requests to bomb Seoul.

It is difficult to assess the influence of Chinese airpower on the

Panmunjom negotiations, as the factors influencing them are debated to this day. It seems clear, however, that Moscow would never have been willing to fight an air war in Beijing's behalf. Without Chinese assumption of control over, and some responsibility for, Soviet aircraft and pilots, and the resulting influence on air combat and psychological benefits for CPV ground forces, the Korean War might have ended very differently.

By the time of the 27 July 1953 armistice, thanks to top leadership support, China had developed and acquired the world's third largest air force, equipped with many advanced Soviet aircraft, supported by a command and logistical system and pilots with combat experience, some of whom would later lead the PLAAF. The PLAAF's thirteen aviation schools had trained 5,945 flight and 24,000 maintenance personnel. Its three thousand aircraft in twenty-eight air divisions had performed 26,491 sorties (42 percent of the number of Soviet sorties) and engaged in 366 discrete air battles. Drawing on the in-combat contributions of ten fighter divisions, two bomber divisions, and eight hundred pilots, as supported by 59,700 ground personnel, the PLAAF claimed to have shot down 330 enemy aircraft (25 percent of Soviet totals) and hit another 95. These achievements came at a combat loss of 231 aircraft and damage to 151, and 168 lost to other causes, and the loss of 116 airmen (only four fewer than the Soviets). This reportedly resulted in a 1:1.42 air–air kill ratio (1.9:1 for the Soviets, although the latter figure had been much higher earlier in the war).[19]

In the ensuing decade the PLAAF continued to develop organizationally. Having raised its first airborne unit in 1950, it formally established an airborne corps in 1960. In 1957 it assumed control of the PLA Air Defense Force; in 1958 it established a surface-to-air missile force and added new antiaircraft artillery and radar units. Its central headquarters expanded, and it established regional headquarters and air corps throughout China. Its twenty-nine schools created regulations and teaching materials based on China's new indigenous experience.

Despite rapid improvements, however, the PLAAF suffered from significant limitations that persisted throughout the war. Its air divisions varied tremendously in their combat contributions. Its command system was overly centralized, its leaders inexperienced. Despite a tremendous emphasis on morale, some Chinese pilots had difficulty coping psychologically with the perilous asymmetries they faced.

Much of what the Korean War gave to the PLAAF in spurring its short-term buildup it took away in terms of long-term strategic justification for its development. The most immediate legacy of the war was the entry of the U.S. Seventh Fleet into the Taiwan Strait, thereby preventing the PLA from incorporating Taiwan physically into the PRC. This eliminated what otherwise might have been a significant impetus for PLAAF development. The Korean experience convinced many of Mao's senior military leaders (for example, Peng Dehuai) that modernization and professionalization were essential, but Mao maintained that a "People's War" of attrition was the correct choice for China. Even though his own son had been killed in an air raid in Korea, Mao concluded that enemy air attack was less significant than ground attack.[20]

The Offshore Islands Campaign, 1954–1955

In the first decades after Jiang Jieshi and the Nationalists retreated to Taiwan, he sent surveillance flights over the mainland (with American assistance), sparking many low-level skirmishes with Communist forces. These included one hundred CIA-supported U-2 flights; the PLAAF shot down five from 1963 to 1967.

The PLAAF's initial mission was to work with the ground forces and navy to seize GMD-held islands. These efforts were disrupted by the Korean War, which removed the possibility of retaking Taiwan by triggering American involvement. By 1954, however, the PLAAF was charged with a similar, if more modest, role: attacking offshore islands to coerce the GMD and thereby express Beijing's will to reincorporate Taiwan. The most dramatic CCP-GMD confrontation was part of the 1954–1955 Yijiangshan Campaign, the only PLAAF operation to date coordinated in depth with other services (in this case, the ground forces and navy) in combined operations. In it, two hundred CCP aircraft in five divisions (one bomber, one ground attack, three fighter), two independent reconnaissance regiments, and three naval air divisions performed reconnaissance, air defense, fighter escort, and strike missions.[21]

On 25 October 1949 thirty thousand Third Field Army soldiers had attempted to take Jinmen via small boats across the ten-kilometer strait but suffered heavy casualties and seized only a small beachhead, which they failed to reinforce, and withdrew. In spring 1954 the PLAN began to shell Jinmen and Mazu, prompting U.S. naval and air force deployment to the region, both to support the Nationalist garrisons and to prevent Nationalist forces on Taiwan from attempting to retake the mainland—a central goal of Jiang's, which he never relinquished during his lifetime. Between March and August 1954 the PLAAF gained control of the airspace surrounding the Dachen Islands and neighboring Zhejiang province on the mainland. In September the PLA amassed forces near the Dachen Archipelago's Yijiangshan Islands (selected because they lay opposite ample mainland railroads and airfields), engaged in drills, and conducted aerial reconnaissance. On 1 November the PLAAF and PLAN staged a seventy-eight-day blockade of the islands, supported by PLAAF and Naval Aviation bombardment, and attacked GMD ships. On 18 January 1955, with an amphibious landing supported by air and naval forces, the PLA captured the main island. During 2–9 February the PLA seized four other islands.

As they had in the Korean War, Chinese leaders adopted a cautious, responsive approach. The CMC imposed defensive rules of engagement on the PLAAF, ordering it not to enter the high seas, not to bomb the Dachens when U.S. ships were in the area, and not to attack U.S. military platforms in international waters or airspace under any circumstances. Even over Chinese land and airspace, PLAAF pilots could attack U.S. aircraft only if they entered Chinese airspace, could return fire only if under direct attack, and could bomb Jinmen or Mazu only if the GMD air force bombed mainland China.[22]

The Taiwan Strait Crisis, 1958

China initiated the 1958 Taiwan Strait Crisis by shelling Jinmen. Mao's strategic objectives included (1) expelling the Nationalist air force from PRC airspace over Fujian and eastern Guangdong provinces, (2) testing the 1954 U.S.-Taiwan mutual defense treaty,

(3) persuading the United States to resume negotiations regarding Korean War POWs, (4) playing a leading role in the socialist world by expressing solidarity for Arab national independence movements, and (5) rallying support for domestic initiatives. August–October 1958 witnessed seven air battles—history's only large-scale air combat between the PLAAF and its Nationalist counterpart. Meanwhile, U.S. ships escorted Nationalist ships to resupply GMD-held offshore islands, and the USSR supplied SA-2 missiles to China. Again determined to avert direct U.S. involvement and limited by the PLAAF's inability to bomb Nationalist-held islands, the CMC imposed the following rules of engagement: do not conduct operations over high seas, bomb Jinmen and Mazu only if Nationalist aircraft bomb the mainland, and initiate attacks on U.S. aircraft only if they enter mainland airspace. In an example of air-based intelligence available to U.S. statesmen but not to their Chinese counterparts, six U-2 overflights during this period found no evidence of "troop movements that would indicate that the PRC was planning to invade the islands," thereby undermining implicit PLA threats to do so in ordering Nationalist garrisons to surrender (unsuccessfully) at the outset of the shelling.[23]

By late October 1958 it had become clear that Washington would not intervene directly and that Moscow would not provide the support that Beijing desired. Likewise, the PLAAF's counterstrike capabilities vis-à-vis Taiwan were uncertain because of the limited range of Chinese MiG-17 aircraft and the need to dedicate half its aircraft to defending PLAAF bases. At Mao's instruction, therefore, the PLA halted air operations and switched to intermittent shelling (this would continue until Beijing and Washington normalized relations on 1 January 1979). Thus ended the latest Chinese military operations to date involving full-fledged air combat. Though the crisis may have been manipulated by Mao to further domestic initiatives, it nevertheless highlighted the fact that PLA limitations and U.S. support precluded Beijing from taking Taiwan and that Moscow would not provide Beijing with a nuclear umbrella—though it did supply much more weaponry than was known in the West at the time.

The Chinese Vietnam War, 1965–1969

Before and during the Vietnam War, China provided military assistance to Communist allies in Southeast Asia. The PLA made incursions into Burma in 1960–1961. In the 1960s it assisted Laos by constructing roads and providing air defense. China supplied North Vietnam with large amounts of weapons throughout the Vietnam War but sought to limit its involvement in the conflict by rejecting repeated North Vietnamese requests for pilots and aircraft.[24]

As the U.S. became involved in Vietnam, China once again faced a significant military challenge on a sensitive border. Concerned in particular with the resulting air threat, on 5 August 1964 the CMC placed the Guangzhou and Kunming military regions on alert and sent additional PLAAF forces to the border provinces of Guangxi and Yunnan, redeploying air divisions, constructing new airfields, and setting up additional radar installations. In late 1965 the PLAAF began deploying AAA units to North Vietnam. This was hardly unprompted; between 1964 and 1968 U.S. aircraft routinely overflew southeast China on their way to Vietnam, which Beijing viewed as a flagrant violation of its airspace. The CMC instructed the PLAAF not to engage U.S. aircraft, even in Chinese airspace, but actively encouraged both PLAAF and PLAN aircraft to attack the BQM-147 drones that the U.S. flew over this area of China from 1964 to 1969 to show resolve, and it claims to have shot down twenty.[25]

Even this nuanced approach proved unsustainable from Beijing's perspective. Until April 1969 U.S. reconnaissance aircraft routinely flew as close as twenty miles from China's coast, and a U.S. unmanned aerial vehicle reportedly touched down on Hainan Island in February 1970.[26] Following the appearance of two U.S. Navy F-4B Phantoms over Yulin Naval Base on Hainan Island on 8 April 1965, the CMC authorized the PLAAF to attack U.S. aircraft that entered PRC airspace. Mao ordered the best PLAAF and Naval Aviation units to the region "to strike relentless blows" against any further intruding aircraft. Starting on 20 September 1965, PLAAF and Naval Aviation forces shot down twelve U.S. aircraft and damaged four. In April 1967 a U.S. Navy F-4 was shot down near Guangxi Province in southern China; this is the most recent instance of a PLAAF aircraft downing a manned aircraft. In May 1967 a U.S. Navy A-4 was shot down in a similar location; this is the most recent instance of a PLAAF AAA unit downing a manned aircraft. Despite Hanoi's entreaties, however, China did not engage U.S. aircraft over North Vietnam, though Chinese aircraft did occasionally penetrate its neighbor's airspace. Instead, China supplied Hanoi with sixteen AAA divisions and offered its aircraft sanctuary.[27]

The Deng Era

Long before becoming China's second-generation leader, Deng Xiaoping served in a variety of military leadership roles during the civil war. In 1975, after regaining Mao's favor, he was named CCP vice chairman, CMC vice chairman, and chief of the General Staff. From 1978 until his last public appearance in 1994, he was China's preeminent leader, despite stepping down formally in 1989 as CCP CMC chairman and in 1990 as State CMC chairman—positions in which he had served since 1981 and 1982, respectively. Shortly after a visit to the United States in 1979, he ordered China's Self-Defensive Counterattack against Vietnam, and in 1989 he ordered the Tiananmen Square crackdown.

Deng restored stability after decades of Maoist turmoil. His post-1978 reforms brought much-needed technology transfer, foreign direct investment (FDI), and export markets. During the sixth Five Year Plan (1980–1985), defense was given priority as the "fourth modernization." China's first aviation sector restructuring had begun in the early 1970s. The worst excesses were halted rapidly. When Lin Biao died and Commander Wu Faxian was arrested in 1971, the PLAAF was freed from the control of two Maoist ideologues, but it was also deprived of a commander until May 1973. Other leadership changes ultimately helped restore the PLAAF and the aviation industry to a more logical trajectory. Maintenance and quality control were acknowledged to have become serious problems. Zhou called for immediate results and in 1971 ordered a thorough reassessment of the industry. But within three years he faced political challenges that limited his power, and after two more both he and Mao would be dead. It was thus under Deng's leadership that these efforts were finally consolidated as part of his larger reforms. Deng sought to improve Chinese airpower and also to assert stronger control over the PLAAF, which he and others viewed as a "potentially dangerous service" in the wake of the Lin Biao incident.[28] Deng was also concerned about the loyalty of the airborne force: during the Wuhan incident in early 1967, central China's political, economic, and transportation hub had "suffered factional strife between the 'Rebels,' who were supported by Premier Zhou Enlai, and the 'Million Heroes,' who were supported by the Wuhan Military Region (MR) command. When Zhou sent two people to mediate the situation in July, the MR commander arrested them and helped arm more of the 'Million Heroes,' which led to more bloodshed between the two factions. The acting Chief of the General Staff, Yang Chengwu, ordered the PLAAF's 15th Airborne Army to intervene on behalf of the 'Rebels' and to rescue the two mediators."[29]

Major PLAAF reforms, including the reestablishment of training and education, began in 1977 with the appointment of the former PLAAF political commissar Zhang Tingfa (1975–1977, 1977–1985) as commander. To fund China's rapid economic development and a shift to smaller, better-equipped forces, Deng significantly downsized the PLA, which had peaked at a level of six million personnel. Since 1949 the PLAAF has implemented six reductions in force (in 1960, 1970, 1975, 1985, 1992, and 2003), all of which were part of larger PLA force reduction programs. Early initiatives were aimed primarily at cutting the size of headquarters staffs by 15 to 20 percent. By the end of 1976 the PLAAF had shed 190,000 personnel from its 1972 peak of 760,000. In August 1985 it further downsized 20 percent by eliminating some establishments, reforming the unit organization structure, and eliminating old equipment. In October 1992 Deng would carry out yet another 20 percent reduction. In the late 1980s the PLAAF was finally fully integrated into the campaign command structure of the ground forces, following their bureaucratic synchronization by geographic area in 1985.[30]

The Sino-Vietnam Border Conflict, 1979

China launched the Self-Defensive Counterattack against Vietnam from 17 February to 17 March 1979, ostensibly because of border incursions, but in reality to punish Vietnam for preparing to overthrow its ally Pol Pot in Cambodia and to halt its Soviet-assisted expansion of influence in Southeast Asia. While moving thirty to forty divisions to the Vietnamese border, China prepared simultaneously to deter an attack by the USSR, which had concluded the Treaty of Friendship and Cooperation with Vietnam in 1978. Encountering heavy resistance when its forces crossed the border, Beijing stated that the PLA would not proceed farther than fifty kilometers into Vietnam. While it prepared fifteen border airfields to accept 20,000 PLAAF aviation, SAM, and AAA troops, and massed 800 to 1,100 aircraft there, the PLAAF was in no position to go to war, having been devastated by the Cultural Revolution. It was charged with major logistics preparations, but it had great difficulty with fuel supply. It deployed J-7s, its most capable aircraft at that time, to frontline airfields to counter Vietnam's limited number of MiG-21bis aircraft, but their operational status was questionable.

To avoid escalating the conflict, which he planned to end within thirty-three days, or contend with better-trained Vietnamese pilots and a lack of proximate Chinese airfields, Deng relegated the PLAAF to providing deterrence and support: it did not engage in air combat and flew no ground attack aircraft or bomber sorties into Vietnamese airspace.[31] Neither side flew missions to support its ground forces directly because neither wanted to escalate the conflict. The PLAAF flew 8,500 sorties over Chinese territory, including area familiarization, evacuation of wounded personnel via helicopter, and postconflict operations. On-station time for border sorties was severely limited. After accomplishing its basic objective, the PLA systematically withdrew twenty-eight days after invading. Severe problems with coordination, command, control, and logistics demonstrated how unprepared for combat the PLA had become. In a separate incident, a Vietnamese MiG-21 crossing into Guangxi Province was shot down on 5 October 1987; this is the most recent instance of a PLAAF SAM shooting down an aircraft.

The Jiang Era

Jiang Zemin (1926–) was hand-picked by Deng to head China's third-generation leadership, becoming CCP general secretary and CMC chairman in 1989 and president of the PRC in 1993. During his decade in office, Jiang increased PLA budgets and directed significant PLA modernization. An electrical engineer by training, and one of the first Chinese leaders to grasp the significance of the information age and its implications for warfare, Jiang built on Deng's technical and economic reforms to fund research and development and weapons programs at a level previously unimaginable for China. Since 1990, China's annual official defense expenditure has increased on average more than 10 percent annually, yielding an official budget of $106.4 billion for 2012 (the second highest in the world after that of the United States). This supports higher levels of weapons and equipment development and acquisition. In September 2003 the PLA initiated its tenth downsizing since 1951.[32] The 2003–2004 downsizing included 200,000 troops, of which 170,000 (85 percent) were officers, including 50 PLAAF flag officers.[33] Jiang worked with the CMC and PLAAF to provide the service with its own strategic theory, although this would not come to fruition until after his retirement.

The Taiwan Strait Crisis, 1995–1996

Chinese air operations in proximity to the Taiwan Strait offer examples of how airpower is already affording Chinese leaders strategic tools that can be adjusted to send a variety of signals, against a backdrop of growing deployments opposite Taiwan. Of note is the fact that PLAAF aircraft did not fly over water until 1996 and flew to the center line of the Taiwan Strait for the first time in 1999.

The 1995–1996 Taiwan Strait Crisis offers the most prominent example to date of such signaling. The PLA fired ten DF-15 short-range ballistic missiles to the north and south of Taiwan (not over the island or in the strait) as part of large-scale military exercises. These exercises, and the accompanying political rhetoric, were designed to discourage independence moves by Taiwan's President Lee Deng-hui before and during his election. This was in accordance with Jiang Zemin's "two transformations," which, following conspicuous U.S. success in the First Gulf War, sought a "Revolution in Military Affairs" (RMA) that emphasized quality over quantity and mandated PLA preparations to fight "limited local wars under high-technology conditions," and a later focus on "informatization," or the use of information technology and networks. It also suggested an increased PLA attention to asserting sovereignty over claimed territory on its maritime periphery.

PLAAF and PLAN aircraft were involved in related exercises but did not approach the main island of Taiwan itself. A large number of aircraft were deployed to airfields opposite Taiwan, and some were involved in the PLAAF's first flights over the strait. Subsequently, in July–August 1999, to show Beijing's displeasure with a statement by Lee Deng-hui about special "state-to-state" relations between Taiwan and mainland China, the PLAAF dispatched numerous aircraft over the strait, and to the center line for the first time. By early August the flights were reduced, probably to preserve the political effect of ramping up sorties to generate public attention in the future. As their capabilities grow, China's air forces will be capable of further strategic signaling options, including circumnavigating Taiwan with bombers or an aircraft carrier, or even implementing an air blockade.

The Hu Era

Hu Jintao (1942–) recently led the fourth generation of China's leadership. Like his predecessors, he chairs the CMC (since 2004) in addition to serving as general secretary of the CCP (since 2002) and president of the PRC (since 2003). Under Hu's leadership the 2,285,000-strong PLA is divided into the ground forces (70 percent of personnel, or 1.6 million), the PLAN (11.2 percent, or 255,000), the PLAAF (13–14.4 percent, or 300,000–330,000), and the Second Artillery (strategic missile forces) (4.4 percent, or 100,000).[34] The PLAAF also has a surface-to-air missile and antiaircraft artillery corps and three airborne divisions assigned to the 15th Airborne Corps. It has multiple academic institutions and research institutes.

Together with naval aviation, the PLAAF in 2011 possessed 2,300 operational combat aircraft of varying degrees of capability. Their range is severely limited by lack of deck aviation platforms (carriers), substantial aerial refueling capabilities, and overseas bases. Still hampered to some extent even today by bottlenecks in China's domestic aviation industry, the PLAAF continues to import large numbers of advanced aircraft and aeroengines from Russia, and has "encountered difficulty expanding its fleet of long-range heavy transport aircraft" and tankers.[35] Most helicopters in the PLA's disproportionately small fleet (totaling 700–800 airframes, including roughly more than 500 for the ground forces, perhaps as many as 100 or more for the navy, and approximately 100 for the air force) are either imports or copies of foreign models.[36] Varying degrees of progress are finally being made in a wide range of areas, however. China has produced its own fourth-generation fighters, the J-10 and J-11B (an all-Chinese variant of the Russian *Flanker*), and is developing the J-15 carrier-based fighter and the J-20 stealth aircraft.

At an expanded CMC conference on 24 December 2004, Chairman Hu Jintao introduced a new military policy that defined the four new missions of the PLA: first, to serve as an "important source of strength" for the CCP to "consolidate its ruling position"; second, to "provide a solid security guarantee for sustaining the important period of strategic opportunity for national development"; third, to "provide a strong strategic support for safeguarding national interests"; and fourth, to "play an important role in maintaining world peace and promoting common development."[37] The last two missions truly reflect new emphases for the PLA, and the fourth is unprecedented. Hu requires the PLA "pay close attention" not only to "interests of national survival, but also to national development interests; and not only to safeguard the security of national territory, territorial waters, and airspace, but also to safeguard electromagnetic space, outer space, the ocean, and other aspects of national security."[38]

Hu has stated further: "As we strengthen our ability to fight and win limited wars under informatized conditions, we have to pay even more attention to improving non-combat military operations capabilities."[39] In an attempt to transform Hu's general guidance into more specific policy, articles in state and military media have argued that the PLA must go beyond its previous mission of safeguarding national "survival interests" to protecting national "development interests," that is, economic growth.[40] High-level PLA officers are now conducting sophisticated analysis of the "nonwar military operations" needed to promote these interests.

As China's 2010 Defense White Paper elaborates, "The PLAAF is working to ensure the development of a combat force structure that focuses on air strikes, air and missile defense, and strategic projection, to improve its leadership and command system and build up an informationized, networked base support system."[41] It is contending with the General Armaments Department and the Second Artillery to assume authority over China's growing military space assets. According to the U.S. Department of Defense, "The PLA's new missions are . . . driving discussions about the future of the PLAAF, where a general consensus has emerged that protecting China's global interests requires an increase in the PLAAF's long-range transportation and logistics capabilities." Yet "it is likely that the Air Force's primary focus for the coming decade will remain on building the capabilities required to pose a credible military threat to Taiwan and U.S. forces in East Asia, deter Taiwan independence, or influence Taiwan to settle the dispute on Beijing's terms."[42]

PLAAF and Naval Aviation forces must thus prepare for the traditional missions of being ready to coerce Taiwan and further China's other territorial and maritime claims in the East and South China seas, while also supporting increasing nontraditional operations. Indeed, China's only major uses of airpower under Hu's tenure have been in this latter category.

Gulf of Aden Anti-Piracy Deployment, 2008–

The dramatic rise of piracy in the waters off of Somalia in 2008, combined with United Nations Security Council resolutions designed to empower other nations to fight that piracy, presented the Chinese with a historic opportunity to deploy a naval force to the Gulf of Aden to protect merchant vessels from pirates. For the first time in its modern history, China has deployed naval forces operationally (as opposed to representationally) beyond its immediate maritime periphery. Since 26 December 2008, on what have been twelve task force deployments thus far, China has sent some of its most advanced naval platforms. These are equipped with the PLAN's most advanced helicopter, the Russian Ka-28 Helix. In testimony to both China's utter lack of experience and its determination to perform on a new world stage, the helicopters on the first mission were piloted by some of the PLA's finest: two senior colonels with several thousand hours of flight experience. These helicopters assumed a frontline role in what have been extremely cautious rules of engagement. If the PLAN detects a "suspicious vessel," it will deploy a helicopter for surveillance and reconnaissance, and for deterrence measures if necessary. During transit to the Gulf of Aden special forces aboard the warships, building on earlier, land-based training, carry out antipiracy exercises with shipborne helicopters, from which they rappel onto the deck to simulate landing on hijacked or pirate vessels. The helicopters also practice nighttime landing operations at sea, a new area for the PLAN.

Though the PLAN has sought to minimize contact with pirates during all three types of operations, it has encountered, and demonstrably deterred, them on several occasions. Of all PLAN platforms, helicopters have had the closest and most numerous encounters. These modest aviation assets have enabled China to safeguard key maritime interests, receive considerable international and domestic approbation for its contributions, and help guarantee it a voice in future regional security affairs.

Libya Evacuation Operations, Spring 2011

The PLA's first operational deployment to Africa and the Mediterranean, as well as its largest noncombatant evacuation operation (NEO) to date, took place in response to increasing unrest in Libya in February–March 2011. The bulk of China's 35,000 nationals in Libya were evacuated overland on buses (to Tunisia and Egypt), by sea on chartered merchant vessels (primarily from Benghazi), as well as by air on chartered aircraft (primarily from Tripoli) and military aircraft (Sabha to Khartoum, Sudan). The deployment set a major precedent because it marked the first time China has sent military assets to a distant part of the world to protect its citizens there. This demonstrates Beijing's growing capability to conduct long-range operations, which it was both incapable of doing and unwilling to do only a decade ago.

It also represented the first use of long-range military transport aircraft to rescue Chinese citizens from a foreign conflict zone. On 28 February 2011 four Il-76 transport aircraft were dispatched to Libya via Khartoum with CMC approval. As of the evening of 2 March 2011, the Il-76s had moved 1,700 Chinese from Libya to Khartoum.

The deployments sent a clear diplomatic message: Beijing was unwilling to tolerate Chinese citizens being harmed by large-scale political violence overseas and will increasingly be able to scale up long-range deployments if necessary. At the same time, Beijing has probably struggled to balance the national pride many Chinese felt about the rescue operation with the fact that the precedents set will substantially increase popular pressure for intervention in future crises.

Finally, this operational experience is valuable but incomplete; China's air forces have not fought any combat engagements in recent years. The PLAAF's Commander Xu Qiliang joined the PLAAF in 1966 at age sixteen, eight years after his service's most recent participation in "large-scale air-to-air combat."[43]

The Future of Chinese Airpower

China has entered the second decade of the twenty-first century as a global economic and political power with growing regional military capabilities. Ongoing territorial and maritime claims disputes on its immediate periphery, as well as ethnic unrest in its western provinces and poverty in its vast interior, continue to necessitate prioritization in military development and the focusing of high-end military capabilities in areas close to home. Yet as the world's second largest economy, with its manufacturing industries requiring tremendous imported resources and 40 percent of its oil arriving by sea, China's interests increasingly extend beyond its shores to resource-rich areas of the developing world and the trade- and energy-rich sea-lanes of the Indian Ocean. China's vigorous soft-power diplomacy and status as one of five permanent members of the UN Security Council can only safeguard these interests to a certain degree. Meanwhile, China is the first developing nation to have produced comprehensive aerospace capabilities. The aviation component, which has so long lagged, is finally reaching internationally capable levels. China's nationalistic, increasingly well-educated citizens will not easily permit their leaders to accept perceived indignities now that Beijing more than ever has the means to defend its interests. How Beijing will decide to develop and employ its military capabilities to safeguard its growing interests will critically influence the course of events in the twenty-first century.

A key uncertainty is how far China's military will operate intensively beyond its shores. To support power projection overseas, both for national prestige and for limited missions beyond Taiwan, China must extend the range of its airpower. This is likely to mean further emphasis on aerial refueling, acquisition of some modest access rights to overseas military facilities, and development of some form of deck aviation capability. With respect to the last, China's former Ukrainian *Kuznetsov*-class aircraft carrier *Varyag* has undergone sea trials since August 2011, and will become operational in 2012. The U.S. Department of Defense states that "China likely will build multiple aircraft carriers with support ships over the next decade."[44] Developing the necessary forces, training, and experience for long-range combat capabilities would be extremely expensive and time-consuming, however. Building an aircraft carrier is one thing; mastering the complex systems that enable airpower projection requires years and precious lives.

Amid this dynamism, one thing is certain: for the first time in the history of the People's Republic, Beijing's leaders will be able to plan ahead, shape events, and choose from a wide variety of capable air assets to support their statecraft. How, when, and where they decide to do so will represent a fascinating new chapter in the influence of airpower on history.

Notes

The views expressed in this chapter are mine alone. I draw heavily on the following seminal sources, which I am grateful for permission to cite: Allen et al., *China's Air Force Enters the 21st Century;* Allen, "The PLA Air Force: 1949–2002"; Allen, "Air Force Deterrence and Escalation Calculations for a Taiwan Strait Conflict"; Zhang, *Red Wings over the Yalu;* Zhang, "Air Combat for the People's Republic"; and *People's Liberation Army Air Force, 2010.*

1. South Korea and Japan have extremely competent air forces, which, in fact, might be better at defending their respective national territories than the PLAAF. What they lack, however, are the PLAAF's potential power projection capabilities.

2. See Walter J. Boyne, *The Influence of Air Power upon History* (New York: Pelican, 2003).

3. Kenneth W. Allen, "The PLA Air Force: 1949–2002—Overview and Lessons Learned," in *The Lessons of History: The Chinese People's Liberation Army at 75,* ed. Laurie Burkitt, Andrew Scobell, and Larry M. Wortzel (Carlisle, Pa.: U.S. Army War College, Strategic Studies Institute, 2003), p. 42.

4. Ibid., p. 8.

5. *Air Force Basic Doctrine,* Air Force Doctrine Document 1, 17 November 2003, 73, www.dtic.mil/doctrine/jel/service_pubs/afdd1.pdf. Interestingly, given the importance of the concept of *airpower,* it is difficult to find a definition in USAF doctrine documents. Joint Publication JP 1–02 does not have a definition of airpower and mentions it only twice in the entire document.

6. China Air Force Encyclopedia Editorial Committee, *China Air Force Encyclopedia* (Beijing: Aviation Industry Press, 2005), pp. 81–83.

7. Ibid., pp. 39–41.

8. Hua Renjie, Cao Yifeng, and Chen Huixiu, eds., *History of Air Force Theory* (Beijing: Liberation Army Press, 1991), p. 316.

9. U.S. Air Force Association, www.afa.org/quotes/Quotes_81208.pdf, p. 6.

10. Kenneth W. Allen, Glenn Krumel, and Jonathan D. Pollack, *China's Air Force Enters the 21st Century* (Santa Monica, Calif.: Rand, 1995), p. 73.

11. Wang Dinglie, ed., *China Today: Air Force* (Beijing: China Social Sciences Press, 1989), p. 481.

12. *People's Liberation Army Air Force, 2010* (Wright-Patterson Air Force Base, Ohio: National Air and Space Intelligence Center, 2010), www.au.af.mil/au/awc/awcgate/nasic/pla_af_2010.pdf, pp. 12–13.

13. Xiaoming Zhang, "Air Combat for the People's Republic: The People's Liberation Army Air Force in Action, 1949–1969," in *Chinese Warfighting: The PLA Experience since 1949,* ed. Mark A. Ryan, David M. Finkelstein, and Michael A. McDevitt (Armonk, N.Y.: M. E. Sharpe, 2002), p. 271.

14. Xiaoming Zhang, *Red Wings over the Yalu* (College Station: Texas A&M University Press, 2002), p. 209.

15. Ibid., p. 139.

16. Zhang, "Air Combat for the People's Republic," p. 272.

17. Allen, "The PLA Air Force: 1949–2002," p. 17.

18. Zhang, *Red Wings over the Yalu*, p. 207.

19. Ibid., pp. 201–202.

20. Ibid., p. 208.

21. Zhang, "Air Combat for the People's Republic," p. 280.

22. Ibid., p. 281.

23. Gregory W. Pedlow and Donald E. Welzenbach, *The CIA and the U-2 Program, 1954–1974* (Langley, Va.: Central Intelligence Agency, 1998), p. 215.

24. Zhang, *Red Wings over the Yalu*, p. 211.

25. Ibid., pp. 289–290.

26. Kenneth W. Allen, "Air Force Deterrence and Escalation Calculations for a Taiwan Strait Conflict: China, Taiwan, and the United States," in *Assessing the Threat: The Chinese Military and Taiwan's Security,* ed. Michael Swaine, Andrew Yang, Evan Medeiros, and Oriana Mastro (Washington, D.C.: Carnegie Endowment for International Peace, 2007).

27. Zhang, *Red Wings over the Yalu*, p. 291.

28. Allen, "The PLA Air Force: 1949–2002," p. 4.

29. *People's Liberation Army Air Force, 2010,* p. 95.

30. Allen, "The PLA Air Force: 1949–2002," p. 8.

31. Ezra Vogel, *Deng Xiaoping and the Transformation of China* (Cambridge: Harvard University Press, 2011), 528.

32. Liu Xunyao, ed., *Air Force Dictionary* (Shanghai: Shanghai Dictionary Press, 1996), pp. 973, 977, 980, 982.

33. "China Cuts Army by 200,000 with Ground Army Ratio to Record Low," *People's Daily Online,* 9 January 2006, http://english.peopledaily.com.cn/200601/09/eng20060109_233979.html.

34. Percentages are derived from International Institute for Strategic Studies, *The Military Balance, 2012* (London: Routledge, 2012), p. 233.

35. U.S. Department of Defense, *Military and Security Developments Involving the People's Republic of China, 2010,* Annual Report to Congress (Washington, D.C.: Office of the Secretary of Defense, 2010), www.defense.gov/pubs/pdfs/2010_CMPR_Final.pdf, pp. 33–34.

36. Dennis J. Blasko, "Chinese Helicopter Development: Missions, Roles and Maritime Implications," in *Chinese Aerospace Power: Evolving Maritime Roles,* ed. Andrew S. Erickson and Lyle J. Goldstein (Annapolis: Naval Institute Press, 2011), p. 154.

37. "Earnestly Step Up Ability Building within CPC Organizations of Armed Forces," *Liberation Army Daily,* 13 December 2004, www.chinamil.com.cn.

38. Liu Mingfu, Cheng Gang, and Sun Xuefu, "The Historical Mission of the People's Army Once Again Advances with the Times," *Liberation Army Daily,* 8 December 2005, p. 6.

39. Shen Jinlong, "Naval Non-Combat Military Operations—Challenges Faced and Countermeasures," *People's Navy,* 1 December 2008, p. 4.

40. Major General Tian Bingren, "The Scientific Development of the Historical

Mission of Our Army in the New Phase of the New Century," *China Military Science* (October 2007): 21–27.

41. *China's National Defense in 2010* (Beijing: Information Office of China's State Council, 2011), http://news.xinhuanet.com/english2010/china/2011-03/31/c_13806851.htm.

42. U.S. Department of Defense, *Military and Security Developments Involving the People's Republic of China, 2011,* Annual Report to Congress (Washington, D.C.: Office of the Secretary of Defense, 2011), www.defense.gov/pubs/pdfs/2011_CMPR_Final.pdf, p. 24.

43. *People's Liberation Army Air Force, 2010,* p. 17.

44. U.S. Department of Defense, *Military and Security Development Involving the People's Republic of China, 2012,* Annual Report to Congress (Washington, D.C.: Office of the Secretary of Defense, 2012), www.defense.gov/pubs/pdfs/2012_CMPR_final.pdf, p. 22.

References

Allen, Kenneth W. "Air Force Deterrence and Escalation Calculations for a Taiwan Strait Conflict: China, Taiwan, and the United States." In *Assessing the Threat: The Chinese Military and Taiwan's Security.* Edited by Michael Swaine, Andrew Yang, Evan Medeiros, and Oriana Mastro. Washington, D.C.: Carnegie Endowment for International Peace, 2007.

———. "The PLA Air Force: 1949–2002—Overview and Lessons Learned." In *The Lessons of History: The Chinese People's Liberation Army at 75.* Edited by Laurie Burkitt, Andrew Scobell, and Larry M. Wortzel. Carlisle, Pa.: U.S. Army War College, Strategic Studies Institute, 2003.

Allen, Kenneth W., Glenn Krumel, and Jonathan D. Pollack. *China's Air Force Enters the 21st Century.* Santa Monica, Calif.: Rand, 1995.

China Air Force Encyclopedia Editorial Committee. *China Air Force Encyclopedia.* Beijing: Aviation Industry Press, 2005.

Chinese Military Encyclopedia. Multiple vols. Beijing: Academy of Military Science Press, 1997.

Cliff, Roger, et al. *Shaking the Heavens and Splitting the Earth: Chinese Air Force Employment Concepts in the 21st Century.* Santa Monica, Calif.: Rand, 2011. www.rand.org/content/dam/rand/pubs/monographs/2011/RAND_MG1100.pdf.

Erickson, Andrew S., and Lyle J. Goldstein, eds. *Chinese Aerospace Power: Evolving Maritime Roles.* Annapolis: Naval Institute Press, 2011.

Hua Renjie, Cao Yifeng, and Chen Huixiu, eds. *History of Air Force Theory.* Beijing: Liberation Army Press, 1991.

Jiang Siyi, ed. *The Dictionary of the PLA's Major Events.* Tianjin: Tianjin People's Press, 1992.

Lanzit, Kevin M., and Kenneth Allen. "Right-Sizing the PLA Air Force: New Operational Concepts Define a Smaller, More Capable Force." In *Right-Sizing the People's Liberation Army: Exploring the Contours of China's Military.* Edited by Roy Kamphausen and Andrew Scobell. Carlisle, Pa.: Army War College, 2007.

Lewis, John Wilson, and Xue Litai. *Imagined Enemies: China Prepares for Uncertain War.* Stanford: Stanford University Press, 2006.

Liu Xunyao, ed. *Air Force Dictionary.* Shanghai: Shanghai Dictionary Press, 1996.

Liu Yalou. *The Collected Works of Liu Yalou.* Edited by Air Force Editorial Group. Beijing: Blue Sky Press, 2010.

People's Liberation Army Air Force, 2010. Wright-Patterson Air Force Base, Ohio: National Air and Space Intelligence Center, 2010. www.au.af.mil/au/awc/awcgate/nasic/pla_af_2010.pdf.

People's Liberation Army Chronicle, 1927–1982. Beijing: PLA Academy of Military Science, 1983.

Saunders, Phillip C., and Erik Quam. "Future Force Structure of the Chinese Air Force." In *Right-Sizing the People's Liberation Army: Exploring the Contours of China's Military.* Edited by Roy Kamphausen and Andrew Scobell. Carlisle, Pa.: Army War College, 2007.

Seventy Years of the PLA. Beijing: Military Science Press, 1997.

Vogel, Ezra. *Deng Xiaoping and the Transformation of China.* Cambridge: Harvard University Press, 2011.

Wang Dinglie, ed. *China Today: Air Force.* Beijing: China Social Sciences Press, 1989.

Xin Ming, ed. *People's Liberation Army Air Force Handbook.* Qingdao: Qingdao Press, 1991.

Zhang, Xiaoming. "Air Combat for the People's Republic: The People's Liberation Army Air Force in Action, 1949–1969." In *Chinese Warfighting: The PLA Experience since 1949.* Edited by Mark A. Ryan, David M. Finkelstein, and Michael A. McDevitt. Armonk, N.Y.: M. E. Sharpe, 2002.

———. *Red Wings over the Yalu.* College Station: Texas A&M University Press, 2002.

———. "The Sixty-Year Endeavor to Increase Chinese Air Power." In *Global Air Power.* Edited by John Olsen. Dulles, Va.: Potomac Books, 2011.

Suggestions for Further Research

Many areas concerning China's use of airpower for military purposes remain inadequately explored. First, the state of education, training, and jointness in China's air forces, including professional military education for its leaders, remains uncertain. Second, though it has certainly improved markedly in recent years, the realism of training conducted by China's air forces is unclear, particularly concerning jamming, minimum altitude, and night flight operations. For instance, Chinese military publications emphasize the importance of flying in a "complex electromagnetic environment," but they fail to clarify whether China's air forces actually train under conditions of their own jamming and understand fully the practical ramifications. If jamming is simulated instead, how will they know what would happen under real conditions? Finally, a third critical question is how does or will China's air forces deconflict aircraft and SAMs working in the same airspace. Do they actually practice this, and how would it work during real combat? PLAAF writings suggest that SAMs and aircraft conduct "combined-arms training," but by U.S. standards this is opposition-force training, as the aircraft attack areas the SAMs are covering. It is difficult to find documentation of SAMs and aircraft working together against attacking aircraft, or of Naval Aviation aircraft flying combat air patrols (CAP) for PLAN ships against attacking aircraft. Can PLAAF and Naval Aviation aircraft actually fly in the same airspace covered by the various services' SAMs? How do or will they actually coordinate so that the SAMs do not shoot down friendly aircraft? Will the fighters fly out and meet enemy aircraft with SAMs covering them, or will the aircraft be the last line of defense in case the SAMs do not shoot down the enemy aircraft? The answers to these questions will help determine the extent to which China's air forces can finally be used as a reliable instrument of statecraft. On a different tack, how and how well have Chinese statesmen been trained to handle modern geopolitical problems? Is their focus on deterrence, peace, or aggrandizement as the realities of airpower?

9

A Century of Airpower

Mark Parillo

It was only a century ago that airpower became a factor of any consequence in warfare and, by extension, to statesmen. Its arrival, and its rapid rise to military utility in World War I, spawned both theories and controversy about its ultimate value. The debates have continued to the present day; they show no sign of abating. Diplomatic and military practitioners, on the other hand, have had to go beyond theory to create the strategies and policies by which peace is kept or war is waged. As our contributors have outlined, the results have been a mixed bag.

Many of the earliest thinkers attempted to understand airpower as something akin to sea power. After all, both involve forces deployed in a medium—the oceans or the atmosphere—that cannot be "occupied" by man-made vessels or other military forces and which therefore are susceptible to only very limited claims of sovereignty. Yes, nations do recognize limited sovereignty on the sea in the form of territorial waters and in the skies as national airspace. Yet the seas and the air remain largely open highways, albeit governed by accepted rules of the road, at least in peacetime. In wartime they are major thoroughfares to be severed through blockade or to be employed for delivering military blows to the enemy. In the great conflicts between nation-states, airpower has been, at least since World War II, the final arbiter of military campaigns, including, we might add, campaigns fought largely at sea. In sum, airpower has succeeded sea power as the ideal instrument for a nation's projection of

273

power, that is, its voice in the international dialogue of power politics, in peace as well as in war.

Like sea power, airpower is militarily valuable because of its tremendous flexibility. Interwar theorists such as Giulio Douhet often clashed over the definition of airpower: tactical support device, as exemplified by the Luftwaffe, or strategic arbiter of war, as the strategic bombing advocates in Great Britain, the Soviet Union, and the United States proclaimed. In the world's navies a parallel controversy raged: Were aircraft valuable appendages for the great surface battle fleets, or were they sea warfare's new dreadnoughts? The latter controversy was resolved in the Pacific theater during World War II, but the former persists to the present day. What World War II unquestionably demonstrated, however, was that the whole debate over airpower as tactical or strategic was itself misplaced, for airpower's true strength lies in its marvelous versatility.

No national air arm showed this more convincingly in World War II than that of the United States. The U.S. Army Air Corps spent the interwar years preparing to conduct independent bombing campaigns to reduce future adversaries to economic and psychological ruin. That meant developing the B-17 and the vaunted Norden bombsight. It meant emphasis in training on formation flying and bombing accuracy. It also entailed undertaking extensive economic studies of potential enemies to determine the quickest way to wreak havoc on the enemy military machine's supporting web of industry and so force surrender from the skies.

Though the strategic bombing campaigns of World War II visited terrible physical damage and human suffering on the foes' populations, they did not obviate the need for the destruction of military forces in the field. Extensive naval and ground campaigns had to be waged over the years, and all of them relied on airpower in one form or another. Probably none was more impressive than the Allies' tactical air forces over the final eighteen months of the war. Soviet Il-2 Sturmoviks, British Typhoons, and American P-47s seemed ubiquitous to the weary Wehrmacht ground forces, so much so that Germany's desperate 1944 gamble in the Ardennes had to be undertaken in the winter months, since by then only foul weather could keep Allied aircraft from chewing up the attacking panzer columns.

The Canadian Bolingbrooke contributed to the defense of American Alaska in 1942. (Robin Higham Collection)

Add to this the highly valuable air superiority mission. Control of the skies means preserving the air for one's own purposes while also denying it to the enemy. It was control of the air that enabled operations such as the 1944 Normandy assault (and perhaps even more so the Normandy buildup phase) to occur at all. Allied aerial tactical support would of course have been far less effective and dependable without the fighters' conquest of the Axis air forces. As the German ground troops used to remark during the 1944 campaign in France, "If you see a silver plane, be careful; it's American. If it's a black plane, that's equally dangerous; it's British. And if you see no planes at all, well, that's the Luftwaffe."

Allied airpower, with a heavy American component, performed other strategic roles besides what Mark Clodfelter calls the "beneficial" bombing of the Axis homelands (that is, to save Allied casualties). Strategic reconnaissance proved crucial, particularly in the war at sea on both sides of the globe. In addition, air supply, though limited in World War II compared to the present day, was a historically new asset that changed the way campaigns could be fought—or planned at all. The Allies employed it to maintain the pressure on the Germans after the breakout from Normandy, and it had a decisive effect on operations in Burma. And there is no telling just how critical the famed "Hump" airlift was in keeping Nationalist China in the war. That dangerous operation was hugely successful; motor supply deliveries over the reopened Burma Road did not surpass Hump tonnages until months after the Japanese surrender in August 1945.

Yet another strategic role of airpower in World War II was air mobility. Several nations had experimented with it in the prewar years, but it was the Germans who showed its potential in their early blitzkrieg campaigns, with successful though costly airborne operations to capture the "impregnable" Belgian fortress at Eben Emael and the island of Crete. The Allies made similar use of air mobility. Airborne drops were a vital part of the Normandy invasion. Three months later Operation Market-Garden briefly held out hope for penetration of the Rhine River defenses and a possible collapse of German resistance by the end of 1944. In East Asia and the western Pacific, Japanese parachute assaults were part of the initial tide of victory after the bombing of Pearl Harbor. The Allies conducted similar operations in their later Pacific counteroffensives to seize strategic positions.

Battlefield interdiction was one more possible use of the "new" weapon. Isolating an area to be seized or an enemy force to be destroyed became a sine qua non of the American dual drives across the Pacific. Though the Japanese fought with stoic heroism at places such as Tarawa, Saipan, Peleliu, Iwo Jima, and Okinawa, their ultimate annihilation became a virtual certainty as soon as U.S. submarine patrols and carrier sweeps sealed off the islands to be assaulted. Perhaps nowhere was this more evident than on Leyte in the fall of 1944, where American airpower turned Ormoc Bay into a watery graveyard for Japanese reinforcements, dooming any hope of a successful long-term defense of the island. A similar story can be told in the European Theater. The chances of constructing a viable beachhead in Normandy were directly proportional to the Allies' ability to cut off the region from German reinforcements during the early weeks of the operation, when the foothold along the coast was most vulnerable to counterattack. Allied bombers wrecked the French rail network so thoroughly that when the breakout from the beaches finally occurred in late July, supply problems hampered pursuit of the fleeing Germans. Supply airlifts joined long-haul trucking, including but not limited to the famed Red Ball Express, as improvisations that allowed the Allies to continue their pursuit of the Germans while the engineers were feverishly rehabilitating the French rail net and airfields.

Airpower was lethal at sea, too, and, again, in many forms. Carriers supplanted battleships as the new capital ship in fleet encounters, but it went well beyond that. Land-based aircraft proved formidable, too, as aircraft usually dominated the area within their range. It was the Americans' "Cactus" air force of single-engine bombers and fighters that held the line at Guadalcanal (code-named "Cactus") against the might of the Imperial Japanese Navy in the dark days of 1942. Aerial reconnaissance proved all the more crucial at sea because of the paucity of surface observers. Aircraft were the best antisubmarine weapon available; their mere presence could deter an attack on convoys. It was B-29-dropped sea mines in Japanese coastal waters that served as the coup de grâce in the blockade of the home islands instituted by the American submarines. Airpower also became so essential to the many amphibious assaults mounted by the Allies in both major theaters that a new phrase was coined to describe modern seaborne assaults: "triphibious warfare."

The U.S. Army Air Corps had seen airpower as the vital element in tomorrow's warfare, but in the very narrowly defined role of precision bombing. The Air Corps had prepared itself for that role, but in the great conflagration of world war, airpower's contributions to victory had been many and multifaceted. In World War II versatility and adaptability proved to be airpower's great strength.

The Royal Air Force's experiences were similar. By the end of the war the British had converted their island into an anchored carrier sitting off the coast of Europe; some six hundred airfields had been built since World War I. With great faith in the deterrent value of strategic bombing, the British saw the big bombers as a defensive weapon. And

An RAF Avro Vulcan armed with Skybolt missiles and a USAF B-52H as part of the Western Allies' deterrence in the mid–Cold War era. (USAF SM 362421)

yet the strategic bombing threat did not deter war. Furthermore, what saved the nation in its "darkest hour" of 1940 was not four-engine bombers but Fighter Command, architects of the best air defense system yet devised and, ironically, destroyers of the earlier British article of faith that "the bomber will always get through." Bomber Command itself had to abandon daylight bombing just a few months into the hostilities, resorting instead to nighttime terror bombings of the German populace, an approach euphemistically labeled "area bombing." Finally starting to yield notable dividends in the spring of 1944, Bomber Command's contributions to victory were only one aspect of British airpower. Aside from the gallant defense of the skies over the British Isles, the RAF mastered tactical support, airborne operations, interdiction, and aerial supply (especially in Burma), alongside, and in some cases before, their American allies. A critical element in this was the flexibility provided by tactical airfields rapidly constructed with American perforated steel planking known as the Marston mat. It was this air-transportable asset that, for example, enabled the "Broadway" base for the Chindits to be opened behind Japanese lines in Burma. And then there was the crucial role played by Coastal Command in the defeat of the U-boats in the Battle of the Atlantic. Airpower's versatility ruled the day or, at the very least, saved it.

Airpower, however, has dimensions that go beyond its military applications in times of conflict. Airpower has assumed the mantle sea power once wore as *the* high-tech weapon, that is, the military asset with the most profound effect on grand strategy, the defense budget, and the national consciousness. Grand strategy, for one, depends on the availability of air bases and the range of the aircraft that can use them. Any assessment of airpower, and the policy makers who wield it, must therefore go beyond the strictly military to the spheres of technology, economics, and culture.

As the arm of national security requiring the highest levels of engineering and technology, the air weapon garners a healthy share of the defense budget. It embodies a large chunk of the collective national resource base and so requires a great deal of scrutiny and, often, debate. In the United States, for example, controversies recently swirled around the B-2 bomber and F-22 fighter-bomber programs and in Britain about the TSR-2 tactical strike and reconnaissance aircraft.

The economic aspect of airpower extends beyond government expenditures. The aircraft industry, given the very high cost per unit produced, is a significant economic force in itself. Consumption of materials, engineering skill, power, and general labor sends ripples through the economy. In more recent times, costs and technical sophistication have climbed to such heights that very few nations still have an aircraft industry sufficient to meet all their needs, both military and civil. Hence, the aircraft industry itself has become a substantial element of airpower. The procurement or sale of aircraft, whether military or civil, has implications for statecraft.

Something similar can be said for the air transportation industry. Just as a strong merchant marine can be a powerful economic, military, and political asset for a nation, so too can the airlines. Though sea transport remains an essential economic service industry, air transport has gained in significance because it has taken over from the merchant fleet the most conspicuous cargo of all—humans. In recent decades, select airline companies have acquired fleets larger than those of some national air forces. In the conflicts in Iraq and Afghanistan, the airlines, as they did in Vietnam, provided express delivery of military personnel and equipment. But aside from such military uses and the obvious economic importance of a nation's air transport industry, to some degree the service reputation of its airlines shapes the image of that nation on the world stage.

The high-tech nature of airpower also has broad cultural repercussions. A nation's presumed facility for science, or lack thereof, enters into policy makers' decisions about high-tech weaponry. In the Eisenhower years there were successive crises of the American self-image of scientific and technological superiority, aside from the strategic implications, caused by the "bomber gap," the "missile gap," and the Soviet launch of *Sputnik*, Earth's first successful man-made satellite. In his 2011 State of the Union address, President Barack Obama referred to "the *Sputnik* moment," still resonant with the American people half a century later.

Airpower may become part of national self-identity in other ways. The air forces are the most glamorous and exotic of the services, and their pilots are the last military individualists, at least in the public imagination. As knights of the air who track their victories in personal duels as a metric of their skill and success, the pilots put a face on the growing depersonalization of industrialized warfare, beginning in World War I, the first great aerial war. Pilots became not only national heroes but iconic figures. The Japanese in World War II referred to them as samurai, the embodiment of the nation's undying cultural heritage of *yamato damashii,* the essential spirit of Japan.

Whether Japanese samurai, neo-Teutonic knights, Britain's "few," or American eagles, airmen are commonly part of national identity, in many cases more so than any other kinds of warriors. The air forces typify the claimed forward-looking, scientifically minded, can-do nature of a given society. Or citizens may identify with the romantic individualism of the aircrews who fight for national security and, on occasion, to defend the historical and cultural legacies of the people.

The identity of the statesmen who must decide how airpower, in its military, economic, and psychological dimensions, should be wielded in pursuit of national goals varies from country to country. Just who those people are is a product of political processes. First, there are ways by which individuals rise to power in a given society. Such routes may or may not favor those who have an understanding of airpower. Second, there are processes by which national affairs are directed. These may range from the dictatorial and autocratic to the democratic and multilateral. Hence, the decision-making authority may rest in the hands of relatively few or very many. Policies may be crafted from the interaction of military and civilian leaders, as was the case at the 1943 Casablanca conference, when the Anglo-American Allies concocted the combined bomber offensive. We have seen in this volume many examples of particular political systems at work; a range of influences shapes national policy.

We should understand, however, that even similar political systems may produce statesmen with markedly different conceptions of the nature and uses of airpower. Many factors may have shaped the states-man's understanding of that force. Reference has already been made to cultural legacies as one such factor. France, for example, has a long history of aviation pioneering; Frenchmen are likely to absorb a sense of ownership about the development and use of airpower, including its nonmilitary aspects, that will be distinct from that of other peoples.

We can add to this strategic and political legacies that may vary from one nation to another. Americans, for example, long honored George Washington's warning against peacetime alliances, typically demobilized as much as possible upon the cessation of hostilities, and thought of the great distances from the other hemisphere as strategic bulwarks. All these traditions have been transcended, but the point is that American statesmen, even some in the present day, have been immersed in this larger strategic weltanschauung as part of the process of growing up in

America. They may have eventually parted ways with its dictates, but such prescriptions were undoubtedly given greater shrift than in the thinking of statesmen of other national origins.

Another component in decisions about the employment of airpower is military geography. Nazi Germany, as a continental power, developed its Luftwaffe with the tactical, ground support applications of airpower in mind; not much else might have been anticipated from a society that had seen land forces serve as the arbiter of its political reality since Roman times. Meanwhile, Britain's contemporaneous Royal Air Force was much more firmly oriented toward strategic air missions. With its traditional strategic imperative of controlling large and often topographi-cally challenging areas along with scattered and sometimes recalcitrant imperial subjects, the economy-minded British Empire pioneered "air policing" in the 1930s in places such as Somaliland, Afghanistan, and Iraq. When World War II erupted at the end of the 1930s, British policy makers thus enjoyed a special strategic legacy that favored the continued prosecution of strategic bombing campaigns, despite the frightful losses and abysmal bombing inaccuracy of the early war years.

As noted above, the processes by which individuals rose to positions of power varied, but they could have a critical effect on how policy makers viewed airpower. For example, the French public, with its long-standing penchant for surrendering power to a "man on horseback," often sup-ported military professionals for policy-making positions. Someone such as Charles de Gaulle of France or Nationalist China's Jiang Jieshi was more likely to grasp the range and breadth of airpower capabilities and limitations because of his military schooling, whereas Mao's or Lenin's military acumen, whether it was great or small, was more the product of instinct than formal training.

And there can be no denying the military complexities involved in the development and application of airpower. Consider, for example, the multifaceted nature of airpower logistics. If the design and manufacture of high-performance aircraft are challenges of the first magnitude, air logistics present further tests of organizational and engineering skills while providing handsome rewards for imaginative thinking. Aside from repairing wartime damage, aircraft require constant maintenance,

A Lockheed C-130 Hercules of the USAF delivering humanitarian supplies. (Robin Higham Collection)

meaning a steady infusion of spare parts and mechanical skill. Providing a constant flow of those resources to air units requires vast production, transportation, and training systems. Statesmen do not need to understand all the technical aspects of these many fields in order to employ airpower effectively, but the chances of making sound decisions increase with a better understanding of the parameters and pitfalls of the logistics processes.

There is perhaps no better examples of this principle at work than what occurred during the years preceding World War II, when so many decisions were being made that would affect the development and application of airpower in the coming global conflict. Though there were British bombers subduing native unrest along the Afghanistan border, Luftwaffe squadrons fighting in the Spanish Civil War, and U.S. Marine aviators learning the finer points of dive-bombing in the civil insurgencies of Latin America, there were few instances of modern aerial campaigning on a scale to test logistics networks. The result was a period of "white noise," a veritable vacuum in which logistics methods were constantly evolving, methods that would soon be tested and found wanting in World War II.

Take the case of basing. Aircraft in World War I could operate from lightly modified farmers' fields, but the planes that fought the next great war required airfields of much greater substance, not to mention far more elaborate maintenance facilities and parts inventories. In a theater such as the Pacific Ocean, where tens of thousands of square miles might contain only a few, widely scattered places suitable for an airfield, the logistics of airfield construction and aircraft maintenance was often the key element not only in military success but in the very plausibility of operations in the first place. There is no question that the U.S. capability by 1944 of producing a functioning airstrip out of jungle or swamp in three weeks as compared to six to eight months for the Japanese was a huge Allied asset. It is small wonder, then, that Admiral William Halsey called the bulldozer one of the three most important weapons in the theater. Nearly as important were innovations such as the Americans' aircraft machine-shop ships, vessels that could produce aircraft parts on demand and thus obviate the need to spend months stocking warehouses at newly captured bases. These ships became important components of the fleet train, an armada of supply ships that could establish a base just by dropping anchor in a harbor newly seized from the Japanese.

Such capabilities did not yet exist when the Franklin Roosevelt administration opted to increase the deterrent pressure on Japan in 1941 by sending B-17 bombers to the Philippines. The movement was far from complete when the Japanese commenced hostilities on the "day of infamy," and so we cannot judge the adverse weight the bombers might have carried with Japanese decision makers. Yet the plan suffered from a certain detachment from logistical realities that reflect the paucity of practical experience with the application of airpower in the interwar years, just as the technological revolution was erupting.

Benito Mussolini of Italy was an interwar leader who emphasized aviation as a symbol of modernity. He sent Air Marshal Italo Balbo with

Pallets of supplies being loaded into a USAF C-5A to reinforce peacekeeping forces or to succor victims of natural disaster and so to effect policy. (USAF 18246)

In this 1982 comparative photo display, an M-1 Abrams main battle tank debarks from a USAF C-5 Galaxy on a self-contained ramp; unloading a wide-bodied commercial liner requires elaborate cargo-handling facilities. (Lockheed RM 2013)

A U.S. Army main battle tank and 175-millimeter self-propelled gun prepare to embark on a cargo test flight for the C-5 Galaxy, June 1970.

a formation of flying boats across the Atlantic to the Century of Progress Exposition at Chicago in 1933; he employed the Regia Aeronautica ruthlessly against the Ethiopians in 1935 and against the Republicans in Spain in 1936–1939. But in World War II Mussolini's ambitions overstepped his capacity to make war. Il Duce's armed forces could not defeat Greece in 1940, hold off British imperial troops in the African colonies, prevent Allied control of the Mediterranean, or resist the Allied invasion forces in Sicily in 1943.

If the Italian dictator did not understand the sinews of airpower, Air Vice Marshal Hosni Mubarak of Egypt, though successful in creating an air force that stymied Israeli aggressiveness, failed as the long-serving supreme ruler of Egypt to comprehend the ultimate nature of statesmanship. In early 2011 F-16 fighters buzzing Cairo could not curb the popular protests that eventually toppled his regime, even after the dictator's stubborn misreading of the level of the populace's determination to oust him.

In the Arab states in general, rulers have seen airpower as both a prerequisite and a symbol of power. In South Asia yet more air forces with a British legacy have emerged as potent weapons in the balance of power. And in the twenty-first century, China is developing its aerial arsenal of air forces, airlines, and aircraft production directed by Beijing toward superiority in Asia, if not beyond.

We may view airpower as the successor of sea power in its range of military and economic importance, but it does not follow that airpower is without limits on its influence. "Space power," as one example, provides indispensable intelligence and scientific resources. "Cyber power," in the form of viruses, hacking, and the like, has been employed for some time now in the pursuit of military and political objectives. The changing nature of political-military struggles also reveals limits to the effect of airpower. When enemies are other than nation-states, such as the stateless Al Qaeda, the path to victory includes many activities and operations for which airpower is a suitable counter. But winning popular support among indigenous populations, spotting and disarming improvised incendiary devices, identifying and eliminating nonuniformed enemy combatants hiding among the civilian population, and winning the support of the indigenes are among the more frequently occurring challenges of recent times that might be assisted by airpower but seldom can be achieved by airpower alone.

Airpower thus has its limitations, and, what is more, airpower will perhaps not remain the trendsetter of national power. Space power has the potential for many other applications, including devastating military ones. Many of these capabilities are now far too expensive to actualize, but there is no predicting when or how much that might change. Or the future may see use of the Internet—"cyber power"—emerge as the leading projector of national power. Perhaps other arenas beyond outer space and cyberspace will supersede airpower.

Insofar as airpower has its limitations, so does this volume. Years or decades from now, we will perhaps need to explore the application of new realms of international power in a publication titled *Statesmen and _____ Power.* At present we can only speculate how that title might be completed. There is, however, something we can predict with some

Winston Churchill learned to fly in 1912 and was much concerned with airpower in policy making until his retirement from active political life in 1955, making him a statesman of airpower for more than four decades. (©National Portrait Gallery, London)

certainty about that volume. While it will explore the capabilities of this as-yet-unidentified sphere of force, it will also note its limits, as we have done here. And there is one limitation that applies to airpower that will also appear in that future volume: human judgment. We will never be able to remove that variable from the calculus of how airpower—or any power thereafter—will be applied. Whatever the future may bring in the march of technology and conquests of new spheres and environments, the new realms will always be limited by the stretch of human wisdom, a limitation that has always been in place. Add to this the inevitable burden of pressure under which policy makers must operate.

The lessons delineated in this volume will still be relevant as the future develops because statesmen are human.

Contributors

Commander Kent S. Coleman, U.S. Navy, is currently assigned to the NATO Training Mission–Afghanistan/Combined Security Transition Command–Afghanistan. He previously has been assigned to the U.S. Strategic Command, National Airborne Operations Center; has served WestPac/Persian Gulf deployments that included Operations Southern Watch, Enduring Freedom, and Iraqi Freedom; and has been a Naval ROTC instructor at Marquette University. He holds a B.A. in economics from Northwestern University, an M.B.A. and M.A. in international affairs from Marquette University, and a Master of Military Art and Science in military history from the U.S. Army Command and General Staff College and a Master of National Security and Strategic Studies from the U.S. Naval War College.

René De La Pedraja received his Ph.D. in history from the University of Chicago in 1977. He resided for many years in Latin America, and currently he is a professor in the Department of History at Canisius College in Buffalo, New York. De La Pedraja has published eight books and numerous articles, mainly in the area of business history. His early interest in merchant shipping eventually brought him to the field of military history. In 2006 he published *Wars of Latin America, 1899–1941*. He is writing a sequel, "Wars in Latin America, 1948–2012," which he hopes to complete in 2012.

Andrew S. Erickson is an associate professor in the Strategic Research Department at the U.S. Naval War College and a founding member of the department's China Maritime Studies Institute (CMSI). He is an associate in research at Harvard University's Fairbank Center for Chinese Studies, a fellow in the National Committee on U.S.–China Relations' Public Intellectuals Program, and a member of the Council for

Security Cooperation in the Asia Pacific (CSCAP). Erickson previously worked for Science Applications International Corporation (SAIC) as a Chinese translator and technical analyst. He has also worked at the U.S. embassy in Beijing, the U.S. consulate in Hong Kong, the U.S. Senate, and the White House. Proficient in Mandarin Chinese and Japanese, he has traveled extensively in Asia. Erickson received his Ph.D. and M.A. in international relations and comparative politics from Princeton and graduated magna cum laude from Amherst College with a B.A. in history and political science. His research, which focuses on East Asian defense, foreign policy, and technology issues, has been published widely in such periodicals as *Journal of Strategic Studies, Orbis, Joint Force Quarterly,* and *USNI Proceedings.* Erickson is coeditor of, and a contributor to, the Naval Institute Press book series Studies in Chinese Maritime Development, comprising *China Goes to Sea* (2009), *China's Energy Strategy* (2008), and *China's Future Nuclear Submarine Force* (2007), as well as the Naval War College Newport Papers *China's Nuclear Force Modernization* (2005).

Patrick Facon holds a doctorate in history and is qualified as a university professor. He is director of research at the Department of the Armée de l'Air of the Service Historique de la Defense and a member of the Académie Nationale de l'Air et de l'Espace (Toulouse).

Robin Higham, professor of history emeritus at Kansas State University, Manhattan, is the author of more than thirty books, among which are *Britain's Imperial Air Routes, 1918–1939* (1961); *Air Power: A Concise History* (1972), a 1973 History Book Club choice; and *Two Roads to War: The French and British Air Arms from Versailles to Dunkirk* (2012); and coeditor, with Stephen J. Harris, of *Why Air Forces Fail: The Anatomy of Defeat* (2006), which was no. 2 on the U.S. Air Force chief of staff's 2009 reading list. Born in London and educated at Bryanston and Hotchkiss, Higham served in the RAFVR, 1943–1947, reaching the rank of flight-sergeant pilot. After the war he graduated cum laude from Harvard, then took an M.A. at the Claremont Graduate School and a Ph.D. at Harvard. He was editor of the respected quarterlies *Aerospace*

Historian, Military Affairs, and *Journal of the West* and taught courses in military history and the heritage of the Western world.

David R. Jones has taught as Department of National Defence Professor of Military Studies (Acadia University) and professor in Strategy and Policy and a Secretary of the Navy Fellow at the U.S. Naval War College, Newport, and at present is an adjunct professor with the Department of Russian Studies, Dalhousie University, Halifax, Nova Scotia. The founding editor of both the *Military-Naval Encyclopedia of Russia and the Soviet Union* (later *Russia and Eurasia*) and the *Soviet Armed Forces Review Annual,* he has published widely on Russian and Soviet history, as well as on the Acadians of Nova Scotia and the Pensacola Ice Pilots hockey team; he is also the author of plays for the stage, television, and radio.

John H. Morrow Jr. is Franklin Professor and department chair of history at the University of Georgia and specializes in the history of warfare and society. He received his Ph.D. from the University of Pennsylvania in 1971. He is the author of *The Great War: An Imperial History* (2004), *The Great War in the Air: Military Aviation from 1909 to 1921* (1993), *German Air Power in World War I* (1982), and *Building German Air Power, 1909–1914* (1976). Morrow is writing a history of the Second World War and a coauthored manuscript on the U.S. 369th Regiment during the First World War.

Richard R. Muller is professor of military history and associate dean at the USAF School of Advanced Air and Space Studies at Maxwell Air Force Base, Alabama. He is a military historian specializing in the history of airpower and the Second World War. He is the author of *The German Air War in Russia; The Luftwaffe's Way of War, 1911–1945* (with James S. Corum); and most recently *The Luftwaffe over Germany: Defense of the Reich* (with Donald L. Caldwell), which received the Air Force Historical Foundation's prize for the Best Air Power History Book of 2008, as well as many articles, book chapters, and reviews. A native of New Jersey, Dr. Muller received his B.A. in history (with honors) from Franklin and Marshall College, and his M.A. and Ph.D. degrees in military history from the Ohio State University. He has held fellowship appointments at Yale University and the Smithsonian's National Air and Space Museum, and he was named the Air Force Civilian Educator of the Year for 2009.

Mark Parillo earned his Ph.D. in history from the Ohio State University and has been a member of the History Department faculty at Kansas State University for nearly twenty years. His scholarly publications include two books and numerous articles and book chapters, mostly on various aspects of World War II. He has served on the editorial review boards or editorial staff of the electronic military history discussion list H-War, the World War Two Studies Association, and the *Journal of Military History.*

Douglas V. Smith, head of the Strategy and Policy Division of the College of Distance Education, United States Naval War College, is a graduate of the United States Naval Academy, Naval Postgraduate School, and Naval War College (with highest distinction), and he holds a Ph.D. in military history from Florida State University. A career naval officer, he was head of War Planning and Long-Range Planning for Commander-in-Chief, U.S. Naval Forces, Europe and United States Commander, Eastern Atlantic. In that assignment he was responsible for the naval component planning for Operation Eldorado Canyon, the Egypt Air interception, and the *Achille Lauro* hijacking recovery. He is the author of *Carrier Battles: Command Decision in Harm's Way,* which is now used by the Stockdale Scholars and in the Distance Education Strategy and Policy course, and editor of *One Hundred Years of U.S. Navy Air Power.*

Jeffery S. Underwood received his doctorate in American history from Louisiana State University in Baton Rouge in 1988. His book, *The Wings of Democracy: The Influence of Air Power on the Roosevelt Administration, 1933–1941,* was published by Texas A&M University Press in 1991. Since 1988 Dr. Underwood has worked as a historian for the United States Air Force and Air Combat Command. Currently he is the historian for the National Museum of the United States Air Force at Wright-Patterson Air Force Base, Ohio. In addition to writing official histories and curating museum exhibits, he has written numerous articles and book reviews for professional journals and magazines. He has also done television and radio interviews for the History Channel, PBS, National Geographic, BBC, CNN, MSNBC, C-SPAN, NPR, CBS, and others.

Index

M-4 strategic bomber, 138
M46 series bomb, 137
M-52 bomber, 139
MacArthur, Douglas, General, 219
Mach-3 XB-70 bomber, 192
Mach-3 XF-108 interceptor, 192
Mahan, Alfred Thayer, Admiral, 2, 232
Malvinas. *See* Falkland Islands war,
    1982
Ma Ning, 244, 245
Mao Zedong (Mao Tse-tung), 257,
    258; airpower and, 239, 242–243,
    249, 251; Great Leap Forward,
    246; Korean War and, 239, 247,
    248–249, 250, 251, 253; People's
    Liberation Army (PLA) (Chinese
    Red Army) and, 239, 243, 244;
    People's Republic of China (PRC)
    establishment and, 242; Taiwan and,
    254, 255; Vietnam War and, 256
Marchandeau, Paul, 72
Marshall, George C., General, 186
Marston mat, 279
Mazu (Matsu), 214, 215, 254, 255
McDonnell Douglas. *See* Douglas
    aircraft
McKinley, William, 178
McNamara, Robert S., 194–195
medium- or intermediate-range missile
    system (MRBM, IRBM), 139, 192,
    218
Mein Kampf (Hitler), 89
Messerschmitt, Willy, 87
Messerschmitt fighter plane, 100;
    109E, 106; 110 night fighter, 109;
    Bf 109G, 109; Bf 109, 56, 95, 96,
    106, 108; factory, 99; Me 109B,
    109; Me 109, 28, *77*
Mexican Revolution (1910–1929), 148
Mexico, 150, 178, 216; air force, post-
    1945, 148–149, 158; air force,
    pre-1945, 148
Michelin brothers, 40

Midway, 211
MiG jet fighters, 155, 161, 248; MiG-
    9, 250; MiG-15, 138, 239, 247,
    249, 250; MiG-17, 255; MiG-
    21bis, 259; MiG-21, 220, 259;
    MiG-29, 163, 164, 166, 167
Mikhailovich, Alexander, 118, 120, 143
Milch, Erhard, 52, *73*, 87, 91, 98, *100*,
    101
Military Air Forces of the Workers' and
    Peasants' Red Army (VVS-RKKA)
    (Soviet Red air force). *See* VVS-
    RKKA (Military Air Forces of the
    Workers' and Peasants' Red Army)
Milosevic, Slobodan, viii, 230
Mirage V fighter-bomber, 160, 162,
    164, 168
missile systems, 189, 191–192, 200;
    air-launched cruise missile (ALCM),
    200; AMRAAM (Advanced
    Medium-Range Air-to-Air Missile),
    165–166; BGM-108 Gryphon
    ground-launched cruise missile
    (GLCM), 200; conventional air-
    launched cruise missile (CALCM),
    200, 204; Pershing II missile, 200;
    SA-7 Grail surface-to-air missile,
    202; SA-24 "Grinch" antiaircraft
    missile, 33; Skybolt missile, *278*;
    SM-62 Snark missile, 192; Soviet
    Union, 200, 201, 202; SS-20
    missile, 200; surface-to-air missile
    (SAM), 162, 202, 239, 252, 259,
    261, 271; Tomahawk cruise missile,
    201; United States, 200. *See also*
    ballistic missiles
Mitchell, Billy, Brigadier General, 92,
    178–179, 180, 181, 185, 187, 188,
    190, 204
Moldavia, 163
Moltke, Helmuth von, 39
Montesinos, Vladimiro, 162–163, 167,
    174n8